A SECRET SYMMETRY

ALDO CAROTENUTO

A SECRET
SYMMETRY

SABINA SPIELREIN

Between

JUNG and FREUD

Translated by

ARNO POMERANS

JOHN SHEPLEY

KRISHNA WINSTON

Pantheon Books 🏛 New York

Grateful acknowledgment is made to the following for
permissions to reprint previously published material:
Princeton University Press and Mark Paterson & Associates: Excerpts
from *The Freud/Jung Letters: The Correspondence Between Sigmund
Freud and C. G. Jung*, ed. William McGuire, trans. Ralph Manheim
and R. F. C. Hull, Bollingen Series XCIV. Copyright © 1974 by Sigmund
Freud Copyrights Ltd. and Erbengemeinschaft Prof. Dr. C. G. Jung.
Reprinted by permission of Princeton University Press and Mark
Paterson & Associates.
Princeton University Press and Routledge & Kegan Paul Ltd.: *The Col-
lected Works of C. G. Jung*, trans. R. F. C. Hull, Bollingen Series XX.
Excerpts from vol. 16, *The Practice of Psychotherapy*. Copyright 1954, ©
1966 by Princeton University Press. Excerpts from vol. 3, *The Psychogen-
esis of Mental Disease*. Copyright © 1960 by Princeton University Press.
Reprinted by permission of Princeton University Press and Routledge &
Kegan Paul Ltd.

Library of Congress Cataloging in Publication Data
Carotenuto, Aldo.
A secret symmetry.
Translation of: Diario di una segreta simmetria.
Bibliography: p.
Includes index.
1. Psychotherapist and patient. 2. Mentally ill
—Soviet Union—Biography. 3. Spielrein, Sabina.
4. Jung, C. G. (Carl Gustav), 1875–1961—Relations
with women. 5. Freud, Sigmund, 1856–1939.
6. Psychoanalysts—Europe—Correspondence. I. Title.
RC480.8.C3713   150.19′5′022   81-18832
ISBN 0-394-51530-7   AACR2

Design by Margaret McCutcheon Wagner

CONTENTS

FOREWORD

THE COMPLEX ENCOUNTER of Sigmund Freud and C. G. Jung, which unfolds in their correspondence and in a relatively few other documents, has its two vivid protagonists—or three, if we include Emma Jung, whose few letters to Freud contain perhaps the most affecting passages in the correspondence. But there is a latent world of secondary characters, of whom we perceive dim glimpses between the lines of the letters, as if behind a scrim. There is the eminent Professor Dr. Eugen Bleuler, director of the Burghölzli, the insane asylum for the canton of Zurich, whose collaboration in the psychoanalytic movement was courted by Freud and Jung, and who for Jung was a perplexing father figure, the target of some of the most unkind words in his letters, though in later life he claimed Bleuler as the primary influence on his psychiatric career. There is the Chicago millionaire Harold McCormick, one of Jung's first English-speaking patients, whose breakdown in March 1910 sent Jung hurrying to him by ship and railway, then returning to Europe barely in time for the Second Psychoanalytic Congress, at Nuremberg. There is the puzzling figure of J. J. Honegger, the young and promising Swiss psychiatrist who was Jung's colleague and protégé at the Burghölzli, and who killed himself in March 1911. There is Otto Gross, renegade psychoanalyst, whom Jung treated during a deranged episode at the Burghölzli and whose maverick theories had a Reichian dash of the erotic. There is Toni Wolff, later to be Jung's supreme anima figure, of whom we are given a glimpse at the age of twenty-three, when Jung, about to take her along to the 1911 Weimar Congress, calls her his "new discovery . . . a remarkable intellect with an excellent feeling for religion and philosophy." And, surely the most intriguing of them all, there is the Russian girl Sabina Spielrein, who appears first as a desperately ill patient of Jung's in the asylum, then as a brilliant medical student who has fallen in love with her doctor, and finally as an established psychoanalyst and writer.

In my task of annotating the letters between Freud and Jung, I spent much effort seeking to trace Spielrein's Russian origins and her career in Western Europe and later in the Soviet Union, where she returned after the Revolution and continued to practice, teach, and write for professional journals in the West. But Spielrein eluded me, though I found a few memory traces. Jung's elder daughters dimly remembered her as a Russian lady who came to tea. From Piaget I learned that she had been his training analyst in Geneva, and he spoke of her with respect. Helene Deutsch had a faint recollection of Spielrein as a small brunette person among Freud's woman disciples during the war years. Spielrein's name vanished from the journals around 1937. Inquiries that I addressed to possible sources in Moscow and in Rostov-on-Don, where she lived and taught at the university, went unanswered.

Now, the discovery of a cache of Sabina Spielrein's papers, hidden away for more than sixty years in Geneva, discloses a figure of forceful and compelling outline. She steps out of the shadow and takes her place on the stage, no longer a secondary character but— if we are to believe the thoughts and fantasies she confided to her diary—a central element in the development of Jung's conception of the transference and, as Dr. Aldo Carotenuto believes, in the formation of his idea of anima and animus. Jung's own image, as we have come to see it, acquires deeper dimension in his ambivalent relationship to this woman. And there are new details for the portrait we have of Freud, as he quizzically regards this disciple of his who stubbornly maintains what Freud could only see as an irrational cathexis to the man who had deserted and betrayed him.

Spielrein, up until the early 1920s at least, was one of the very few who preserved a dangerous rapport with both Freud and Jung. The others who were similarly eclectic, or ecumenical, included Ludwig Binswanger, who led his own school of depth psychology, and the American psychoanalyst Smith Ely Jelliffe, who finally gave up his long effort at evenhandedness, lost patience with Jung, and adhered faithfully to Freud. While the emotional basis of Spielrein's link with Jung was conspicuous, she was also a worthy theoretician who sought to employ Jungian insights in her Freudian studies. In a way that we see as somehow pathetic, she wanted to reconcile her two masters, to the extent at least of fostering a mutual respect for each other's views of psychodynamics and of therapy. With Freud there was not the least concession to Jung's position. Jung's view of Freud continued throughout his life to be complicated, to swing between reverence and resentment. There is a story sometimes heard in Zurich that, after the *Anschluss,* Jung sent one of his closest colleagues to Vienna to urge Freud to come to Switzerland—an overture that Freud quite evidently rejected.

In the few glimpses of her personal life that we can find in her diary and letters (and fleeting they are: who was her husband, Scheftel? what became of her daughter, Renate?), a woman emerges who, today, suggests the heroine of a novel: a Russian of an evidently well-to-do and enlightened Jewish family, a girl afflicted by neurotic symptoms that rival the Wolf Man's, intellectually brilliant, sent to Europe's psychiatric capital, Zurich, both for treatment and for university study; caught up in an infatuation for her analyst and teacher, yet pursuing and completing her medical studies; a marriage, seemingly brief, and a child, but we know little of that episode; prestige as a member of the circle close to Freud, yet still in friendly contact with Jung until the 1920s; and, in the Soviet Union of those turbulent years, an independent soul as teacher, therapist, theoretician—until she dropped from view at the time of the banning of psychoanalysis in the U.S.S.R., which was also the time of Stalin's purges.

Though so much that is new and unforeseen is disclosed in Dr. Carotenuto's book, the relationship between Sabina Spielrein and Carl Jung must—without access to Jung's letters to her, which cannot yet be published—remain somewhat obscure. Spielrein's diary and her letters, even if fragmentary, display the intensity of her sometimes ambivalent feelings toward Jung, whose response Carotenuto analyzes as love or, given its evidently unfulfilled character, as "symbolic love." Freud, as the third limit of the triangle, is the requisite counterfoil to Jung and the supportive figure to whom Spielrein can confess her devastating adventure.

With the discovery of these documents of a singular life, an extraordinary woman, possibly one of the lights of psychoanalysis, has been resurrected. Her writings, hidden in dusty bound journals, out of sight for half a century, must again be read and studied. Aldo Carotenuto's work of reviving Sabina Spielrein and providing a framework for her is a service to the scholarship of depth psychology.

William McGuire

ACKNOWLEDGMENT

Grateful acknowledgment is made to Anna Freud
for her permission to include the correspondence
between Sigmund Freud and Sabina Spielrein.
Unfortunately, we have not yet received permission
to include the letters from C. G. Jung to Sabina Spielrein.
I hope that this will be possible in the future.

A.C.

INTRODUCTION

IN DECEMBER 1974 I began working for the Istituto di Psicologia of the University of Rome, giving a series of lectures on the thought and analytical practice of C. G. Jung. For a number of years I had been lecturing on analytical psychology at various institutions, but on those occasions my audience had consisted of student analysts, who were already sufficiently acquainted with the material I was presenting. With the students at the university matters became more complicated; for teaching psychoanalysis to people with no direct analytical experience is a risky proposition, even when actual clinical cases are used as illustrations; at best there is the risk of the material remaining incomprehensible, while at worst everything appears so clear as to transform the students into "wild" psychoanalysts.

In order to overcome at least some of these problems, I decided at the time to anchor any theoretical analytical schematization to Jung's probable deeper motivations, committing myself once more to the felicitous definition of "creative illness" proposed by Ellenberger.[1] I hoped—and the results did not disappoint me—that during a series of theoretical lectures, even students lacking a previous knowledge of psychoanalysis would understand that it was not so much a question of technique as, rather, an operation that must necessarily pass through personal experience.

In 1976 these lectures became a book, *Senso e contenuto della psicologia analitica*, which expounds, in the light of my clinical work, the most important points in the psychology of C. G. Jung.

As we know, one of the cornerstones of Jungian psychology is the phenomenal description of the inner heterosexual modality that for convenience has been called the *anima* or *animus*, depending on whether the reference is to a man or a woman. That is to say, by the terms *anima* and *animus*, Jung sought to indicate the unconscious countersexual image present in every human being.

But even a superficial reading of the pages in which Jung describes this experience is enough to give an inkling of the profound and traumatic personal events to which he may have been referring.

It was in 1974, with these considerations in mind, that I held a comprehensive seminar for my colleagues of the Associazione Italiana per lo Studio della Psicologia Analitica on that extraordinary book, *The Freud/Jung Letters*. As we are aware, the existence of this correspondence became known only in 1955, with the publication of Jones's second volume on the life and work of Freud. The vicissitudes of these letters are fully described by William McGuire, to whose introduction I have referred for all particulars.[2] In reading the book I was especially struck by an interesting clinical case that Jung described to Freud as early as the fourth letter (23 October 1906). It concerned Sabina Spielrein, with whom Jung would seem to have experienced the fundamental transference-countertransference phenomenon. For many months I reread, analyzed, and carefully checked the correspondence against *Memories, Dreams, Reflections*, arriving at the conclusion, as I wrote in my aforementioned book, that "the case [of Sabina Spielrein] is exemplary in that it demonstrates Jung's encounter with the image of the anima, an encounter that later most likely influenced his theories on the subject."[3] My book, published in February 1977, was read by my friend and colleague at the University Carlo Trombetta, lecturer in psychopedagogy and a close student of the thought of Claparède. Trombetta was much taken with what I had written, and the reference to Sabina Spielrein reminded him that he had come across this name in the past, in the course of his historical researches on Claparède. Trombetta later spoke of my book to Professor Georges de Morsier of Geneva, whose memory had miraculously preserved the references made in the text to the subject of Jung and Sabina Spielrein.

In October 1977 Carlo Trombetta received a telephone call from de Morsier, who informed him that some documents had been found in the cellars of the Palais Wilson, the former headquarters in Geneva of the Institute of Psychology. From a superficial examination, it looked as though they had to do with Jung, Freud, and Sabina Spielrein. Would Carotenuto perhaps be interested? A few weeks later all the material was in my office.

In my book I had made certain assumptions about the importance that Sabina Spielrein had had in Jung's life, but my conjecture was based solely on perceptions derived from specific passages in his works, from the correspondence with Freud, and from *Memories, Dreams, Reflections*. With the documents in my possession, the originals of which are now deposited in a bank vault, I had proof at last that my conjectures were well founded. The documents comprised the correspondence between Sabina Spielrein and Jung (forty-six letters from Jung and twelve from Sabina), the correspondence between Spielrein and Freud (twenty letters from Freud and two from Sabina), and Spielrein's diary from 1909 to 1912, besides letters from Bleuler, Rank, Stekel, and other people less well known. Since all the material was handwritten, I was faced with the necessity of first having it typed. Only Freud's letters offered any great difficulty in deciphering, but this was overcome by Elisabeth Kargan, who read Freud's correspondence word by word into a tape recorder. I have pondered the documents at length, and from my reflections has emerged this book, in which I have sought to give some interpretations of the affair.

Sabina Spielrein, who was born in Rostov-on-Don in 1885 and probably died in the Soviet Union around 1936–37, had been one of Jung's patients; he met her in the Burghölzli, the psychiatric hospital in Zurich, in 1904. Suffering from nervous disorders, she had been taken by her parents to Zurich for psychiatric treatment. The treatment clearly achieved a certain success, for Spielrein in due course received her diploma in medicine, with a thesis on schizophrenia. She later became a psychoanalyst in the Psychoanalytic Society established by Freud, whom she came to know personally. In psychoanalytic circles she is remembered as the fore-runner, along with A. Stärke, of the idea of the death instinct, which in later years was to become the point around which some of Freud's speculations revolved. Of the people who knew her, Helene Deutsch, Jean Piaget—who had been her pupil—and Mrs. A. Niehus-Jung are still alive as I write.*

Jung, still an inexperienced analyst, found himself involved in a transference-countertransference relationship with Spielrein. He even wrote about it to Freud, who tried to help him as best he could; Sabina, too, when her relationship with Jung became un-bearable, was to seek Freud's help. Since, however, the friendship between Freud and Jung was already deteriorating, Sabina found herself in the middle of a very complex love-hate situation that saw the three principals struggling and even tearing one another to pieces, all trapped in a human predicament. This view of things in no way detracts from their stature as scientists, or from the image we preserve of them in our minds; the only thing affected is that tiresome and scarcely credible "luster," cold and polished as the marble of a monument, that serves to extinguish rather then rea-waken memory, gratitude, and love. Indeed, the subtle emotions that emerge from the documents impart to the figures of the pro-tagonists a human aspect of incredible fascination.

Sabina's diary covers a fairly brief period, 1909–12. Other por-tions have probably been lost, but that is not to say that they may not eventually turn up. The diary depicts her emotions and feelings toward her analyst, seen sometimes as a devil, sometimes as a hero. Any girl who keeps a diary about her analysis would very likely use similar language. It is possible to glimpse in every line the description of the transference, i.e., that special atmosphere that unites patient and analyst during an analytic treatment and allows the patient to face up critically to the influence of the past on his or her present life.

SPIELREIN'S letters to Jung are written on sheets of white paper of regular size, except the one of 27 November 1917, which is written on graph paper. Five undated fragments from letters are

---

*Jean Piaget died in 1980. — TRANS.

probably from 1911–12. I have used ellipses to indicate the missing parts, as at the beginning of the letter of 15 December 1917.

The last letter to Jung bears only the designation "28 January" and is probably from 1918. In these letters an unknown hand has underlined the names of Freud and Jung and made annotations in French.

Of the letters to Freud, only the first (30 May 1909) is complete. The other, written in several installments (between 10 June and 20 June 1909), lacks a few pages. Here, too, I have used ellipses to indicate the missing portions. In addition, there are five undated fragments, which may have formed part of the same very long letter. I have pointed out in a footnote the probable connection of certain fragments. The letters to Freud are written on small folding cards and may actually be rough drafts, since there are a number of crossed-out words and corrections.

Of the twenty letters from Freud to Spielrein, from 1909 to 1923, seventeen are written on sheets of two sizes (regular and prescription) with the letterhead "Prof. Dr. Freud" in the upper left and the address "Wien, XI. Berggasse 19" to the right. The other three letters (9 February, 8 May, and 28 August 1913) carry the letterhead "Internationale Zeitschrift für ärztliche Psychoanalyse." Freud's letters are complete and all bear dates, except for a note addressed to Vienna and therefore datable to 1912, the year Sabina Spielrein was in the Austrian capital.

The diary, which runs from 27 August 1909 to 11 July 1912, consists of a ruled notebook and a number of loose pages, some of them from the same notebook. Some pages are missing.

Finally, some data on Jung's letters to Sabina. Here we have thirty-four letters, five of which are undated. Two carry the letterhead "C. G. Jung—Privatdocent der Psychiatrie" at the upper left and "Burghölzli—Zürich" to the right, and twelve "C. G. Jung—Privatdocent der Psychiatrie" to the left and to the right the address "1003 Seestrasse—Küsnach—Zürich." Jung has corrected the house number by hand on the letterheads of seven successive letters (instead of 1003, it became 228); a single letter bears the new number printed. Then there is a letter written on the stationery of the "Hotel Erbprinz—Weimar," and two headed "Internement des Prisonniers de Guerre en Suisse. Le Commandant de la Région

Anglaise." Nine more letters are written on plain paper of four different sizes; one of these, larger in size, is stamped at the top: "C. G. Jung. MD. LLD. Seestr. 228, Küsnach—Zürich." In addition, there are eight brief missives written on plain cards, of which five are undated. Finally, there are four visiting cards, undated, only one of which bears an inscription: "Dr. Med. C. G. Jung—Küsnacht—Zürich."

In the text I have used italics to indicate any words underlined in the manuscripts. I have added explanatory notes—documentation and bibliographical references—and, whenever possible, I have provided brief information on the people whose names are mentioned.

These letters by Jung, Freud, and Spielrein, and the diary as well, were completely unknown, nor was their existence even suspected. This partial publication of the unearthed documents thus represents a discovery for the world, one that I hope will stimulate further research on Sabina Spielrein.

I NOW HAVE the duty of thanking many people who have helped me in my research: Gerhard Adler (London), International Association of Analytical Psychology; Helene Deutsch (Cambridge, Massachusetts), International Psychoanalytical Association; K. R. Eissler (New York), director of the Sigmund Freud Archives; K. Ernst (Zurich), director of the Psychiatrische Universitätsklinik Zürich (Burghölzli); Ernst Federn (Vienna), co-editor of the *Minutes of the Vienna Psychoanalytic Society*; Anna Freud (London); Adolf Guggenbühl-Craig (Zurich), president of the International Association for Analytical Psychology; Imre Hermann (Budapest), International Psychoanalytical Association; Edward D. Joseph (New York), president of the International Psychoanalytical Association; A. Niehus-Jung (Baden); Huldrych M. Koelbing (Zurich), director of the Medizinhistorisches Institut der Universität Zürich; A. B. Kogan (Rostov-on-Don), State University, Rostov-on-Don; Jeanne A. Lampl–De Groot (Amsterdam), International Psychoanalytical Association; P. J. Van der Leeuw (Amsterdam); Hans Lobner (Vienna), editor of the *Sigmund Freud House Bulletin*; William McGuire (Princeton), editor of *The Freud/Jung Letters*; C. A. Meier (Zurich), International Association for Analytical Psychology; B. Petrakoba

(Rostov-on-Don), editor-in-chief of *Komsomolets*; Paul Roazen (Downsview), York University (Ontario); J. Spanjaard (Haarlem), International Psychoanalytical Association; Richard F. Sterba (Grosse Pointe, Michigan), International Psychoanalytical Association; Isidore Ziferstein (Los Angeles), associate clinical professor of psychiatry, University of California.

Special thanks, of course, go to my colleagues Paolo Aite, Giuseppe Faraci, Antonino Lo Cascio, Mariella Loriga, Giuseppe Maffei, Marcello Pignatelli, and Silvia Rosselli, who for three days in the splendid setting of Argentario discussed my book and gave me valuable suggestions and advice. I must likewise thank Mrs. Jannette Bouctor, who resolved a number of problems of interpretation in the holograph texts.

My thanks also to Fiorella Bassan, Rita Maglione, Lanfranco Marra, Anna Pintus, and Carlo Romano, whose discussions with me of certain points led to greater clarity in the final draft of the book.

Finally, as always, I must express my gratitude to my dear collaborators and pupils Luciana Baldaccini, Daniela Bucelli, and Paola Franco Magliano, who were at my side throughout the writing of the book.

Aldo Carotenuto

The past is fragile. Handle it
as though it were red-hot iron.

Goethe

PART ONE

DIARY
and
LETTERS

I

The DIARY of SABINA SPIELREIN (1909-1912)

Translated from the German by Krishna Winston

[. . .] were linked. Yesterday, too, for instance, when the landlady pressed me to her heart, kissed me, told me she liked me so much, I was such a good person, etc., I was deeply moved. Do I deserve this? Can anyone really love me this way? It stirred me deeply that this woman, who has so many worries of her own, can enter into my feelings, can share my sorrows, without my even mentioning anything to her. I should have liked to tell her a great, great deal, but I could not bring out a word. I just hugged her and then commented on the curiously eerie lighting in the hallway. I was glad to be by myself again; even today I cannot quite face her; I feel somehow inhibited. I would like to do such nice things for this woman and cannot find a single kind word! Inwardly so deeply moved—outwardly so dry in manner!

I am tired.

Berlin, 27 August 1909

Arrived in Berlin last night. To my surprise, Uncle Adolf was waiting for me in the lobby of the Hotel Kiel, where I am now staying. His name will come up again. My room is certainly spotless, but not homey: spare, simple furniture, tasteless yellow wallpaper. The window looks out on the opposite wall of the building, which forms four sides of a little square courtyard. No greenery anywhere! Cramped and barren! But I did allow myself to make a little improvement this morning. If one wants to be completely honest—one must also be able to note things down which give a little insight into the psychology of so-called modest girls, to which category I also belong; it lasted only a short while, now it is over, and . . . well, it makes me uncomfortable to write about it. Let's overcome this reluctance: when I went to wash this morning, I closed the curtain, but in such a way that there was a gap through which someone could look into the room. I did not do it on purpose; but by the time I was at the washstand and noticed the mistake, I did not feel like changing it. As I recall this, I can feel myself blushing; here I believe—I would never be able to think such a thing, and yet it was only half an hour ago that I was standing at the washstand and thinking: it's so nice when someone admires me; down to the waist I am not embarrassed; I took pleasure in having the contours of a grown woman, I was happy that my skin is soft, my curves lovely and well developed. Even if I have a very ordinary face, I can still be attractive. What can be more beautiful than a healthy young girl, if she is "maidenly"?

28 August 1909

To finish up briefly with yesterday's topic, I want to mention that I could never stand by the window that way on purpose. The conscious has to be circumvented in some subtle manner, and then . . . one can indulge oneself a little. When I was fully dressed, except for my belt, I noticed that a nice young gentleman was gazing into my room; I felt myself blushing deeply, and this mild manifestation of the unconscious, which I noted quite objectively, pleased me very much. For a moment I hesitated. Modesty won out, and I hid behind the curtain. A little later an older gentleman looked out of the upper building and . . . how wonderful! A wave of deep disgust washed over [. . .]

[. . .] gruesome loneliness. Yearning for love, fear of emotional atrophy. .... I find myself recalling the rolling, moist, verdant area north of Lake Constance with its picturesquely distributed stretches of evergreen forest. And then the marvelous lighting effects when the sky is somewhat cloudy. And yet I always felt so heavyhearted when I submerged myself in the atmosphere of the solitary cottage surrounded by that green carpet. I could never surrender completely to a peaceful life in the bosom of my family. Perfect stillness makes me anxious. I have to have people with passionate strivings around me, I have to experience the life of many individuals, I must be inspired by mighty and profound feelings, I must have music, art. In truth, I could never be satisfied. And what about my old ideal of wandering through the world like the ancient Greek philosophers, surrounded by a crowd of disciples, teaching them outdoors, in harmony with nature? I would want to teach them genuine love for everything in nature, not forced sentimentality. My imagination painted pictures for me of how we would sit at sunset among the rustling golden ears of grain and after our day's labors enjoy a modest supper of bread and cucumbers. "No pomp . . . no divine splendor, let love alone remain blissful in joy and sorrow," I would say now, be it tumultuous, be it tender, be it calm and broad, but true, great love is what I would wish to teach my disciples. Is there Someone who knows this? If [. . .]

[. . .] but life is so hemmed in by the stupidest formalities, which one must honor, no matter how petty, if one does not wish to be stamped out. Well, all this is well known. Enough for today, I think. I could not express the main thing, and that is that my friend loves me. More about that later.

21 September 1909, Kolberg

Always later . . . everything later, and now, too, I say—later. Just now I am surrounded by family and do not have a moment to myself. Even now I can hear the voices of Mother and my little brother, who are playing together. I have fled to the terrace, because I find my room most uncongenial; it is next to Mother's room, and I need solitude. I must be alone, must be able to commune with myself. My spirits are so dismally low. Perhaps everything would be much, much better if I did not have so much worldly wisdom in me, and if I could therefore simply "jump into" a situation. "Jumping into" something does not always have its drawbacks, and a lovely experience does leave one with a lovely memory, even if disappointment ensues. I found the best description of this in Peter Nansen's *The Diary of Julia.*[1] The book gave me great pleasure. What tormented me as I read it was that I cannot write so beautifully myself (I mean in terms of language). My heart is still youthfully fresh, my intellect already very old, and this constant examining, weighing, caution, mistrust [illegible]—they are all [. . .]

Friendship. Can it alter so suddenly?

Mother says it is impossible for my friend and me to remain friends once we have given each other our love. A man cannot sustain pure friendship in the long run. If I am nice to him—he will want love. If I am always cold—then the [illegible] will hurt his feelings. That depressed me so, so much! Oh dear, what should I hope for? If I could move Fate, if I could be sure that a plea spoken before witnesses would be fulfilled, I would pray here: dear Fate, allow us, my friend and me, to be exceptions, allow us to meet each other always radiant with pleasure, to support each other in joy and sorrow, to form one soul, even *à distance,* to reach out our hands to each other in the search for the "higher, farther, wider," or, as my friend says, "the good and the beautiful," that we may be a support to many who are weak. Allow me to be his guardian angel, his spirit of inspiration, always spurring him to new and greater things. Do I perhaps ask too much? If it is too much, well, it need not always persist with the same intensity, but at least until I find someone who will take his place, someone whom I can call my husband in highest bliss. And may I remain good old *friends* with my present beloved. Is that possible? What awaits me when I return to Zurich? I am afraid to think about it. Why can't I be happy? Why should I go to bed day after day with the most sorrowful thoughts in these last days of my youth? Oh, no, please, Guardian Spirit, allow there to be a pure, noble friendship between us, in the sense in which I understand the word; allow this feeling to satisfy me completely and to become a ray of light in my solitude!

He loves her; she is loved by him. That is the story of my parents. In her youth my mother had loved someone else. Her love was returned. They became engaged, used the intimate form of address, exchanged blissful letters when they were separated. And? . . . They had to part. Why? Relatives were opposed. They told the bridegroom all sorts of tales about his bride. The latter was too proud to defend herself. He hurt her feelings with his ridiculous suspicions. It was not working out any more. She did not want to be his relatives' plaything, and she told him one day not to be so insolent as to speak to her of love. Thus the break came about. My mother felt her life was ruined; the world had lost its color for her, a new love seemed impossible. Around this time she met my father, who soon won her. Mother was impressed by his intelligence, his firm and noble character, his tender concern for her. He also knew how to win over Mother's parents. In spite of all this, Mother did not love him; three times he was told "no." He did not give up. The fourth time it was "yes." They became a couple. One could hardly imagine two more different people.

[. . .] required hours of solitary work and now wanted recognition from the outside world, at least from Prof. Bleuler. So not a single person around with whom one could talk. Who knows what is more valuable. If I am cut off from contact with life, that means that I do not fit into life, that I am lost and done for forever. As soon as Prof. *Bleuler* left, I did not even want to pull myself together any longer. I wept in torrents, paying no attention to the fact that several people were nearby. What did that matter to me? What was left for me in this world? I must admit that it gave me pleasure to weep. I was longing for some comfort and was happy that everything came pouring out for once.

Some change had to come about, specifically a change for the better. All week long (just changed hotels for the second time) before I was supposed to hear about my dissertation,[2] I was hopelessly depressed: I feared the worst. I begged my guardian spirit to preserve me from losing my wits, and the very night before the fateful event I had a dream that I was with Father and Mother and

heard my father say I had come into the world to accomplish something great; I should just continue to work calmly and patiently. In
the dream I began to read a book; upon waking I was still engrossed
in it; I got up and continued with my work, as if I had never been
tortured by doubts. Only later did I find anything remarkable in
this seamless transition between dream and reality, and even conscious consideration of the phenomenon could not destroy my
calm. The father represents the ancestor component in a person, a
component that is often clairvoyant, in any case means much more
for the fate of the individual than any momentary conscious attitude. If this component was particularly strong that crucial night,
it must have had its reasons! The individual could suspect that
something decisive would occur the following day. And that in fact
happened. Despair gave me courage. I ran to my friend, with whom
I had not wanted to speak for a long time. For a good while I found
no words, until I was finally able to tell him of my desperate
situation and ask him to read my dissertation, if for no other reason
than that he figures in it. He laughed at *Prof. Bleuler* as an analyst
and said surely I had not come to make fun of a person whom I
liked so much. We arranged that in September I would ask for my
dissertation back from *Prof. Bleuler* and send it to my friend. This
perfidy toward my old professor tormented me constantly. Later I
would confess it to him, but that will not make him feel any less
wronged by his triumphant rival, who only ten years ago was his
humble student and now, as a "scientific giant," as Prof. Bleuler
himself calls him, derides his old teacher.

Of course I will do it, even if it means treating Prof. Bleuler this
way. But what should I do? The most important outcome of our
discussion was that we both loved each other fervently again. My
friend said we would always have to be careful not to fall in love
again; we would always be dangerous to each other. He admitted
to me that so far he knew no female who could replace me. It was
as if he had a necklace in which all his other admirers were—
pearls, and I—the medallion. At the beginning he was annoyed that
I had not sent my paper to him long before, that I did not trust
him, etc. Then he became more and more intense. At the end he
pressed my hands to his heart several times and said this should
mark the beginning of a new era. What could he have meant by

that? Will we see each other or not? I am much too proud to go to him, and he cannot come to me, because of a number of important circumstances. How will things develop?

8 September 1910

So why am I filled with agitation again? Why this pain? Things were going so well lately. Even earlier today I was still feeling young and strong and rejoicing in being young. I walked today for the first time along the Limmat, on the lonely path that runs parallel to Promenadenstrasse. Everything was gleaming in bright sunlit colors, after so many gloomy days. It was especially wonderful to look through the branches of those great old trees that bend almost down to the rushing water. Unfortunately I had to hurry back to my dissertation, i.e., to the "exam ordeal." And even more unfortunately, I called on a woman colleague, to find some relaxation and help her overcome her ennui with life. Another colleague came by, a woman who irritates me, then a Russian doctor from the surgical clinic, a little, redheaded, thoroughly unprepossessing fellow. We got into the usual silly conversation about men and women: pointless, knowing remarks, just to have something to say; and the whole world suddenly struck me as so dreary. So this is supposed to be youth, the strength and blossom of humanity? Is it possible I shall never escape to a different milieu, with people who love life as I do, who know how to find beauty in everything and don't just make pretty mockery of everything? If only they would at least say something new and clever! What is it I want? Yes, there comes that difficult question again. My guardian spirit was right in his promise that everything I wanted would be fulfilled, if by wanting one means that for which all of one's nature unwaveringly longs. Scarcely had I uttered my worries about the fate of my dissertation, scarcely had I expressed the desire, which seemed impossible to fulfill, that I should not need to play this traitorous role toward Prof. Bleuler, when the wish came true: the very next morning I went to see Prof. Bleuler. He was quite friendly toward me again and said that he had only been able to look over one-tenth of the dissertation, but this tenth was fine, and for the rest he would rely on me. He asked whether I wanted to publish the paper in a Freudian journal, whether I myself wanted to talk with Dr. J. about it or would leave that to him. I chose the latter. So that great burden is gone; I need not lie and can write to Prof. Bleuler that I am sending my paper to Dr. Jung. And now: will it really be published? Maybe there is no space left, especially for such a long paper. Why am I so anxious to see it in print? Well, because of course that provides a small measure of satisfaction. "Small"—because in general I am very mistrustful and would like to add: *"se non è vero è ben trovato."*[3] But then it would have to be *"ben trovato"*! Sometimes it seems to me that the scholarly world which reads the article will see me as a know-it-all who wants to point out every folly to the entire world. No, seriously, my paper does contain some interesting and stimulating material, and for that reason it will be good if it is read, even if it is not an extraordinary piece of work. It is also the joy I would give my parents which [. . .]

[. . .] makes me await publication in the journal with longing; they are also thoughts toward which I have a certain critical distance; they are more like reveries about how through my work I might manage to meet more interesting people, etc.

And my friend? Should I express the same wish with respect to him that I uttered earlier? Oh, yes, what is it I should wish for? My dear, good friend! The hardest thing is just to wish for something consistent!

9 September 1910

Dear God, how happy I really am! Just received a letter from Prof. Bleuler: "Dear Fräulein Spielrein, I should like to ask you to send the dissertation to Dr. *Jung* in Küssnacht, so that he can decide whether it is suitable for the *Jahrbuch*. With best wishes, Yours most sincerely, Bleuler."

That is better than I could ever have dared to hope. The dear, good Little Father! So he did not forget! What should I write to him? I should like to say so many things, how grateful I am to him, but my respect for him prevents me from saying much.

Now there is one more worry: whether Dr. Jung will find the article suitable for the *Jahrbuch*. Oh, Guardian Spirit, if only I could have some assurance quickly! Is it possible that even I may find a lucky star? Is it possible that a tiny bit of truth can be discovered in my "fantasies"? Thank you, thank you a thousand times, dear Fate.

11 September 1910

"Now, Wanderer, we set out. You must stay calm and clear! For you are lost—if you give in—to fear!"

Yes, those were two bad nights. My love for my friend overwhelmed me with a mad glow. At some moments I resisted violently, at others I let him kiss every one of my little fingers and clung to his lips, swooning with love. How foolish to talk about it! So this is I, usually the soul of pure, clear reason, allowing myself such fantasies. How am I supposed to withstand this savage force? Here I sit, weary from all the tempests I have endured, and repeat to myself: not this! Better an absolutely pure friendship, even *à distance*. That he loves me is certain, but "there is a but," as our old natural-history teacher used to say, and that is that . . . my friend is already married. We came to know each other, we became fond of each other without noticing it was happening; it was too late for flight; several times we sat "in tender embrace." Yes, it was a great deal! Then my mother intervened, conflict arose between her and him, then between him and me. I simply could not break with him under such circumstances. A few months later, when I was feeling stronger, I caught up with him after his lecture. At first he wanted to hurry away, because he thought me his bitter enemy and perhaps feared a scandal. The foolish child. I reassured him, told him that I did not want to "start" anything with him, that I had come because he was very dear to me, because I wanted to see him as a fine, noble person and therefore wanted to confront him with his horrid behavior toward my mother and me. His manner changed at once; he showed deep repentance, talked about a malicious person who had been telling tales about us that made my friend think I hated him and was going about maligning him. To think that such disgusting people exist, and that he could believe all that!

Well, we parted as the best of friends, to meet again as the best of friends. If earlier I doubted the intensity of his feelings, now I have seen only too clearly how he loves me. Perhaps in the past he still had a bit of mistrust for me, which then made way for untarnished faith in me. When he gave me his diary to read, he said in a very soft, hoarse voice, "Only my wife has read this . . . and you." He said no one could understand him as I could. Because he happens to have a wife, it often seems unfair that my diary, in which I speak of our love, takes up where his earlier one left off. That may be true, but I also have a good excuse for acting as I do. Our love grew out of a deep spiritual affinity and common intellectual interests. "What intelligent eyes!" he sometimes sighed, or tears came to his own eyes when I explained something about, for example, Wagner's psychological music, for he had thought, felt, written (in unpublished works, too) the very same things. And I was ready to die for him, to sacrifice my honor to him. It was my first love. Not to live with him, or at least for him, for the child I wanted to give him, seemed impossible. I wrote poems for him, composed songs about him, thought only of him day and night. And yet his wife,[4] who, as his diary makes clear, hesitated for a long time before marrying him, because in spite of her love she gave thought to her own comfort and did not want any wild-eyed "slave to an ideology"; his wife is protected by the law, respected by all, and I, who wanted to give him everything I possessed, without the slightest regard for myself, I am called immoral in the language of society— lover, maybe *maîtresse!* He can appear anywhere in public with his wife, and I have to skulk in dark corners. I myself would not want our love to be trumpeted through the streets, partly out of consideration for his wife, partly so that the sacredness of it not be sullied; but still, it has always pained me that we must conceal our feelings. — True, he wanted to introduce me in his house, make me his wife's friend, but understandably his wife wanted no part of this business, so that *"volens-nolens"* most of it had to be kept secret from her. I often feel the force of my passion and of our spiritual kinship so strongly that I ask myself whether I should not try to snatch him away from his wife, especially since my guardian spirit tells me I can do anything I wish, and has so often proved it to me in cases in which I should never have thought it possible (some examples later). But: should I want this? Could we then be happy? I think—neither of us could, for the thought of his wife and children would leave neither of us any peace. I am far from being his wife's enemy; I can only too well understand her position toward me, and although I hardly know her, I do believe she must be a good person, if my friend chose her. How often I have had to suffer because of her, how often I have asked her forgiveness in my thoughts for the pain I brought into her quiet home. Altogether, my love brought me almost nothing but pain; there were only single moments, when I rested in his arms, in which I was able to forget everything; at such times, even if I reminded myself of all the tragedy of our situation, I could not be jolted out of my blissful mood; even the cynic mocking in me—"human beings certainly are curious machines"—made no difference.

And now? He is close to me again. At least (if I am so fond of him) I could give him a little boy, as we used to dream of? Then he could go back to his wife. Yes, if only it were that easy. I have already suffered so much that now I think of myself a little more, I dread the pain of parting, dread the loneliness that would follow, perhaps for my entire life, for by the time the child is one year old, I might be 27 already. And how can I hope for a new love if I have a child? And my scientific ambitions would also suffer: with a baby I would be accepted nowhere. And that would be in the best of cases; what if I did not even get pregnant? Then our pure friendship would be destroyed by the intimate relationship, and our friendship is what is so terribly dear to me.

Well, then, I shall try to become fond of someone else, if that is still possible. I want to be loved and respected by him, I want to unite my life with his, so that I shall not merely have the brief brilliance of a meteor, with present and future anguish, so that my pride as a woman does not suffer constantly, so that I also do not suffer on account of others. Yes, if only it were possible! It is not easy to give up the thought of the baby boy, my longed-for Siegfried, but what is to be done? Yes, my dear, good friend! Things are not easy for me now, but I see no other way out. Therefore—be firm and do not give way to idiotic emotionalism. From the bottom of my soul I wish that my friend may deeply respect me, love me, and always feel it as I do now. We could become dangerous to each other. And now—may he be happy! If only I might hear sooner about the paper I sent him. The suspense makes me unable to calm down, especially since I confidently expect I shall go through more turmoil in connection with this.

14 September 1910

Yes, that was indeed turmoil! There has been much turmoil up to now, and there is infinitely more still to come. I received a nice note from him right away, in which he addresses me as his Dear friend and concludes with Your friend. He said many passages in my paper had thrown him into raptures. Yesterday another letter arrived, and it had an entirely different tone: he is miffed that everywhere I omit his name, as if intentionally, do not cite his works, and in the end even make fun of him a bit. Good God, if only he had an inkling how much I have suffered on his account and still suffer! Is it surprising that I was afraid to read his works, fearing to become a slave to emotion again? Is it so extraordinary that I unconsciously even fell into a negative attitude? In his most recent letter he called me "Dear Fräulein" and closed with "Sincerely, Dr. Jung." At first I almost collapsed with grief when I read it. Then I calmed down, and was even pleased that he reacts so strongly to my behavior that he wanted to wound me with that cold tone. My pleasure then turned into wild passion, and in the morning was the opp[. . .]

[. . .] beautiful house, but he seemed not to hear it and immediately took up my case, which pained me greatly. On his table I noticed a letter addressed to me, but my emotion was so great that I did not retain anything of it beyond the salutation, "Dear Fräulein" and the conclusion, "Sincerely, Dr. Jung." I explained to him as well as I could that I like him but cannot help it that my proud nature resists his excessive power over me. Everything went off peacefully. He suggested that I work through the dissertation with him, so that it can be accepted by the *Jahrbuch.* He said the case was so interesting that I would be accepted into the Psychiatric Society. After some hesitation (because of the psychic torment I would undergo in his presence), I agreed. So this wish, too, which seemed so utterly unrealizable, can also be fulfilled, and yet my unsated heart contracts painfully, for the main thing is missing, and this main thing is love. Oh, again this "What to do?" I hardly believe that I could love anyone the way I love my friend. I fear my life is ruined. The only salvation would be for him to be mine, but since that is impossible because of his wife, and I cannot wish her the pain of being abandoned, only one solution can be hoped for, and that is that both spouses should grow weary of each other and that his wife should run off with some "Frenchman." Yes, that is of course a childish, crazy wish, well-nigh inconceivable in connection with a Swiss woman, and yet in that crazy night I could not comfort myself except by imagining this little drama. What wouldn't I give to have it be possible! Now, Wanderer—be firm! Whatever may happen—for the time being, settle down to work. I am ashamed that I have wasted so much time. Courage. Ah, yes—courage!

[?] *September 1910*

The genius within me calls me "damp poodle." Oh, Guardian Spirit, give me the strength to bear all this! Several times already I have put up unconscious "resistance" to my friend: last Saturday, too, I did so, that is, I had arrived by trolley at the steamboat landing by the railway station at the very moment the ship was about to pull out; but this time I became furious and, disregarding the inner voice that warned me about falling, I jumped out of the trolley and . . . fell. I fell on my left knee (left, according to Dr. Stekel, means an incestuous desire) and ripped my skirt and bent my umbrella. In this condition I ran to the ship, which I just managed to catch. "Aren't you a damp poodle!" said something inside me, and I felt at that moment that I certainly am. The session with him made me more tired than ever before. In the waiting room his children came running to meet me, two sweet little girls and a little boy.[5] Yes, I felt as if I had been plunged into cold water; I could barely talk to the little ones. In front of the children I was small, powerless, and any "desires" seemed revolting to me. What did I want, after all? I sat down humbly, spoke rationally, and all the while . . . if anyone could have seen how inwardly I was swallowing one tear after another. He laughed at my accident with the trolley and said I should not go about fulfilling "anxiety desires." I laughed, too, and thought to myself, "Damp poodle." Oh, how all this annoyed me! To be one among the many who languish for him, and in return receive his kind gaze, a few friendly words. To gaze up at him and rush to fulfill his every wish, so as not to bring down his wrath upon oneself! For if one once fails to take his vanity into account—one must do bitter penance: he assumes a frigid, official tone, and who suffers from that? Not he, of course: a slight annoyance can be banished with work; love for one woman can be replaced by love for another; and then one is also sure that this one woman will finally be humiliated and she will be the one to endure tormented days and sleepless nights, the silly little girl. Later I realized that I well deserved the name "damp poodle" for my excessive zeal: when my proud nature revolts, when the temptation to make him dangle an hour or so is this strong, it should be listened to if one would avoid having a broken umbrella. Shortly before these events I dreamed that my mother's umbrella was already old, and mine, on the contrary, new and elegant. Now it is no longer so fine, and every time I catch sight of the miserable object, I have to exclaim, "Damp poodle!" to myself. This, too, must be overcome! We discussed so many interesting issues. He suggested that I publish my second study[6] along with his and Dr. Honegger's;[7] he found the linkage "sexual instinct–death instinct" well worth working out. I clung to my interest in scientific research, I dreamed up scenes of my future success, and in this way I forced myself to return to "reason." Today there were two things that destroyed my composure again. In the afternoon I went to the art exhibit. I felt completely lost among all the pictures. The only way I could receive pleasure from it would be if I were not tortured by the most embarrassing thought that this huge field is *terra incognita* to me, that I actually know so wretchedly little. Is it even possible for me to fill these gaps? After all, I'm not so young any more. Am I still educable? Even if I want to attend university lectures in art history and mythology, might not my memory fail me when called on to remember and especially organize so much material? May I not already be a hopeless case? Will I be able to do systematic work? I came home in this glum mood and forced myself to sit down with my pathology text. It is hardly surprising that I had great difficulty concentrating and, after faithfully plowing through my assignment, found my mind in a complete muddle. I ascribed it completely to my friend, because in those first days I was able to work so well. Now the idea occurred to me that if I continued in this way I should never be able to prepare for my exams; maybe I ought to give up my visits to him. But on the other hand: what would become of my dissertation in that case, etc. When I was out walking, I met Frl. Aptekmann.[8] She was once a patient of my friend's and is now "one of the many." He told me she was not one of those he could love. I feel she is not particularly intelligent. Still, she is beautiful and a decent girl, for which reason I gladly acceded to her wish to make my acquaintance. She has no inkling of my position vis-à-vis him, she does not even know that I have anything to do with him now. She loves him and believes that he loves her. "Blessed is the one who can believe." In his letters to her he uses the salutation, "My dear colleague"! She asked him whether she might come to see him tomorrow. Since I am with him in the mornings, he had to give her an appointment at 6 P.M. She is going because of her thesis, which he is supervising. She said she had sensed that he would have her come in the evening, and it would be very cozy. She was so happy about it—her eyes gleamed, her cheeks glowed. I did not want to cause her any grief; I said with a smile, as if Dr. Jung were just anyone to me: "Ah, you see! That has deep significance! I wish you success!" or something of the sort. But, but! This dark night into which I sank soon afterward. Tuesday at 6 P.M.! Won't that be the hour at which I used to go to him, generally oppressed in spirit, to be sure, but sometimes also so happy! And now I can come early in the morning, am drained, weary, because I must renounce love. She, on the other hand, hopes, and glows with passion. Who knows; me he considers "dangerous"; he is on his guard with me, and the love for me which he suppresses may find a new object in her. After all, I did the same thing with Dr. Lutz once! But maybe more of that some other time. "So you have outlived your attractiveness," I thought, and remembered the various women loved by Mark in *The Diary of Julia*. Oh,

Guardian Spirit, preserve me from such a terrible experience. I simply cannot be one of the many. It is an absolute necessity to me to see his love for me aglow from time to time, and under the right conditions I can channel it into a calmer form. It is a necessity to me to know that he did not exchange me so soon for another girl, and a fairly unprepossessing one at that. Didn't he once give me his soul? Now I am fairly calm, am going to bed, and wish myself a truly peaceful night, so that tomorrow I can face my friend with pure joy in my heart and see the same in his. I wish that from the bottom of my soul! I wish, wish with all my youthful faith that I may never be a "damp poodle" again.

[?] September 1910

How happy and foolish I am, so much so that I do not even appreciate my own happiness, instead throwing myself with so much energy into emotion that I soon grow weary and then see everything facing me as dreary. So now, too, I am in this mood *post factum;* I want to resist it, thanking my guardian spirit with all my soul for fulfilling this last wish.

Evening

Yes, I am happy, sometimes so happy that I would like to embrace the entire world and sometimes ... I would like to bellow with despair. Downstairs someone is playing, "And if ever your sweetheart" ...! Yes, my dear, good friend. I love you and you love me. The thing I was longing for only recently has been fulfilled: he revealed his love almost too clearly. How did this come about? Last Tuesday he could not receive me. The wire he had sent arrived too late, so that I was already in Küssnacht. Here I learned from the maid that the doctor could not be seen, etc. How poodle-damp I felt then! Also, it was raining. I started for home without knowing when the next steamer was due; one had just left, so I would have had a whole hour to wait. I could not take the ship home; the ship had too many emotional associations for me; I chose the train, where I sat all hunched up, choking back my tears. But I was furious! So that's what you call friendship! He could not even take the trouble to come downstairs and apologize for having me travel all the way out to Küssnacht in vain. If I had a million, and a husband to boot, I thought, then of course it would be another matter, but as it is, I was just his pupil, his student, and a Russian into the bargain. What special respect did he owe someone so insignificant? "Just wait," I thought; "if nothing is sacred to you now, so be it; I'll tell my colleague everything!" But as I approached the house, my resolve faltered. It has always been my principle not to act in the first flush of anger, and this time, too, I derived only good from this principle. I sat down to the work I had earlier planned on doing, that is, reading his paper.[9]

After only a few lines I was completely entranced by him again; it struck me as so silly to have to talk with this brilliant person about such trivialities as his own bad manners, when we had so many really interesting topics of discussion. I decided to give him a good tongue-lashing for wanting to turn his friend into a slave, and then to drop the subject: I shall simply take what he has to give; can I help it that his works lift me so far above all petty personal concerns that my own joys and sorrows dwindle to childish frivolities in my eyes? I now felt completely at peace. I told my colleague only how impolite Dr. J. had been to me, without divulging any details of our relationship. In the evening I learned I had done my friend an injustice; that very day he had had a little girl[10] and could not leave his wife. This information was understandably both gratifying and painful, yet I had myself well in hand and went back to work. When I looked at myself in the mirror before going to bed, I was taken aback; that couldn't be me, that stony gray face with the uncannily grim, burning black eyes staring out at me: it was a powerful, baleful wolf that lurked there coldly in the depths and would halt at nothing. "What is it you want?" I asked myself in horror. Then I saw all the lines in the room go crooked; everything became alien and terrifying. "The great chill is coming. . . . " So I went to bed. The next morning I felt transformed. The air was cool, and I breathed in the coolness ecstatically. I found myself yearning for a perfectly clear, cold summer day on the North Sea, the world broad, clear, and calm before me, and I myself one with this cool tension, like the sea breathing in great waves. "Do you want to?" something in my depths asked. "Oh, yes!" I replied with rapture, without knowing what it was all about. The trees, the grass, the people strolling by along the seashore, everything seemed grouped in a particularly picturesque fashion. I felt destined for something great, felt above all petty concerns. This feeling persisted until noon, when my first encounter with a real, live person dispelled the entire "mood." But a slight trace remained, for my friend's paper transported me again to superterrestrial regions. The next day I saw him. We were supposed to sit down to work. Instead we discussed sexual instinct–death instinct, the portrayal of second thoughts in the form of death, the theories of dementia praecox, and the world of our ancestors. We talked on and on. My friend listened to me with rapture, then showed me his paper, not yet printed, and a letter to Prof. Freud and Freud's reply.[11] He showed it to me because he was deeply stirred by the parallels in our thinking and feeling. He told me that seeing this worries him, because that is how I make him fall in love with me. I saw almost too well what I mean to him. It gave me the greatest satisfaction. "So I am not one among the many, but one who is unique, for certainly no girl can understand him as I can, none could surprise him this way with an independently developed system of thought that is completely analogous to his own. He resisted, he did not want to love me. Now he must, because our souls are deeply akin, because even when we are apart our joint work unites us." Yes, as I said, one can easily suppress one's erotic feelings in return for this beautiful, noble friendship. He urged me to write my new study on the death instinct, but I said that I first wanted to finish the one I am working on.[12] Tomorrow I shall see him again, and we have resolved to keep to the task at hand. For now my only wish is that we may remain "friends" tomorrow.

9 October 1910

Many things happened. More of that another time, perhaps. Now I can sing the same song as before, that I want to love. The night is so wonderful, so treacherously warm. In the distance, plaintive notes of a violin float on the air. Siegfried, my baby son! Someday you must express what your mother is feeling now. You must be able to find yourself a worthy father! Should this not be the case, if all my intelligence and heightened sensitivity has been granted me only to help me more readily perceive my uselessness for life and watch the dream of my youth melting away, then . . . I cannot go on living.

I shall be very cautious in my assertions, but I do believe I am capable of destroying myself with cyanide in the presence of the idol of my youth. In my own affect I have no fear of death! But enough of this sorry fantasizing. I still have a few years left, I must not despair yet—courage!

18 October 1910

Instead of working—writing my diary! No, in the long run this will certainly not do! Today I want to try a new approach . . . first describe what happened. "It was . . . it was . . . a wonderful dream," in the words of the song I composed. Yes, and this dream was Siegfried. Should I tell everything in order? "Oh, Guardian Spirit, may my yearning be divine in origin!" I had to exclaim in the words of my friend last night, for this was what robbed me of my night's rest, the thought that I might be one of the many, that my accomplishments might not surpass the ordinary, and my "higher calling" might be a ridiculous dream which I must now pay for. The question is, where does this need to believe in a higher calling originate, this need so firmly rooted in me? It may be in part inherited from my father,[13] but we know—or, rather, those who accept the role played by the father in the individual psyche know—that the father must have an *analogon* in the mother who chooses him. And that is how it was: my great-grandfather and my grandfather were both rabbis, and therefore—God's elect. I still remember my great-grandfather, from when I was 3–4 years old, simply as a large, friendly man in black. What made a much deeper impression was what I heard about him: he was a highly honored rabbi in Ekaterinoslav. In our town he was borne through the streets by the people. Many stories were told about his prophetic abilities. I par-

ticularly remembered the story told about his death: he had calmly
predicted the time of his death, to the minute. He did not die, but,
rather, took his leave of us and went to God, who was calling him.
My grandfather is still alive. He has become senile, but remains
cheerful and loving. My grandfather loved people. His house was
always open to all comers. Numerous relatives lived in his house
and were permitted to take as much money as they needed. There
was none left for the dowry for his daughter, but that did not
trouble him: he firmly believed that God would provide for his
daughter, and he was right. He probably also did a great deal for
strangers. There were stories about how one time he defended
someone in court, how another time he overpowered two boys
trying to beat up a woman on the street, how yet another time he
gave his last three rubles to a poor woman, etc. It is significant that
my father speaks with great respect of my grandfather, something
he does of no one else; he admires his intelligence and his great
capacity for love. It is significant that no one has anything but
praise for my grandfather; "your dear grandfather," "your good
grandfather," "your sweet grandfather," people say to me, even people I do not know. It is also noteworthy that my grandfather could
permit himself to deliver speeches in public places like courtrooms
that would otherwise not have been tolerated in Russia. One might
think that this spirited, steadfastly cheerful person would have
gathered nothing but roses in his life, and yet this was by no means
the case. As a young man he already suffered a disappointment.
Women doted on him, since in addition to his life-loving nature he
was also very good-looking. He chose one among the many: the
daughter of a physician. The doctor, as a representative of the
Christian community, was considered an unbeliever. My great-
grandfather could not tolerate that, of course. The dream of my
grandfather's youth had to be relinquished, and he married a girl
his father selected for him. My grandmother was a loving, long-
suffering woman. Apparently she was not terribly intelligent. Of
my grandparents' four surviving children the first, a son, is stupid;
the second, a daughter (my mother), very intelligent; the third, a
son—limited; the fourth, a son, very intelligent. All the children—
very musical, like my grandfather. Was my grandmother also musical, I wonder? My grandfather must have unconsciously retained

the image of his first love, for he considered study of the Christian sciences more important than anything else. His daughter was supposed to study, only study; she was not permitted to help around the house. In spite of all the threats directed against him as a rabbi, he sent his daughter to the Christian *Progymnasium* (which then became a *Gymnasium*) and also saw to it that she was educated at the university. Mother, who learned everything easily and eagerly, was his pride and joy. How did this complex manifest itself in my mother? [Sentence almost illegible.] Her first sweetheart, to whom she was engaged, was a physician. As mentioned earlier, the two were forced to separate. So intelligence and the medical profession are represented in my mother's first love. This man was not particularly religious, but for Grandfather he was no longer the unbeliever whom Mother should properly have sought out, if the analogy had held. Mother was very much afraid of falling in love with a Christian or of being loved by a Christian. What happened? One man who perished out of unhappy love for her was a Christian, a respected figure in Saint Petersburg: she told him that she would never marry a Christian, because that would destroy her parents; the next day he shot himself. For a long time my mother did not want my father. He was presented to her by my grandfather. Why? My grandparents were impressed by his intelligence and his piety. And this very piety was a double-edged sword, for on the one hand my father may have strong religious feeling that takes the form of vague belief in a destinylike force, perhaps also in a sense of calling, but in the eyes of the "true believers" my father is a downright heretic. As already mentioned, my mother did not find satisfaction in love for her husband. Now for the third generation. I am the oldest. I believe no one could have been happier than my grandfather when he learned I had decided to study medicine. Up to the age of 13 I was extremely religious; in spite of numerous contradictions I perceived, in spite of my father's derision, I dared not give up the idea of God. Relinquishing God proved extremely difficult for me. What resulted was a void. I kept my "guardian spirit." When I dreamed in my loneliness of a girl friend, I always pictured her as being a Jewish girl, who would be the best student in our class after me. And such a girl actually turned up. At first she was my *"pontifex maximus,"* as my father liked to tease me. I was sure she was smarter and a much, much nobler person than I, and I loved her with all the intensity of childish love. That lasted a while (one year). Then I became somewhat disappointed in her and chose a Christian girl as my best friend. It is worth noting that both girls were unmusical. Later I withdrew completely from other people; when I was in sixth grade, after the death of my little sister, my illness began. I took refuge in isolation and left my two girl friends to become best friends. In earliest childhood they had been playmates; then they had not seen each other for a long time; I got to know each of them separately, and had loved each separately for a while, different though they were. And then I brought them together and withdrew.

19 October 1910

Certainly it is foolish of me to take out my diary instead of settling down to work, but unfortunately I would not understand a word of what I was reading in any case. So it is better to abreact my feelings promptly. I left off with the first female pair. My two girl friends have had very different fates. The Jewish girl is already happily married to a Christian (a Dutchman); she bore two girls, one of whom died. The Christian girl is still single. Her libido tried to attach itself to my brother,[14] then to his best friend. But she never got beyond friendship with mild overtones of tenderness. The men she chooses are all Jews.

Of my two friends, I consider the Christian girl to be more intelligent, but she rarely manages to do more than play the role of the "appendage," which she played for her girl friend. She often intentionally presents herself as a dear, stupid little ninny. She fears powerful storms of emotion; she transforms life into a jolly game and thus far she has not put the stage of childhood behind her.

The Jewish girl's husband, with his blue eyes, blond hair, and his merry disposition, is reminiscent of his wife's girl friend. He made a very pleasing impression on me, although he seemed somewhat weak and childish. But he is certainly a dear.

Now the second pair, which is actually chronologically the first pair, and male. Fifth form in *Gymnasium*. My history teacher. A Christian. The little [illegible] at first calls forth deep revulsion in me. After his first lecture his high intelligence and the serious, sad expression in his black eyes vanquishes me. Precisely because I would like to be especially earnest in his presence, I am unable to control myself and burst out in convulsive laughter at the sight of his odd grimaces. This brings us into conflict. I receive several black marks in the class record. (Bad conduct?) Later this problem evaporates when my eagerness for knowledge opens up a whole new world, and simultaneously my crush on the man who opened up to me previously unknown vistas grows by leaps and bounds. I want to make some sacrifice for him, I want to suffer for him. My Jewish girl friend also likes this teacher best. She, too, admires his great intelligence. We read history and cultural history together. We two are the only ones in the class who receive the highest grade from him—a 5. One time he has every person in the class make a presentation on a particular historical period. He begins with the weaker pupils and ends with the stronger ones. My friend chooses the battles that the Russians waged under the leadership of Alexei Michaelovitch.[15] I choose the development of various religious views during this period. This was the time when I took a lively interest in the psychological aspects of religion. I also arranged to have lessons in Ancient Hebrew, so as to read the Bible in the original. We probably both received a 5. The teacher saw me as the more intelligent one. He considered my intelligence exceptional. Our acquaintance began one time when I took my brother along and went to ask him about some extra reading for myself. He was not at home, but immediately afterward he came to my house. Such were my joy and my esteem for him that I could barely find words. He was equally embarrassed. We both stood there like "two candles," as Bombuchna, watching through the door, commented. I was looking for a friend to whom I could bare my soul. Perhaps he was looking for the same thing. But I wanted him to take the initiative, because I myself was much too proud and shy, and besides, I viewed him as a divinity. But he was as shy as I was, and cut all sorts of capers out of sheer embarrassment, as I later realized all too well, such as leaping around in the room roaring into a phonograph loudspeaker or pursuing me all the way to my room with an opera glass because I considered myself ugly and felt extremely ill at ease when anyone looked at me closely. I was also afraid to be alone in the room with a man without Mother, while on the other hand I wanted to take private lessons with him so we could talk uninhibitedly, animated by our common thirst for knowledge. But nothing happened, because my love for him cooled. Perhaps one reason for this was that he shared my parents' psychological theories in many respects and thus soon lost his aura of novelty and beauty for me; but to a great extent his own awkwardness was to blame; in the end he simply became a bore, taking some perfectly ordinary topic and worrying it all evening. After my departure his need for a confidante found an outlet in my mother. He had come to love her, too, and when she left for Paris, he jumped out of a window, intending to take his own life. He was diagnosed as suffering from dementia praecox. His competitor for my affections was the Uncle Adolf I mentioned earlier, an exquisite example of father-transference. He is by no means as intelligent as my teacher, but he has my father's noble character and a decidedly artistic bent. I have already described how it went. My uncle also finally fell in love with my mother. What is interesting is that I was infatuated with both of them around the same time, so that Mother once asked me: "Which of them do you really love? Your teacher or your uncle?" I no longer remember what I replied, but I am tempted to think I said, "My teacher." Later, when I went to Warsaw, my uncle won out, only to be replaced soon by my present friend, who has more of a hold on me than anyone else thus far. My uncle, as I mentioned, was married and had two daughters. My teacher remained single. The two never had any dealings with each other. But the fact that both of them loved my mother shows that their fates had one point in common. As far as music is concerned, my father is the only musical person in his family. My uncle loves music, but he "has no ear," i.e., he himself cannot even [illegible] [. . .] should. The Christian girl was, and still is, up to her ears in love with the friend who dominates her. Even if they never had a sexual relationship, the stronger woman did exploit her womanly charms to maintain her power over the foolish girl. Thus I heard her say once, "V., don't you feel like admiring my body any more?" At the same time she was also trying to make her colleague be more feminine, even to find a fiancé for her, but she herself undid everything she had achieved. She thought if she found a husband for the girl, the girl would have to appreciate her kindness, for without her no one would love her; she simply generously handed on one of her less valued admirers, since she already had a fiancé. I am sure that she stayed with her colleague as long as she did because she could borrow money from her; they always lived together; that way most of the expenses were assumed by the other girl; such things would be trivial in the context of a real friendship; but she cannot be a friend without thinking of her own profit. Her relationship to her present husband is also significant. He is an Armenian, thus a Christian, a very honest, hard-working, and correspondingly limited person (a medical student). She loves him as much as she is capable of. I am only surprised that in her happiness she feels so little urge to make the people around her happy. When I saw my friend well disposed toward me, I glowed to the depths of my soul with happiness—and that was [. . .]

[. . .] how two so different people could find their way to each other. She—a person who blends in with the crowd, and I—a hermit. She, who approaches life from the practical standpoint, and I—the idealist. Thus it came about that even when she was still well off, she scolded me for throwing away money when I did not want to bargain in shops. She called me and my father psychopaths because I wanted to follow the rules and pay for the surgery course I was attending, instead of auditing without official permission like most of the others. The episode that brought about our definitive break occurred a year ago. It was a simply terrible period for me, for I had separated from my friend and was battling the forces of darkness which wanted to rob me of belief in my ideals. I wept practically night and day, when I was not numbing myself with meaningless mechanical work at the hospital. During this period she moved to the psychiatric clinic as an intern. There she had a large, airy room, and plenty to eat, which meant a good deal to her. In addition, she was sure she was the most impressive female there, because she considered the other women physicians thoroughly insignificant. (Whether that is true—I do not know.) Things were going well, and therefore she did not give me a thought. Actually I am being unfair. She did think of me sometimes; sometimes she wished she could help me out of my dilemma, as I had helped her out of hers. She did not know, however, that with me different methods are called for, that the crucial thing for me is to see my ideal salvaged. Besides, we should never have been friends if we had not had some good moments, for which I am grateful, but in her, selfishness had the upper hand. So one time she wanted me to skip the only lecture course I was still attending faithfully despite my wretched state, merely in order to correct the style of an anamnesis she had compiled. If it had been a question of an important event in her life, I would have done it. As it was, I felt she was trying to monopolize my valuable time; and I said I could not miss class because I would lose my sense of the course's continuity, and there was no reason why I could not read her paper in the breaks during the histology course. She turned away and would not speak to me any more. I thought—she is coming, but she did not come; instead her girl friend came to see me and was at a loss for words; she was probably happy we had quarreled. And my mother told this same friend shortly before she departed that she would rather leave me alone in this desperate condition than ask such a colleague to look out for me. A long time passed before we were again on speaking terms and—"may Heaven forgive me" for suspecting that she made up with me with an eye to the help I could give her with her dissertation.

Now—the lowest common denominator of my two girl friends—was ingratitude. The Jewish girl forgets entirely that she owes her psychiatric knowledge to a large extent—if not completely—to me. She forgets the analyses I undertook with her, the knowledge of the literature she received from me, our discussions of various cases. True, recently I ceased to be so generous with my instruction, since I no longer saw a friend in her, but only a rival who was constantly trying to draw information out of me. Even so, from time to time I opened up with her, because I reproached myself for not wanting to help a person develop and hoarding my wisdom out of vanity. Now she is finally writing her dissertation and giving it to another girl to correct, so that Prof. Bleuler, who knows my style, will not guess I have been helping her. She stresses to me that she is doing her work on her own, and as confirmation she cites the very parts I explained to her. Thus, for instance, I explained to her the signif-

icance of the association of sin with the apple. I reminded her of
the apple in the Bible.[17] She then asked Pat about this point. It
turned out I was right. She gives my explanation as the basis of her
argument. Fortunately I did not tell her *why* I had thought of the
Bible, because then she would go around parading as her own some
ideas that mean much more to me. That business with the apple
was worth clarifying; it simply annoyed me as an indication of her
attitude toward me. Now that is over and done with. I just thought:
my friend, who will be the next to read her dissertation, will certainly not suspect that before she undertook the analysis, she was
instructed by me about a number of matters. He will compare her
analysis with mine, which, to be sure, is much more complicated,
and he will think that mine is nothing special after all, if some
people know how to do analyses straight off, without lengthy prep-
aration. In my imagination I already saw my friend in love with
her, I saw her sitting next to me at psychiatric congresses, she—
proud and contented as wife and mother, I a poor psychopath who
has a host of desires and can realize none of them; renouncing love,
my soul rent with pain. It certainly is a great relief to write a diary.
One gains self-confidence, for I have not yet lost faith in my powers. Secretly my new study, "On the Death Instinct,"[18] is taking
shape within me, although in my first despair I wanted to give up
on it and then . . . the thought of the extent to which my wish for
influence in dementia praecox is justified. So: patience!

The Christian woman to whom I once devoted so much time—
I was forever comforting her in her unhappy love for her girl friend,
forever making peace between the two, whom I called Father and
Mother—this silly goose hates me now. She was always jealous of
the friendship between me and the woman who dominates her.
And now she claims that I tried to separate her from the other
woman, while actually I was the one, and still am, to bring them
together and to rejoice at seeing them together.

As to their later fates: the Jewish girl married a Christian, as I
mentioned, a man whose honest character, selfless loyal love, and
capacity for hard work, along with limited intelligence, remind her
of her present girl friend. The Christian remained single.

As far as music is concerned, the Christian is very musical, even
if only in a certain sentimental vein; the Jewish girl is not exactly

tone deaf, but neither is she particularly musical. She was always
pestering me to play romances; that is the style for her, something
that is actually worlds apart from really beautiful music.

Now—pair No. 4.[19] That is the present masculine pair. The
Christian in it—my friend; he is a doctor, married. Other elements,
such as the strong religious sense and the sense of calling, are
things of which he possesses more than enough, for his father was
a minister! At the time our poetry began,[20] he had two girls, and
the potentiality for a boy within him, which my unconscious fer-
retted out at the appropriate time in "prophetic dreams."[21] He told
me that he loved Jewish women, that he wanted to love a dark
Jewish girl. So in him, too, the urge to remain faithful to his religion and culture, as well as the drive to explore other possibilities
through a new race, the drive to liberate himself from the paternal
edicts through an unbelieving Jewess. His friend is Prof. Freud—a
Jew, old *pater familias*. I do not know whether it is reality or fantasy that Prof. Freud has six children.[22] Here, too, the Christian is
the "son" of the Jew. The latter is older and more independent. But
at the same time my friend is my little son, so that *volens-nolens*
we are married to Prof. Freud. I do not love Freud, because he robbed
me of my most beautiful possession, namely my friend. Now my
friend will perhaps fall in love with Freud's daughter. Why should
I go on torturing myself? What must be will be. The only strange
thing is that I feel not the slightest trace of friendship for Frl. Freud.
She has the advantage of having a father who is widely known. I
have no such advantage and must rely on my own strength, for
which reason I have a much more difficult time of it. But I intend
to cling to my belief that a great destiny awaits me. And now, what
course will events take? I just played the piano. There is so much
fire and so much love in me! *I feel the unshakable conviction:
Siegfried lives, lives, lives!** No one can rob me of that certainty but
my own death. Now, here's what I thought during that critical
night. During the day I had been at a physiological low ebb and
therefore because of Siegfried sought to avoid all excitement. In the
afternoon I wanted to pay a call on a girl whom I do not know well
yet, in order to pass the day as cheerfully as possible and find some

*Underlined in the original (see Introduction, p. xviii).—ED.

respite from the *Weltschmerz* which I am always trying to help my woman colleagues overcome. But things worked out differently. In the morning the Jewish girl from the third pair came to me; for the sake of briefness I shall call her Frl. B. Her first romance was with a Jewish doctor; now she has another and is already in her sixth month. This and the discussions about our work made me very agitated. I was overcome with the fear that I might be useless for life or might even remain infertile. That afternoon I went to see my new acquaintance. Instead of a calming influence I found only wails and complaints. The girl bemoaned the fact that love does not even exist and envied me for still having my sunny belief in it. "The main thing is belief," she said. "If only you believe—you can find everything. I no longer believe." I took this as Fate's way of cheering me up. Oh, I do believe firmly in the existence of love. Haven't I emerged from all my tempests with my beautiful [illegible] view of the world unscathed! I believed in the possibility of a sacred love; to be sure, whether that will last long is the question, but while one loves, one can love with all one's heart: so I went home. Here a colleague was waiting for me, a woman who has been terribly depressed recently. She has given her heart to a doctor from the eye clinic. For her it was the first love. For him? . . . They just went on together, since he did not find her suitable for marriage. And she? . . . She is a girl from a very good family. She withstood him for quite a while. She wanted to leave him and could not. And so things continued until she realized the hopelessness of struggling, and it all happened. For a while her pride was hurt. But on this particular day she was glowing. She was not contented, but happy, and how happy, even though she knew that a separation was inevitable. She spoke of parting from him in love, and I supported her in this, because I saw the same need in her as in myself: to preserve the beautiful moments as they were. She could not liberate herself by dragging her beloved through the mire, as was simplest for Frl. B. Now I was left alone and thought about how beautiful love is when one can surrender entirely to the emotion, when one has a person completely to oneself, even if only for a time; when one can be sure that one's love and happiness do not bring sorrow to anyone, as was always the case with me. No, better to be involved with someone who is not married! And if possible, someone with whom one could establish a settled life. I would give all that is best in me to such a person. We would go hiking outdoors and spend the long winter evenings in our warm, comfortably furnished parlor. In the evening I will sit on the sofa and knit, while he reads to me from his work. We will think and feel in concert. We will try to develop all the noblest and finest qualities in each other. From time to time I may surprise my beloved husband with a little essay I have written on my own, and he will receive it like a dear child. And this esteemed and beloved man will then become the father of my Siegfried. This brave hero, who will rescue me from all the conflicts gnawing at me, who can say to me, "For you I did battle with the raging waves; now I come, brandishing my oars, as victor. You shall be my prize!" (from the poem I composed with my friend after our first poetry). And shall I be able to love him, my savior? And how about my friend? He will remain dear to me, very dear, like a father. I shall introduce him to my husband as my old friend and give him a kiss in my husband's presence. If he is so proud and certain of his power over me that he can do the same toward my friend, I will know how to reward him! He can bask in his victory. But should he grow jealous like an ordinary person, I will always ridicule this weakness in him. But no! He will be above such petty feelings! My friend will also be godfather to my first son. My husband will choose my mother. Such were my golden daydreams. But in crept an evil spirit who hissed: what if all this is just a dream, if you are destined to remain an old maid? I fell into a rage and swore a sacred oath that in that case I would voluntarily renounce this wretched existence, that I would go to my friend, to whom I owe my Siegfried ideal, and would poison myself in his presence with Ken.[23] So . . . I took this oath and soon was overwhelmed with terror. I became obsessed with the thought that perhaps I should poison myself now in order to forestall possible, even probable disappointment. The thought became more and more insistent, and I began to be terrified of myself. I felt as though I were struggling with evil spirits that my friend dispatched in my direction, as if I were struggling with him. That would be a difficult, probably impossible struggle. I can take that step only with his assent. He must give me his blessing.

24 (23) October 1910

Almost 3 in the morning. I cannot sleep. The two of us love each other as much as it is possible to love. If only he were free! But he is not, and given the circumstances, let me record my firm decision: I want to be free of him! I still want to live and be happy. Now I must make a cold compress for my head, since my wild yearning makes me feverish. Dear Lord, I should like to have some peace, at least at night, so that I may gather my forces to begin my new study, "On the Death Instinct"! So "come at last, Reason!" Let me be free at least for a few months, ye dark gods! Oh, Guardian Spirit, let me not come to harm in these storms of emotion. I am absolutely determined now that I want to be free.

9 November 1910

Since yesterday, when I saw him, reason has abandoned me again. Reason! Is there any such thing? Can one even be reasonable when one loves this way? Describe calmly what happened? What he said to me? Yes, the stronger poetry[24] probably occurred a week ago Tuesday. He said then that he loves me because of the remarkable parallelism in our thoughts; sometimes I can predict his thoughts to him; he told me that he loves me for my magnificent, proud character, but he also told me that he would never marry me because he harbors within himself a great philistine who craves narrow limits and the typical Swiss style. He also said that from time to time the thought of changing his fated course occurs to him, that the idea of possessing such a splendid woman as me was certainly almost too tempting, but . . . there is a "but," and this was the philistine within him. I tried not to contradict him. What good would it have done? He has a wife, after all! Now he really must put up some resistance to me. But I am fairly certain he would marry me if he were free, for he is capable of enthusiasm for greatness. I saw that yesterday, which is why savage passion seized hold of me again. I should explain that something foolish happened. He had scheduled the discussion session that follows his lecture for the very day on which Prof. Krönlein was to be buried.[25]

So only one gentleman came, and my friend had to cancel the session in embarrassment. Yesterday he told me about it and also complained to me about how isolated he felt in terms of worldly recognition. And I?—I felt like a mother who only wanted the best for him, and the cleverest advice I could think of was that he ought to use the prestige of his distinguished lineage and his wealth to win people over and obtain his professorship. True, in saying it I was making fun of the philistine in him, but I was severely punished for my suggestion, for my friend took a lofty position and said he would never accept such compromises. He already knows that he will never become a professor, that he also has many enemies and is thrown back on himself, but for that very reason he will remain firm, for true greatness always sprouts in dark corners; in time that which is genuine gains the upper hand. He was so magnificent and strong that I felt myself put to shame; for the manner in which he spoke was the manner in which *I* ought to speak to him in those moments when his courage deserts him. He told me how he had once spoken up for Prof. Freud and dressed down the council members at a meeting. That helped. Oh, I do feel it helped that he spoke to me so spiritedly, with such faith in his work. The previous time he had talked like a peasant, of course in order to show his disdain for the entire cultivated world. That was what he wants. Adieu, my little son! Fare thee well!

26 November 1910

So come once more, companion of my sorrows, for I would certainly not be writing this if my heart were not bleeding again. Yes, now I am about to stand for my examinations; I should like to take the written parts on the 15th or 16th of December and the oral parts on the 16th of January. Soon it will be the eve of the great event, and I will be thinking of my friend's thoughts, which he once solemnly recorded: "Today is a particularly solemn day: the eve of my final examination; I am in a state of calm expectation, my soul afire with suspense." Yes, that was a solemn moment! And I? Is the examination also a solemn moment for me? I must admit that I do not know what I am feeling. For me the examination is really only a necessary evil. My thoughts range far beyond it and . . . the grim "And?" oppresses me. Yes, the first goal I want to reach is that my dissertation may be so good that it will assure me a place in the Psychoanalytic Society.[26] Much more important to me is my second study, "On the Death Instinct," and there I must admit that I greatly fear that my friend, who planned to mention my idea in his article in July, saying that I have rights of priority, may simply borrow the whole development of the idea, because he now wants to refer to it as early as January. Is this another case of unfounded distrust on my part? I wish so fervently that might be so, for my second study will be dedicated to my most esteemed teacher, etc. How could I esteem a person who lied, who stole my ideas, who was not my friend but a petty, scheming rival? And love him? I do love him, after all. My work ought to be permeated with love! I love him and hate him, because he is not mine. It would be unbearable for me to appear a silly goose in his eyes. No, noble, proud, respected by all! I must be worthy of him, and the idea I gave birth to should also appear under my name.

On the one hand it is good that Father has come to stay with me until I take my exams, for his presence puts a brake on my feelings, just the right thing for a "studying machine," but on the other hand it means the end of my freedom, since I have no time for myself, because I have to be with him, and this necessity galls me. Father wants to take me back to Russia, and I do not want to go. My father wearies me with his individualistic, realistic philosophy which would strip away the magic from my grand passions. I don't want to go to Russia! The German language, which I have adopted for my journal, clearly shows that I want to stay as far away from Russia as possible. Yes, I want to be free! Where shall I go? What shall I do with my life? These are all banal questions. For now— work! What do I want now? Always the same thing: to see my friend's love for me aglow once more, yes, that is my unshakably firm wish! Furthermore, I want this love to calm me and strengthen my altruistic, motherly feeling toward him. I cannot say much now. The effect of having my father here is that all my feelings are bottled up inside me. To my woman colleagues my father expressed the view that he has absolutely no objection to an illegitimate relationship. Indeed, he respects a woman who does not fear public opinion and can tolerate isolation. Of course he would not like to see his daughter unhappy, but otherwise he would have no objection to her experiencing such a fate. He talked a good deal on this subject, and my heart grew increasingly heavy, simply because the possibility of "poetry" with my friend still exists, but on the other hand my pride rebels against such thoughts. Why? — Because I cannot be a mere "diversion."

1 November 1910[27]

A new room! What if it might also bring me new happiness?

8 December 1910

Tomorrow I have my first final examination. I have already abreacted all my grand emotions by playing the piano. Today I played all day and thought of Siegfried. I am afraid to think any further, because then I will get a terrible headache.

My whole being is suffused with love. I would like to create something great and good. Help me, Guardian Spirit! Help me, Fate. Show me the noble ideal that I should love, show me my field of action, and I will bear the joys and sorrows obediently. If only this wretched examination ordeal were over! Help me, Fate, in my striving for true love. "Be calm! Perfectly calm!" Come what must, so long as it is beautiful! May my soul be filled with peace now! No fear, no doubts! When my examination is over, I will confess honestly how it all went, and may Fate forgive me if I cheat a little for the sake of a higher goal; everyone else does. I shall simply copy my essay topic for the exam. My friend could not do it. He did take along books, but he could not bring himself to copy. Yes, he was nobler than I shall be in this situation. Here I am not worthy of him. Yes, I am ashamed of myself and that is why I have this ferocious headache. Now I am honestly admitting to my weakness, embarrassing though it is to me, and I promise to overcompensate as much as possible. Forgive me, Gods! Grant me a good night's sleep! I promise faithfully to dedicate my strength to all that is truly good. What still torments me is that I cannot give my father the love he deserves and therefore am partly passive toward him, and partly express my feelings in a negative way, but fundamentally I feel that I have an unusually good, wholly unselfish father, to whom I owe much gratitude. How can I repay him for his concern, his kindness? I shall see what I can do! "Be calm! Perfectly calm!" So come, Sandman,[28] and sing the little girl a little lullaby. Tell her the fairy tale of the hut in the Far North and dispel this grinding anxiety and the unnecessary pangs of conscience. Be off, black terrifying vulture. "Softly, softly, sounds through the room. . . ." Should I slip away with my violin like the little girl giving ground before the triumphant woman? No, I see myself being swept away in the grand ballroom in the arms of my beloved. Who might this beloved be? That I do not know! I am afraid to think of it. Do what you will, Fate. My first goal is to do well on my examination. Especially—plagiarize well! Ugh—for shame! My friend said in parting that I will write an excellent exam because at present I am in league with the devil. May that be true. My friend and I had the tenderest "poetry" last Wednesday. What will come of that? Make something good of it, Fate, and let me love him nobly. A long, ecstatic kiss in parting, my beloved little son! Now—may luck be with me! What a difference between his diary entry and mine on the eve of the final examination, in spite of the colossal similarity between us. How remarkable the difference in the way he, the man, and I, the woman, contemplated the tasks ahead of us! With him the sacredness of his profession occupied the foreground, with me the sacredness of love. Now—to bed!

14 December 1910

Tomorrow—the second written examination. Oh, Guardian Spirit, do not desert me! Each time I become so dizzy that I am afraid I will keel over. Curious dizziness. It means that one is about to do something improper. I know that, but my goal must justify this little swindle. I promise myself this once again and go to bed.

21 December 1910

When will this torture end? I admitted everything to my friend, but he reacted quite differently from the way I had expected; he was happy that I, too, had committed a little swindle and said that he had often done such things in school. He also said that in questions of love I would be honest, in contrast to him, who is dishonest in this realm. Instead of showing me calm love, he fell back into the "Don Juan role," which I find so repellent in him. Although he considers me honest in love, he said I ought to belong to that category of women made not for motherhood but for free love. What should I say? I blush deeply as I recall it. I was profoundly depressed and said many foolish things. Do not let me perish, Guardian Spirit! I want to love someone with all my soul, someone who can return my feeling with all the strength of youth; I want to be a wife and mother, not just a diversion. I want him to see what I am capable of, what I am worth. I want him to love me madly and want to be able to defy him. I want him to see how I am capable of loving and how I can rise above the feeling. But I do want to love someone! Where is the man I could love?

15 January 1911

Wonderful snowy weather! Tomorrow I have my first examination, for I cannot call the previous swindle an examination. After a rather long period of depression I am completely calm again. I want to look Fate hopefully in the eye, for my thoughts are fixed on the good. Many evil spirits may be struggling in my soul, but when I love life unabashedly, the "evil ones" will be bested. What does one mean by "evil ones"? Etc., etc. Let us leave philosophy aside for now. All right, Fate, I entrust myself to you!

19 January 1911

"He is gone, and 'tis good thus."

Good at least that my parents are now happy. "Ah, yes, what will happen now?"

Now, Fate! And this is my final word. I remain defiant, disregarding the dreadful anxiety that robs me of sleep and appetite and drives me crazily from one place to the other. . . . I remain defiant, because I have something noble and great to create and am not made for everyday routine. This is the life-or-death struggle. If there is a God-Father, may he hear me now: no pain is unbearable to me, no sacrifice too great, if only I can fulfill my sacred calling! "He must be a hero"; for it is your will and "the will of my father Wotan." Better death than disgrace. May these words be carved into me like words into a solid gray cliff. Now there is no more fear, because fear is not worthy of a victor; I do not even feel pain any more; I eat, sleep, work, because I am no longer myself, no longer my wish, but unshakable, firm, divine will. Calm superiority reigns in me, I am free of "tension" in the depths of my soul, an indication of the capacity for powerful deeds.

Just as before my final examination, I cry: "Help me, Fate, for my mind is fixed on the good, and my will—is the divine will!
[. . .] could hear, when the apparition vanished. It is very unfortunate, because as the descendant of several generations of religious men I believe in the prophetic powers of my unconscious. One can actually get so close to this "God" that one can speak with Him and learn what He wishes, that is, what is the most useful outlet for the total energy of countless generations, which one calls individuals. So what do you wish, God? Or, stated more correctly: what have you decided in your councils, ye Gods? Reveal to me your final purpose, and may it be done!

If one's little bit of conscious strength meant anything, I ought to be wishing for happiness, and I cannot understand why I am so terribly depressed, as if there were no hope of salvation for me. Could it be because the gods are contending against one another deep within me? Is it a premonition of my end, or is this pain a sacrifice of the sort every great work requires? Will the time come for me, too, when I am undividedly happy? I cannot be condemned to eternal torture?! Now I want to think and speculate as little as possible. I shall attempt to leave myself entirely in the hands of divine might to see whether I do not receive some message.

28 February 1911

Either the gods are too weary and therefore not very productive, or my conscious mind is too critical to take in anything of beauty, but I can hardly believe in the prophetic truth of my last dream. Real prophetic dreams have a glow and leave one in a solemn, lofty mood, but this dream passed like one of many, probably because it emanated from a minor divinity who also had something to say and chose the interval in which the Titans were gathering their forces in silence and therefore would not interrupt his chattering. And this little god collected old, shopworn material and spun his tale. The action takes place in the mental hospital. The building has three (instead of two) floors. The people involved are: Father, Mother, my older brother (who, as has been mentioned, always represents my friend in my dreams), my little brother, and another, analogous child. The little brother comes down with spotted fever. The parents send you and your big brother into the next room to watch over him. You become terrified of contagion and of death and can simply not understand why your parents, who are always so kind, are unwilling to make sacrifices themselves in this case, instead exposing their children to this risk. When the little one needs help, you go in with your brother. You reproach the brother with being very superficial in his diagnosis: why in the world should the little one have spotted fever when he has neither a fever nor a rash? Thereupon your brother shows you that the little boy has a swollen abdomen, as in *Typhus abdominalis,* and also several blue spots on his back. You are still a little suspicious [. . .]

Vienna, 7 January 1912

Vienna! Almost a whole year has passed, and what a difficult period! A reader would ask: "How did it end?" There was no ending, many things happened, and still no conclusion. Away from Zurich and to Montreux on vacation (Chailly sur Clarens), from there—to Munich for art history, and here, where in complete solitude I finished my paper, "Destruction as the Cause of Creation." Because Dr. Jung recommended that I publish the paper elsewhere, it will appear in the *Jahrbuch* after all, but half a year later than necessary. We are friends. My first article was a great success. Now I have actually become a member of the Psychoanalytic Society, on the strength of my dissertation. Prof. Freud, of whom I have become very fond, thinks highly of me and tells everyone about my "magnificent article," and he is also very sweet to me personally. Everything I wished for up to now has come true, with the exception of one thing: where is the man I could love, whom I could make happy as a wife and the mother of our children? Still completely alone.

I have two woman patients whom I am treating free of charge. Both of them are doing well; particularly one (a singer) improved very quickly; she writes me long letters and poems full of my praises. She was born out of wedlock to a count, and her fate touches me deeply [Siegfried]. May all go well with her! What else? During my vacation I was in Rostov for two weeks.[29] I was practically buried under an avalanche of affection, from my parents, Bombuchna, acquaintances, relatives. There I gave a lecture on psychoanalysis. The president thanked me for the "excellent lecture" and asked me to give a few more, but I . . . Dr. D. said I was leaving the next day. Secretary Br. plans to write an article about my lecture in the newspaper of Prias Kr.[30] Everyone loved me and appreciated me, still loves and appreciates me, and I . . . am so lonely! And now—to work! May all go well here for now.

28 January [1912]

Finished the article and sent it off to Jung. What will become of it? I don't want to think gloomy thoughts any more. Now I want to be happy!

17 February [1912]

How did it go? Exactly as with my first article, in fact even worse.

Küssnacht,
5 February 1912

Dear Colleague:

I hereby confirm the receipt of both your manuscripts. With best wishes, Yours sincerely, Dr. Jung."

That is how my friend writes to me. I thought and felt a rush of things. I do not have the strength to report how I answered him. Today there was another unpleasantness. I could take no more. I wrapped my collar protector around my neck and with ecstasy saw myself released from this wretched existence. "Just another . . ."— "No, let's wait a bit," just as it says in my poem. A deep compassion for my parents overcame me; I hesitated, looked into the mirror, and found that the blue-gray woollen scarf suits me well. I thought of how lovingly my mother used to wrap a scarf around my neck to keep me from catching cold, how she raised me to this point, and then . . . her only daughter . . . because of a . . . Oh, because of a man who has smashed my whole life, or perhaps I am lying, because if anyone were around who resembled him and who were mine, I should be madly happy! But of course that is an empty delusion! Sooner or later—I will have to end this miserable existence, and yet I am healthy, strong, intelligent, with a soul capable of flaming love. Isn't that stupid? So should I delay once more the end to this comedy? At the moment I can contemplate suicide without the slightest trace of fear. Last night I dreamed that a girl (obviously my fate) looked at my hand and told me I would marry an older man when I was 27. A prophetic dream! For Dr. Tausk recently looked at my hand and declared solemnly that I would experience something when I was 26 or 27, that my fate would take a new turn. Jung married at 27. So this age is the determining one for me. But how remarkable that Tausk should see this age as decisive for my fate! If Jung is already happily taken care of, his double should whisk himself away—because double happiness is dubious; perhaps I am his tragic negative? Accursed!

Now—work—

22 February [1912]

"God wanted to make him a hero, but the course of events made a fool out of him." A sad sort of god! (Schnitzler—*The Young Medardus*)[31]

A dream a few days ago. I am sliding down a mountain, arrive at a railroad station—whose name I have forgotten (I think it had an "ine" ending). It was like Switzerland. I meet Frl. Aptekmann, a patient of Dr. Jung's, who is going to take her exam soon and is looking very pale. She took her exam shortly after me, and left Zurich. I feel malicious pleasure at the effect of Dr. Jung's treatment on her. I ask her about Dr. J. She says he has already become director. To this I remark with anxiety, indignation, and scorn: no, Prof. Bleuler is the director. "He, Prof. B., is only allowed to go down to the coal cellar now." Prof. Bleuler in my dreams also means Prof. Freud, because I am always confusing the two names. "Coal cellar" seems on the one hand to suggest that poor Prof. B. has been relegated to a miserable and painful little role, but it also has an erotic significance: "No ashes, no coal can burn with such glow / as a secretive love / of which no one must know." Cellar = subterranean grotto = womb, a symbolism I constantly encounter in my patient. Further analysis superfluous. Now Prof. Freud is the one who causes me to glow; if Dr. J. were also the director, his love would leave one cold (Frl. A.).

11 July 1912

On the 14th of June[32] I married Dr. Paul Scheftel. To be continued. Our dreams after a tumultuous night. My dream: I have to pour tea for Father and Mother. First I will pour it into a bottle, then into glasses, but I cannot find a glass, because the glasses are dirty and most of them cracked. I think I found only one glass, but not two, and then I was prevented somehow. Frau Ter-Oganessian (formerly Frl. Bubiguy) with an ugly little girl, and then the child became utterly lovely.

Dream material—yesterday afternoon my husband asked me to pour him a glass of tea quickly before he went to the synagogue for

his father. I planned to do it, jested a bit with him, not realizing
that he was in such a hurry, and he left without having his tea. In
the evening I pretended to be a little baby. Frl. T.-O., as mentioned,
with whom I constantly experience analogies in our erotic fate.
Circumstances surrounding my marriage were the same as hers.
With her—a quarrel with her husband's mother. With me—the
same, because his mother felt slighted by him and left without
seeing him. Now she has a one-year-old girl, Asia.

At night—"Freud" [. . .]

II

LETTERS from
SABINA SPIELREIN
to C. G. JUNG

*Translated from the German by
Krishna Winston*

[. . .] concern us. One speaks as one must, one acts as one must; often one is drawn in, even when enormous complexes stand in the way, and one speaks of desire. Now the other groups come into play, the so-called moral sentiments; they are the most pitiful, because their predestination is suffering, because they are forever embroiled in the most cruel dissension with one another. For morality strives to adapt to what is "advantageous," and how one interprets that shadowy concept is simply a matter of taste.

—"Make someone suffer? Never!" —"Well, isn't what I am striving for a source of suffering to me? Do I even want it for myself? The battle for existence," etc.—"That is called stealing, robbery, ingratitude," etc.—"If you would protect your geese, watch over them well," and all that. . . . Each of the two parties is justified in telling the individual, "You are disgusting, you are self-centered," etc., with individual variations.

Rob the children of their father? That strikes closest to home, because I can never walk roughshod over a child. Do you imagine I received an answer to that? Before I go any further, I want to mention that it never occurs to me to want you for a husband, to steal you from your family. Now: one of our relatives was divorced from her husband when her little girl was already several years old. The father married a second time and had several more children; the mother also remarried and had another daughter. The first girl loved her mother and sister more than anything else in the world, but she also loved her father and for a long time carried his picture around in her bosom, until her mother took it away. She became an opera singer, was very successful, and . . . around this time she made the acquaintance of her brother, and the two young people soon grew to love each other (but not in the sexual sense). She now wanted to see her father, who, it is said, is a well-known doctor in Saint Petersburg, but around this time she got a letter from someone describing the relationship of her father and mother, in which the person said of the mother [. . .]

[*Fragment of an undated letter,
written before 1911*]

[. . .] happy that I did not mail my first letter, which was as harsh as my mood yesterday. Now I have just taken a little walk with the musician; my head is clear, and I want you to feel the same way. My chief purpose is always to cultivate everything glorious in you, and for that to happen, it is of course essential that you love me. The moods in which you are closest to your ideals coincide with your love for me: I am your "first success"; your doubts about your own powers, etc., manifest themselves in resistance to me; when you doubt, you become nothing but a doctor to me. What I want is for you to be great!

My new acquaintance is the son of a tailor; completely on his own he made himself into an artist, and now he wants to devote himself exclusively to composing, so far as circumstances permit. I have not told him anything about myself; but he feels I have so much understanding for art that he cannot fathom why I stick to medicine. My fellow examination candidate, the anthropologist, also felt my true field was art history, not medicine.

With the musician I discussed the Swiss a bit (he comes from Bohemia), then he brought up Goethe and said that Goethe had been enchanted by Switzerland, but not by its inhabitants, who seemed much too rigid to him; the musician thinks the stiffness of the Swiss will relax in the course of a few generations. Blessed he who can believe!

He also told me stories about a number of musicians, among them Haydn, whose father was passionately fond of folk songs, which he played by ear on the zither. I'm just the same; my favorite song is:

> Wand'ring is my greatest pleasure,
> Off I start when e'er I can.
> Should you try to cause me sorrow,
> *Off I'll shake it* like a man.
> Lovely ancient songs I'll sing you,
> Standing in the cold, unfed,
> Plucking strings to serenade you,
> *Know not where I'll rest* my head.
> Many a beauty looks with favor,
> Says she might give me her heart,
> If I only *weren't unworthy*,
> If I played a finer part.
> May the Lord grant you a husband,
> Well equipped with house and farm,
> If we two should come together,
> I fear my singing'd come to harm.[. . .]

[*Probably written during the
first months of 1911*]

Dear friend,

I have just come from Dr. Burger's lecture (art history).[1] He is a person of high intelligence and also of biting wit. There is nothing in this world that he cannot ridicule brilliantly, with the exception of "eternity" and "infinity." He is a thoroughly irresistible, decidedly dangerous character. Today he talked, among other things, about why a small foot can arouse the senses, and how painters know how to exploit this attraction. Yet he is not banal in the slightest; on the contrary, he conveys these suggestive ideas with such fine strokes that one is really moved to exclaim, with Nietzsche,

"Let him who has ears to hear, hear!"[2] Today he analyzed Kaulbach's illustrations to *Reinecke Fuchs*, and wonderfully.[3] The favorite butt of his scorn is philistinism, but he mounts his attacks so cleverly that his listeners never notice that they themselves are being made fun of, and they applaud him with thunderous stomping. For such lectures one definitely needs psychological subtlety, so much so that I found myself thinking at the end: isn't this the person you wanted to recommend me to? Must I wait for the recommendation until my dissertation is finished?[4] Why must I show anyone the dissertation? People will certainly believe I have written one, especially since everyone here is quite accommodating and friendly. Next semester I am going to Vienna,[5] so I would like to ask you to write my recommendation in such a way that it can also be used there, if need be. Or should I go straight to Prof. Freud? Of course I am waiting with impatience for my dissertation, or, if you will, "with admirable patience," because I have no way of knowing what has happened with the conclusion, and yet up to today did not want to betray my concern. But I await your study with no less suspense.[6] I shall tell you soon why that is so.

[Probably written during the early months of 1912]

Dear one,

Receive now the product of our love, the project which is your little son Siegfried.[7] It caused me tremendous difficulty, but nothing was too hard if it was done for Siegfried. If you decide to print this, I shall feel I have fulfilled my duty toward you. Only then shall I be free. This study means far more to me than my life, and that is why I am so fearful. You promised me you would publish it in July, if it is worth anything, of course. And it certainly must be worth something, since so much love and persistence went into it. I sat there many days and nights with Siegfried and worked. Siegfried has an enormous creative thrust, even if he was temporarily consigned to a shadowy existence in the realm of Proserpina. Seif[8] was also very interested in the study. Now I of course await your response with great trepidation, and for that reason you certainly will not make me wait too long, will you? I do not want to disturb your peace and quiet: on the contrary, the dissertation is supposed to add as much as possible to your well-being. I can have someone go over the language for me;[9] the other unevennesses in the presentation are things I will be able to correct, because love for Siegfried will help me. I would be very grateful to you if you would just point out the obscure places to me and perhaps also indicate if I have slighted the work of any scholar.

Generally speaking, the mythological part probably turned out considerably better, because there I was alone with Siegfried, whereas people kept disturbing me while I was working on the first part; then came a passage directed against Siegfried, and after that I could organize my thoughts only very imperfectly.

                                                [*Probably written in 1912*]

Dear one,

Deepest depression, hopelessly lost, and what have you. Probably my unconscious had a premonition of what was to come when, after sending off my dissertation, I was filled with one intense sensation: I do not produce anything worthwhile and have no reason to exist in this world. Then I sat down to Stekel's interpretation of dreams,[10] and listen to what the good man writes ("Life and Dying in the Dream"—a chapter in his book, *The Language of Dreams*, published in 1911): "Where death appears, the life urge can also be found. In the fairy tale about Godfather Death,[11] the doctor asks Death to replace his waning life flame with a new one. What does Death answer? I cannot. One flame must go out before another can be lit!"

From this phenomenon Swoboda derived his law of the preservation of life.[12] There is a balance between life and death, he says, as a result of which the release of sexual cells—for not every sexual act leads to the creation of new life—causes a temporary diminution of life, death in some form and to some extent. He rightly refers to Celsus:[13] "Seminis emissio est partis animae junctura." Thus one can see why coitus so often appears in dreams as dying. Then Stekel analyzes several death dreams. What do you think? Two possibilities remain to me—(1) in a prefatory note I point out that, as was actually the case, my paper was supposed to appear in the previous *Jahrbuch*[14] and had already been delivered to the editors when I learned of Stekel's recent book, *The Language of Dreams*; I had also mentioned my new project in the study on "Dementia praecox."[15] A finished outline of it already existed. I wrote this larger study because Professor Bleuler did not want to acknowledge my ideas,[16] and you above all should know that this paper was projected at a time when I did not yet agree with Freud's theories and wanted to prove to you in letters [. . .]

27 November 1917

Dear Dr. Jung,

I am taking advantage of a slight cold to write, since one does not get around to it otherwise. I read your book a good while ago[17] and would like to discuss several quite unrelated questions with you. This discussion must be spread over a series of letters.

LETTER NO. I   WILL TO POWER OR SEXUAL DRIVE?

You see that I have above all altered the term "drive to power"; this is no quibbling over semantics but a clarification of concepts. Natural history recognizes only two drives, the drive for self-preservation and the drive for preservation of the species. For this reason the "will to power" could of course be as significant for neurotic states as the "repressed infantile wishes of a primarily sexual nature" of which Freud speaks. This we shall soon see. I want to furnish you with a concrete example, something I experienced recently with my little daughter, and then we can discuss it. When she was 3½ the little one came down with influenza and coughed and vomited uncontrollably. I suspected acute poisoning accompanied by bronchitis and therefore sent for the doctor. The little one was very sweet with him, so much so that he promised to take her for a ride in his automobile when she got well. Only once, when she had a high fever, did she cry at the top of her voice when he came, which greatly angered him. The next time he came she was the soul of friendliness and whispered to him, "Je serai gentille! Tu viendras demain!" ["I'll be nice! You'll come tomorrow!"] For several days thereafter he did not come, because she was better.

Then one evening in deepest sleep she suddenly had one of these attacks of incessant coughing, and woke up vomiting. I was already considering the possibility that a neurosis might be involved—but nevertheless sent for the doctor again. He pointed out to me that while he was examining the little one she held perfectly still; he felt a good part of the business was purely nervous in origin. The next morning the little creature said to me, "Quand Molli tousse— alors Maman a peur, le docteur vient et fait toc-toc sur le petit ventre de Molli!" ["When Molli coughs—Mama is scared and the doctor comes and goes tap-tap on Molli's tummy!"] Of course I replied that she was very much mistaken; I now knew that it was no great matter, and so her coughing would at most be tiresome to me; I would simply go away; and she could also not see the doctor until she was well. This brought the conscious process into play, and she kept trying on purpose to make herself cough. This went on for a day, and then the whole thing gradually petered out. There is a prehistory to all this: when she was barely one year old, the child had her first bout with the flu, with severe coughing and vomiting. Once her papa had to get up during the night and give her water by the spoonful. Shortly afterward he left on a business trip, and on the doctor's advice I sent the child to the hospital for observation. Certainly an organic illness was present, but soon thereafter the symptoms intensified; the child would cough for hours, always at night. It should be noted that when this happened I always stayed quietly in the next room. I also asked Prof. Bleuler, and he thought there must be some wish concealed behind the coughing, but with such a tiny creature one could unfortunately find out nothing. What happened later tells us the child hoped that by accentuating the symptoms of her illness she could call her papa and have him near her. At 3½ the "neurosis" makes use of the same symptom complex which brought her her papa when she was one. Now she uses it to lure the father substitute, the doctor. To judge from her own words, she finds the physical contact, the tapping of her little stomach, very pleasurable. She also likes to bare her stomach, and she cries joyfully as she does so, "O, Molli prend des bains de soleil!" ["Oh, Molli is sunbathing!"] She also has a definite streak of "voyeurism": she makes her dolls take sunbaths, too, and she tries to unbutton ladies' blouses. Are these already the beginnings of the sex drive, or something quite different, which in any case displays a marked analogy to the adult sex drive and creates pathways, so to speak, along which the future instinct will develop?—This question cannot be answered and seems unimportant to me, insofar as in both cases we confront primitive forms of an instinct that, in the course of development, will turn out to be the sexual instinct and in neurotics will manifest aberrations corresponding to childhood urges, etc.

Now *Adler* would say that the child wants more power and more protection and therefore produces the symptoms.[18] But I might point out that the "symptomatic action" was closely connected with her father's departure, and that of all the mechanisms at her disposal the child always chooses the one that brought her papa back the last time. It should also be noted that during the previous illness the little one had to lie in bed motionless; she was not allowed to speak or eat, and the only compensation for this most unpleasant situation was that her mother sat there, also silent, by her bed, and that the doctor came once a day. Otherwise no one came. What sort of power does that imply? Wouldn't it be much more logical from the point of view of the drive for self-preservation to give up the vomiting so as to be able to eat everything, including her beloved chocolate? Tranquillity, freedom of movement, play with other children, favorite foods—everything is sacrificed in return for more attention from those whose love one desires. To express my own personal opinion, I would include the instinct for self-preservation in the instinct for the preservation of the species; the need to survive merges imperceptibly with the need to die and be reborn. In its initial stage, the instinct for self-preservation completely coincides with the instinct for preservation of the species, although with very tiny creatures one cannot yet determine whether they love the mother's breast, for example, because it satisfies the need for nourishment, or whether this love is already so emancipated that one loves the breast "physically," for itself, or, what I think most likely, because it satisfies hunger and in addition provides warmth and peace, and for this reason the physical contact becomes pleasurable, which is already the beginning of sexual feeling. And the sense of power? What else is it but the need to attract more attention and love to oneself? And the sense of insufficiency?—One suffers from a sense of inferiority because one feels one has less claim to recognition and love; one cannot survive or procreate; this applies both to the unfulfilled, repressed wishes and to their sublimation products. Freud has often told us that many of our patients would get well—if reality were more on their side. "Flight into illness" is a generally recognized concept, just as, according to Freud, neurotics need their illness and therefore *do not want to relinquish it.* They need it because it is easier to find infantile gratification and, of course, indeed especially, because illness can also bring real advantages. Take, for example, the neuroses displayed by pensioners.[19] The new element you introduce is that a pathological symptom can also point toward a new pathway. This idea has been expressed in this form only by you, as far as I know. Freud did say that a neurotic symptom is at the same time an effort at curing oneself or adapting, but, *if I understand him correctly*— he did not mean to suggest that a symptom reveals new, valuable pathways to us, as you see it. Without its having in any way refuted Freud's position—this would be an *invaluable insight, and I look forward with great eagerness to discussing this and many other matters with you.* Unfortunately this letter is much too long, and I must close.

I would ask you, since it is very important for me, i.e., for my future research, that each time you send back my letter along with your reply. Will you do that?

I can only assure you once more that your new scientific views interest me very much and that for this reason I would like to discuss everything with you in order.

Best wishes!
S. Scheftel

Address: Lausanne, Av. de Solange, Castel Vesta

3 December 1917

FOREWORD

Dear Dr. Jung,

As I reread your letter, I see that I probably did not understand you correctly. Please have the patience, however, to peruse the enclosed letter, which was written earlier, and four additional questions.

1) What do you mean when you speak of "living something symbolically," since you consider the symbol something real?

2) How does one live something symbolically?

3) What good do we derive from a symbolic life?

4) If a symbol tells me, for instance, that I have a "heroic posture"—I know that already, without the symbol. What does analysis of the symbol reveal to me? I have forgotten the fifth question. I will also understand these things far better after receiving a written explanation than from your book,[20] where they are treated fairly laconically, forming part of an inner monologue.

Thanking you in advance,

As ever,
S.S.

Dear Dr. Jung,

For a number of years I was one of your best, if not your best pupil. It is perfectly self-evident that after a period which I needed for developing a new component in myself I should again take an interest in your scientific progress. I intentionally offered you a concrete case because I would like to know (1) whether in this case you consider the Freudian interpretation correct, (2) whether you can apply the Adlerian interpretation here, and if yes—how would you explain this case from the standpoint of the "will to power"? (3) How would you personally interpret this case? If you would not attempt to interpret it without analysis, how would you probe if you had the opportunity, and what, for instance, might emerge in the process? Would it correspond to your view that a child is always an extraverted type, and that children's conflicts always manifest themselves in their emotional life (for the moment I shall leave aside the theories of the emotions)? I derive this from your writings on cultural history, because they speak of the development of the types. . . . In the extravert neurosis probably also points toward a new pathway. It would be valuable for me to know what new pathway is announced by the symptoms appearing in my little daughter.

To come back to Freud: it is very instructive for me that you and Freud accuse each other of the same thing, that is, of applying biological assumptions to psychology. And yet neither of you interprets instinct as something biological. Freud studies chiefly the psychological manifestations of an "instinct," i.e., feelings of pleasure or displeasure which give rise to corresponding wishes. *In this respect* Freud certainly aligns himself with "ego psychology." The dear ego! He assumes sensations of pleasure and displeasure as the source of all psychic occurrences in us, in the case of neuroses the deeply repressed sexual "wishes" (feelings). According to him, we all strive for the pleasurable and suppress everything which is unpleasurable. *Only in the realm of sexuality are we usually not allowed to strive for the pleasurable, indeed, we are not even permitted to admit this striving to ourselves,* because these wishes are very powerful and arouse strong resistance in us. Hence the conflict and the special repression of sexual feelings, or, rather, "wishes." Freud is of course interested in the universal psychic mechanisms, and he demonstrates that the energy that might be expended in gratifying sexual urges harmful to the development of the individual can be set free and "transferred" to higher goals. This he calls "sublimation." *That is why, according to Freud, neither Nietzsche nor Goethe stopped at the stage of repression; rather, they sublimated their baser urges, withdrawing the energy invested in them.* A person cannot be a painter, a musician, a doctor, a mathematician all at once. Freud contented himself with the task of tracing these universal human processes in their normal and pathological manifestations; and in my opinion he solved this task brilliantly (in spite of the conceptual weaknesses and exaggerations). You do agree, do you not?

Now a new question arises: what force pushes us toward sublimation? What force enables us to sacrifice infantile wishes in favor of maturer ones? As an empiricist, Freud does not even touch upon this question in his works. *Adler,* it seems to me, makes an unjustified leap when he simply ignores Freud's observations and sees neurosis as consisting only of conflicts within the will to power. *Your ideas* are decidedly better founded, for they use Freudian principles as a starting point and outline, in *Transformations and Symbols of the Libido,* how in the phylogenesis, too, the original investment of libido was sublimated (domesticated); then you present your own work on the subject. You say that the libido is already domesticated to such a degree, i.e., so firmly attached to various cultural projects, that conflicts can arise at the very heart of these cultural values, just as the suppression of any one of these cultural projects (life tasks) suffices to create a neurosis. Now, if any life task goes unfulfilled, and if its allotted quantum of libido goes unused, this libido regresses to infantile, even phylogenetic ideas, shaping corresponding wishes (which because of the repression have no outlet but in the realm of the unconscious). *Have I understood you correctly? If so—I believe that we have here a very interesting and fruitful insight.*

If you only knew how infinitely many things I had to tell you! But time to close, since otherwise the letter will grow too long. Again I would ask you, as always in this correspondence, to return my letters to you.

Best wishes!
S. Scheftel

4 December 1917

Dear Dr. Jung,

This letter—concerning the translation of your works. You probably know that Herr Medtner wanted to send me the translations for vetting.[21] After which he would look them over and make the corrections. Well, I tried going over one essay, which was very poorly translated, both in style and in content. I worked extremely hard and had to retranslate almost every sentence from scratch; finally I sent *the stuff back to Herr Medtner* (on his request). Now Herr Medtner reproaches me jokingly with being pedantic to the point of insulting him. I am grateful to him for this criticism, but now I have a sneaking suspicion that the other translations are also poor, and that with my pedantry, *which I consider necessary*, I will only find myself constantly in conflict with people. Another crucial point is involved: knowledge of the language and of the scientific terminology are two different matters. When I gave my lectures in Russia,[22] I finally worked up a certain terminology, but if one wants to perform such an important task as translating the works of a scholar, one must at least try to find out what one's predecessors have done, i.e., whether a body of terminology has not already been established; this makes our work considerably easier and brings us closer to accuracy. This does not mean that we cannot correct weaknesses in the existing terminology. I mentioned this to Herr Medtner, but unfortunately neither of us can lay hands on any book on analysis translated into Russian.[23] If we now spontaneously create a Russian terminology on our own, it will probably have many inadequacies, and will also have the disadvantage that readers already accustomed to one terminology will have a more difficult time assimilating material in the new terminology. It is, of course, very unpleasant to do a faulty job, the more so since I approach your works with the same honesty and good will with which you approached my first study. My advice, then, would be— to wait until we have enough literature in Russian and capable translators, even if the translation were considerably delayed as a result. Unnecessary haste and superficiality never produce anything worthwhile, and besides, because of political events in Russia the ground is not ready for scientific matters, so we can take our time. What do you say?

Greetings from
S. Scheftel

[*Fragment*] *15 December 1917*

[. ...] which could have the will to aggression (power). I took refuge in the surgery department, which means that I renounced any aspiration to personal creativity and simply fixed my sights on becoming a competent worker. And then came a totally unexpected reaction, with a force I could never have suspected was present in me. This was the sublimation in musical composition of my desire for self-surrender. As my skill increases—I feel freer, more independent, and I feel that I can once more work scientifically, perhaps with an unprecedented tranquillity and mental sharpness.

After this example I turn to your theory of types.[24] It seems to me that your "introverted type" is the one in which the will to *power prevails*, whereas with the extraverted type the need for *self-surrender is stronger*. This predominance of one inclination or the other—of which we are aware—always constitutes the deciding factor in judging a type. In normal parlance, the emotion that accompanies self-surrender goes by the name of "love"; this emotion is altruistic and therefore displays finer shades of differentiation in regard to one's relations with one's fellow human beings than the emotion one feels when asserting one's *ego* (or the will to power). Therefore the extravert is rightly seen as the "more feeling" person in dealings with others (I always stress that it is only the predominance that is the deciding factor for the conscious conception).

But in my opinion the introverted person certainly also has emotions, but these emotions are *primarily* of a sort different from those of the extravert: while the extravert, who strives for self-surrender, projects his personality onto the Other, and is primarily aware of a sense of participation in the Other's being—the attitude of the introvert must be the opposite of this sort of relationship. I shall not dwell further on this point, since various problems in connection with the genesis and the nature of emotion come into play, problems that have not yet been worked out. I would only call your attention to an inaccuracy that might result in your and Freud's views being conflated and misunderstood. When Freud speaks of "repression," he means something entirely different from what you mean, since you speak of the contrast between repression of emotion and repression of thought in the two types. (1) A *drive* can be *repressed*, likewise a tendency (in the dynamic sense), a "need," or a "wish." But "emotion" is a *product* of consciousness; one can have unconscious "predispositions," "wishes" (adding "as if," i.e., the unconscious acts "as if"), actions, etc., but not *unconscious emotions*. This does not exclude the possibility that emotion can arise out of subconscious motivation. (2) Without going into what I myself consider correct—Freud means by "repression" an active process, as it were, the result of a struggle and a "conviction" handed down by one's internal censorship organ. You, however, use the term "repression" in the sense of suppression, which is the involuntary result of the predominance of one component. In my view, you should retain the term "suppression," for it does not distort the meaning of your explanations and because Freud uses the term "repression" in an entirely different sense, which creates great confusion among the vast majority of readers. (3) *An emotion cannot* be repressed—but it can certainly be suppressed (i.e., prevented from coming into being). (Here again you see the difference in terminology.) Now, how does this occur? Here are two diagrams, illustrating the extra- and the introverted types:

I. Extraverted type

| a | need for self-surrender | a'b |
| c | will to power | d |

subconscious | threshold of consciousness

II. Introverted type

| a | | b = feeling oneself into the object |
| c | | c'd = withdrawing from the object, i.e., objectification |

subconscious | threshold of consciousness

These two diagrams seem perfectly transparent to me. Let us take the introvert, Type II. Line *ab* is the need for self-surrender (immersing oneself in the object). It prevails over line *cd*, i.e., the will to power, specifically by the equivalent of *c'd*. This amount crosses the threshold into consciousness. Line *ab* is held down by line *cc'* and therefore remains in the subconscious. Since now the predominant part is *c'd* = will to power—its appearance on the surface of consciousness is not connected with feelings of "love"; there arises a "thought type" in which an emotion corresponding to line *ab* is suppressed. But this suppressed quantum of emotion remains present in the form of a "predisposition." It could happen with a hitherto introverted person (although this is not the case with everyone) that, as a result of cruel blows of fate or, on the other hand, a happy love experience, his need to be consumed by love (self-surrender) is so greatly intensified that it comes to prevail over the will to power; then we have an extraverted type, and the quantum *ab*, which now occupies the surface of consciousness, creates feelings unique to itself, which up to then were present only as a "predisposition," i.e., more accurately speaking, were not present; when this occurs, the "will to power" in quantum *cd* of the first example is suppressed, probably likewise with corresponding "emotions" (here it is a matter of the terminology employed, which for the time being I shall neither defend nor question).

Have I grasped your theory of types correctly, and have you any objections to the way I interpret this theory?

And now let us return to Freud. As I already mentioned above—Freud examines instinct, not in its separate components, but as a whole. When he speaks of "repressed wishes," he means first sexual pleasure in the narrower sense, and then everything connected with it, i.e., not only the vague need for love (surrender) but also all the selfish urges that could be subsumed under the rubric "will to power." A proof of this: once I brought Freud a piece of analysis which I had already deciphered: the notion (in my dreams) that I could give a lecture as interesting as one by Freud or Jung; but the same symbolism also revealed fulfillment of the wish to create a great Aryan-Semitic hero. Freud not only agreed with this interpretation; he also found the analysis most interesting and profound. *In Freud's writings the multivalence of symbols is often explicitly stressed.* To judge by what I heard from Freud and learned from his writings, I find that Freud's theory already includes what are considered to have been Adler's "innovations," *I mean the idea of the suppressed "will to power." But insofar as Adler disregards the entire Freudian edifice and concerns himself with only one component, the "will to power," he is decidedly narrower and more one-sided* than Freud. In the case of my little daughter, it is only too apparent that the little one would like to have the doctor as a father substitute; her "symptomatic actions" as well as her otherwise lovable behavior toward him, the undisguised joy she manifested when he appeared—all showed that the little one liked him and wanted his love.

You say, taking the Adlerian position as a point of reference: "The child wants to have the doctor with her and arranges her symptoms not for the sake of pleasure but in order to achieve her project." The following objections can be raised: (1) if the child wants something and this wish is to be fulfilled—*the fulfillment of the wish already includes pleasurable feelings;* therefore the child is striving for something pleasurable. (2) The question remains: what end does the child hope to achieve when it wants the doctor to come? Let us assume (in this particular case it is not true) that the child merely wants to prove her power by demonstrating that she is strong enough to lure the doctor to her by means of various stratagems. This would be a poorly sublimated masculine component ("masculine protest") in her. A repressed wish to be great and powerful—could this be something we have heard nothing of in Freudian psychology? Actually *Freud does not restrict himself to this interpretation* and says that a symptom has several determinants and must reveal many other aspects of a person's instinctual life.

Now comes your view of the matter, and here I take another position, insofar as you say something substantially different. Whether the teleological standpoint is correct can be neither contested nor proved, since it is a question of feeling and belief. But this is not the essential issue. *Our subconscious clearly contains warnings, hints, and signals for the direction our future life should take,* and I can unequivocally second Goethe when he says, *"A good man in his dark bewildered course / will not forget the way of righteousness."*[25] I do believe, however, that one cannot sufficiently emphasize that this does not take place in the "unconscious" in Freud's sense but in the "subconscious." In this "side-conscious" the thoughts suppressed in the "sight-conscious" by preconceptions as to the correct direction gather and take shape; at the same time, important problems are solved here, and here ancestral wisdom and ancient symbols are stored.—I could say a great deal to you about this—but will leave it aside for the present. —

In my study "Destruction, etc." I always replaced the expression "unconscious" by "subconscious," or wanted to replace it, without yet realizing, I believe, that Freud means something fundamentally different by "unconscious" from what I meant when I wanted to replace his term "unconscious" by "subconscious." As your pupil, I was used to conceiving of the "unconscious" in your sense of the non-conscious, and only later did I realize that you and Freud meant entirely different things by the expression. A certain "urge," "need," "wish" in us, connected with our deepest, darkest instincts, tries to discharge its pent-up energy in dreams, making use of subconscious imagery to portray its wish as fulfilled. This entire "remolding" of the subconscious (unconscious) thought realm takes place in the preconscious, because the dark, "repressed" wishes as such are not even allowed into the subconscious ("side-conscious"). *If we now analyze a symbol of the preconscious*—we find on the one hand all the repressed wishes of the unconscious, which strike our conscious mind as immoral and intolerable; on the other hand, *if we analyze in the opposite direction,* we find in the side-conscious (subconscious) the profoundly ethical, guiding preoccupations and all the ancestral wisdom of which we are unaware simply because our conscious mind is but a miniscule part of this mighty system of coordinates, that part which we need in a given moment for adjusting to the present. And what is that, the *"present"*? Do you agree with this conception of the unconscious and the subconscious?

Best wishes!
S. Spielrein-Scheftel

20 December 1917

Dear Dr. Jung:

I shall try to explain my mental construct to you. You are acquainted with the hypnagogic phenomena which Silberer first described.[26] I begin with the notion that they constitute the first stage of the subconscious thought process. For his part, Prof. Bleuler asked me whether I ascribed symbol formation to the effects of self-censorship or not. I replied categorically "no," because use of symbols belongs to the very essence of the subconscious (subliminal) thought process. Whenever fatigue, narcosis, or any other form of intoxification weakens "directed" thought—"symbolic" thought sets in. Observation of the hypnagogic phenomena teaches us that the subliminal thought process converts thoughts into symbols, not only visual symbols but also acoustical, dynamic "thought symbols," etc. *The subliminal symbols are universal and more archaic than the corresponding conscious thoughts.* But there is more to the subliminal thought process, as I wish to demonstrate by means of an example: when I am very tired I find myself thinking of various things I plan to do; these musings yield a hypnagogic figure, a polygon, along whose perimeter I "creep" (this image dates back to the year 1904). The polygon took shape when I traced out lines corresponding to directions I might take in my actions. This amounts to symbolic portrayal of a conscious thought process. Now comes a continuation that I did not think out consciously; the polygon changes into a wire mesh; I try to scramble up it, but each time a silent, dark-haired girl seizes me by the feet and drags me down; this section of the dream merges into or follows a part in which I see a beetle that has fallen into a spider's web; I touch it with my finger, and each time it must begin again from scratch or at least is set back considerably in its efforts. When I analyze this, the thought immediately presents itself: "You would like to climb, and the devil seizes you by the feet and drags you down." These are words from something by Gorki.[27] This current of thought (the continuation) did not filter down from the conscious mind to beneath the threshold. It flowed along independently of the conscious mind from the very beginning; *it belonged to the "side-conscious" or the "subconscious,"* if you prefer this term. In this way the subliminal train of thought (the notions) reveals not only our conscious but also our subconscious or side-conscious thoughts. After what has been said, it should be obvious that analysis of the subconscious presents us with the most interesting problems which we must work through in subliminal symbolic language because our directed thought suppresses them. *To prevent misunderstandings,* I emphasize explicitly that it is not only lack of time that causes us to consign many of our "complexes" to the subconscious, but also lethargy, insecurity, etc.—in short, reasons of personal affect. Thus I pushed the complex "music" out of my conscious because it aroused too many tumultuous emotions and I had no real confidence in my ability in this area. Subliminal symbols revealed to me that in my subconscious I was preoccupied with my musical vocation. Now: even though one pushes the above-mentioned sort of complexes out of one's conscious—they are completely *"capable of being raised to consciousness,"* since they are not condemned and banished *like the instincts.* They are not barred from the conscious by any "censorship" in this sense. In contrast, there exist certain organic, brutal urges which so starkly contrast with our conscious ego that one feels "human" precisely because one has finally succeeded in dominating these "wishes" to the point that one sees not a trace of them. This pertains particularly to infantile sexuality, the Oedipus complex. A powerful instinct for self-preservation and personal development resists acknowledgment of these "wishes." This is—what Freud calls "censorship." In normal persons these "wishes" are sublimated, i.e., these animalistic survivals are drained of *most of* their energy, which is transferred to "higher" regions, or at least to normal amorous activity. This takes place under the influence of the "higher needs" in us, which draw off energy like a magnet. Yet the traces of infantile sexuality in us do not entirely vanish; energy is constantly surging back into the old paths, and in the process pleasurable feelings are aroused whose source cannot be allowed to enter our conscious. Any part of the life of the psyche that is born of instinct presents simultaneously a symbolic expression of this instinct, and because the (outgrown) infantile sexual "wishes" in particular are prevented by censorship from speaking the language of consciousness—they likewise employ a subliminal symbolic language. *But even without censorship they would have their subliminal language,* because the conscious is only a "focal point," which can absorb only very little. "Censorship" merely manages to keep these "wishes" *unconscious;* in contrast to those psychic tendencies discussed earlier, a mighty barrier is created between these "thoughts in the depths" and conscious thoughts. Now I would like to portray all this in a diagram. This diagram depicts the following: everything not in the conscious is subconscious. In the cone *abc* the life of the individual psyche broadens into the "collective psyche," the more so the deeper it goes. The unconscious part of the subconscious likewise forms its sphere of influence somewhere below or to the side (hence the two representations), i.e., it sends out impulses which are psychically active and can give rise to images. Just as the "body emotions" described by Scherner[28] are portrayed in the subconscious (hence symbolically)—so, too, these infantile impulses will lead to the formation of symbolic images. A powerful force (censorship), which I depict here as surface *ac,* separates these "psychic contents" somewhere in the subconscious, represses them, and prevents their emerging into consciousness. This area in the subconscious (graphically speaking) is the preconscious. Possibly it is more correct to speak of a censorship zone and to call the "preconscious" the "subconscious." That I have not yet decided. Through

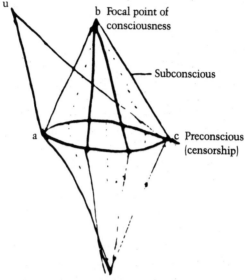

u

b Focal point of
   consciousness

— Subconscious

a   c Preconscious
                                    (censorship)

Unconscious (which is best considered
a special part of the subconscious,
blocked off by the censorship zone)

the processing they undergo in the censorship zone, the offshoots
of the repressed impulses are first given a suitable moral guise;
they receive this simply because they cannot penetrate directly
into the conscious (as an indirect result of censorship). *This is my
view of the matter; it differs from Freud's by the nuance that Freud
does not give consideration to the subconscious as a separate en-
tity.* The subconscious possesses a high degree of moral cultivation,
since it is the repository of the entire history of human development. Thus the subconscious processes the impulse and often
sublimates it by directing its energy (except for small remnants)
toward "higher goals." Analysis of the subconscious reveals this
mechanism to us. I picture *the genesis of the dream symbol* as
follows: several factors are involved, four of which I am familiar
with, and these are: (1) and (2) conscious and unconscious psychic

contents, (3) "body emotions" (see Scherner), (4) *repressed* wishes, i.e., infantile wishes emanating from the unconscious, and other wishes condemned by internal censorship. All these factors contribute to the formation of a specific symbolic image. *Any complete analysis would have to reveal at least these four factors;* in the example with the girl who drags me down, I analyzed the conscious and subconscious thoughts; a Freudian analysis presents no difficulties to the initiate; I no longer remember the "body emotions"—organ sensations—I experienced at the time. One might think that an awkward position of the feet during sleep might help explain the choice of symbolism; of course all sorts of things might be responsible, like heart pains of a purely physiologic nature, for example, which can produce anxiety dreams, etc., etc. The four mentioned symbol-forming factors influence one another, probably on the basis of interlocking innervation. N.B.: the process of symbol formation always occurs in the subconscious. The conscious also employs symbols, for we think in symbolic images, but it rarely generates symbols for a specific purpose; it usually draws on symbols seated in the subconscious, which must therefore have, in addition to their conscious import, an import which is subconscious, "unconscious" in the broadest sense (i.e., including body sensations). To repeat once again: I view as *subconscious everything which does not fall within the scope of the conscious;* one would have to exclude a portion isolated by inner censorship; this is the "unconscious" in Freud's sense. The practical matter of differentiating among the factors revealed by analysis seems to me to offer no major obstacles in most cases: if we are in the territory that the conscious tolerates, among matters of a higher nature, if we are dealing with higher thoughts or emotional conflict—then we are in either the personal or the collective subconscious; but if we encounter hair-raising things that belong to the realm of outgrown instincts or something that seems equally shocking because it appears in an inappropriate context—then we are in the unconscious proper. The range and the power of the unconscious vary from person to person. One cannot say which is "higher" and which "lower," the subconscious or the "unconscious." They are simply different, in a certain sense contradictory, realms. In practice what matters is less the precise classification than one's intuitive understanding of the patient, because practical psychotherapy is a healing *art*. You say that, too, after all. We need scientific findings only for the sense of direction they give us. Now I shall leave the question of emotion and other matters for my next letter. P.S. What does "standard deviation" mean?

With best wishes,
S. Spielrein-Scheftel

Addendum:

The symbols are reversible, i.e., one can as well say, for instance, that the subconscious symbolizes the conscious as vice versa. Take, for example, the idea of a difficult problem in the conscious mind; its parallel image in the subconscious is that of sinking into a dark sea. The accepted explanation is that we view the subconscious image as a symbol—but if we direct our attention to the subliminal realm, i.e., if we view it as "reality"—then all our conscious thought merely constitutes a barely successful attempt at portraying this reality in some symbolic form. Let us consider the same image of sinking into a dark sea from the viewpoint of the subconscious and the "unconscious" (—repressed part of the subconscious); from the vantage point of the "subconscious wishes," this subconscious image is a symbol for the repressed desire to return to the womb (i.e., the "unconscious" employs that particular subconscious image, and transforms it into a "wish fantasy"). From the viewpoint of the nonrepressed subconscious one would have to state the reverse: the dark sea is a symbol of the idea of a difficult problem once it enters the subconscious, and at the same time a symbol for many other, related, ideas in the subconscious; the fantasy of returning to the womb is likewise only a symbol, which also portrays, let us say, a difficult situation or the libido's surging back into infantile channels. From the standpoint of the "organ emotions" one might say that the image of the dark sea, as well as difficulties with a conscious task, are merely an expression and image of some impediment, to the breathing, for example. The notions that occur to one then would be symbolic offshoots of the original symbol. *Where does the right interpretation lie?* Everything depends entirely on what conclusion we wish to derive from an analysis of the subliminal symbol, because the formation and selection of a symbol are clearly influenced by the most varied forces within us.

That is enough for now—

21 December 1917

[...] a symbol is the product of compromise, constellated by processes taking place in the subconscious and the unconscious, which for their part receive elements consisting of remnants of conscious life and subconscious "organic sensations." While the conscious and the unconscious probably have much in common in regard to thinking and also feeling (down to a certain depth) and therefore constitute an uninterrupted range of "consciousness"— the "subconscious" is much more "alien." But more about this next time in connection with the question of emotion.

6 January 1918 (16 January)

Dear Dr. Jung,

Since the holidays, the "Monday morning blues" have set in. "Tant pis!"—otherwise one never starts up again. Your last letter made me happy, because I can see that our thoughts are moving toward each other, and I think we may yet arrive at an understanding.

The terminology I employ for the agencies of consciousness is only a provisional one, and possibly I will find more useful terms after discussing the matter with various personages. I simply wanted to show you what I think, i.e., that *you and Freud* take the same material—let us call it subliminal—and analyze it in opposite directions. You analyze that entire part of the subconscious which approaches consciousness, while Freud descends in the opposite direction, analyzing the "unconscious." You say: *"If censorship is removed, i.e., if repression is analyzed, is there no more unconscious?"* I translate this sentence into the conditional and agree— *then there would be no more unconscious;* but can something that has been "repressed" even be analyzed? Let me show you what I mean by that, so that our discussion does not bog down in terminological difficulties.

Many a neurotic who knows perfectly well that he harbors incestuous desires for his father can nevertheless fall into a fit of hysteria upon seeing his father naked at the washstand. How can that be explained? When he cloaks the phenomenon in the symbolic term "incestuous desires," he apparently bypasses genuine unconscious desires; the unconscious can thus release very little of its energy, and such an insignificant amount can be liberated from the sway of censorship that the sight of the naked father calls forth neurotic actions, indicating the existence of subconscious conflicts. *So what occurs during analysis?*—Let us take an example: a young girl who immediately after her engagement was afflicted with violent neurotic vomiting was freed of this symptom by analysis. She then recognized the connection between her feeling of nausea and infantile incestuous desires, and she was able to eliminate these associations from her new desire to possess her bridegroom. This new desire manifests itself in a variety of ways in her conscious and subconscious mind. Even so, the girl constantly dreams about it in symbolic disguises and often in a completely infantile form. Why should this be? (1) Must anything that actively occupies our consciousness find a subliminal equivalent? (2) Do these psychic contents undergo further processing in the subconscious because the conscious mind can devote only a relatively slight amount of attention to them? These subconscious solutions of problems, along with other problems that they create, are likewise depicted subliminally (i.e., symbolically in dreams). (3) By analyzing the link with incestuous wishes we have liberated some of the psychic contents from repression—to be sure, a very slight portion—and thereby placed segments of the "libido" at the disposal of "higher goals." This liberated quantum of libido sufficed to make the girl able to lead a normal life. But this is not to say that in her desire to possess the bridegroom the girl is no longer repressing anything; on the contrary, a considerable amount is probably still being repressed; it remains linked with infantile desires and will find partial expression in subliminal symbolic disguises. For this reason, insights gained from analysis and contents of the conscious can appear in dreams as symbols for "unconscious desires." When any difficulty arises—for instance, a quarrel with the bridegroom—the earlier symptom can occasionally reappear, in spite of the analysis: the link between the wish to possess the bridegroom and naïve psychic attitudes was still too weak to prevent regression of the libido to infantile desires in the face of a small obstacle. *A relatively complete absence of repression would be possible only with a thoroughly perverse type who could indulge in the most monstrous acts with his parents, etc., without experiencing the slightest inner resistance.* Even here a certain genetically inherited quantum of repression would probably be present, perhaps less the result of "human" inhibitions than of the simple instinct for self-preservation, which of necessity must draw a line somewhere.

Analysis does not aim to completely eliminate all repression. A certain amount of repression is needed, more or less, depending on the strength of the individual's instinctive life, to make him "capable of functioning." Too much can be as harmful as too little. The question of *how much* must be left to the competence of the doctor. Depending on the personality of the patient and more especially that of the doctor, analysis of the "unconscious" can rob the analyzed material of its energy or "saturate it with blood." Probably the neutral attitude on the part of the doctor which Freud recommends is the best one for the average patient, for: if the doctor registers disapproval in the course of the analysis, he increases the patient's resistance and repression; if he displays too much pleasure—he encourages the patient in his self-indulgent tendencies and "saturates his desires with blood." These two extremes are especially risky in an analysis involving a doctor and a patient of different sex.

Now there is a further step, and this would be your method: Freud says one should now leave it to the patient to find a useful application for the newfound energy. You, on the other hand, feel that one should continue the analysis (analysis of the subconscious) in order to reveal to the patient his "higher goals" (vocation). This question can be better resolved from experience than *a priori*. At first sight it seems to me that the Freudian method is better suited to the average patient, whereas yours applies to strong people who are capable of sublimation (here I still have in mind a doctor and a patient of different sex, because as a rule the danger of fixation is greater). In actual practice things never work out the way one decides in theory that they should. Freud certainly does give thought to how his patients can apply their newfound libido after analysis. Freud's pupils are like his children: he shapes them according to his will. Once, when for purely scientific reasons I showed Freud the analysis of one of my "Siegfried dreams," he expressed his pleasure at how successfully I had done the interpretation, and then added: "You could have the child, you know, if you wanted it, but what a waste of your talents, etc." These simple words exerted a tremendous influence on me. If Freud could intervene in my fate this way, when I was not even that close to him, it is certain that he played a much greater part in word and deed in the fate of his patients and supported their sublimation projects. He did not, however, undertake to analyze the subconscious in your sense, i.e., methodically, since when one analyzes the unconscious one involuntarily also analyzes a portion of the subconscious, and vice versa.

Now there arises another important practical consideration: *what is more important for the patient* (if we exclude the harmful side effects of therapy), *to be acquainted with his higher or his lower tendencies?* Simply to be able to answer this, one must trace the genesis of neurotic symbol formation. *Is neurosis a phenomenon occasioned by fixation or by regression?—Both.* One might even say that an unpleasurable experience or failure to fulfill a life goal causes the libido to regress to infantile contents and thereby produces a neurosis; but if one looks more closely one sees that a person actually experiences that toward which he is predisposed by his make-up. There is true profundity in the saying that everyone is the architect of his own fortunes; some people want to be happy and others want to be unhappy, if one takes "wanting" in the metaphysical sense. There are some people who always fall in love with free, youthful individuals and love those who love them; others fall in love with older, married individuals and love only when their love is not returned. For the second category, the predisposition toward conflict is present in their entire attitude toward life, even before a traumatic experience. The same is true for the "higher tendencies." *What, in the last analysis, prevents a normally developed person from fulfilling his life goal?* Fear of life?

Feelings of inadequacy: where do these come from? Why, for instance, did I not begin methodically to sublimate my libido in music more than ten years ago, as I am now doing? In fact my diary is peppered with remarks about "superfluous feelings that were abreacted" in music. It would be obvious to anyone that this was no pose but an expression of a most urgent inner need. The suppressed need found expression in occasional outbursts and with such vehemence that you once told me I might lose my mind if I allowed myself to make music. Thus much time had to pass before I sent you the dream in which I appeared as a painter and wanted to rely on my "unconscious." Without hesitation I then answered my own question as to what I most wanted to do: compose. And I composed, and my teacher was deeply stirred by the freshness and intensity of my songs; I am still working at it and making progress. *Why did this not occur earlier?*—Because I was afraid of life, afraid of thrusting myself forward, afraid of the "demonstration" of my most intimate feelings, which I allowed myself to show only to you, and then in a very awkward manner, sometimes stiff, sometimes excessive. Whence does this attitude toward life come, an attitude that also transmitted itself to my sublimation tendencies?— It comes from fixation of the libido in an infantile attitude. *An infantile attitude toward life creates conflicts, and these result in the regression of the libido, after it has already been sublimated, so that earlier wishes are "saturated with blood" and previously asexual elements are "sexualized" ex post facto.* Now the evil spirit forces its way, in suitable disguise, into the subconscious, where it arranges a compromise with the "higher tendencies." This compromise is the subliminal symbol. At a certain level of consciousness it displays an individual character, and then, the further one progresses, the more archaic it becomes. The contents of the individual *conscious* become transformed into the collective conscious, individual problems appear as age-old problems, etc., and from them individual problems and their solutions again crystallize; sometimes one can trace them all the way up into the conscious.

I need not set forth for you the value of Freudian analysis. You know what this method achieves in the treatment of patients, and you also know what cultural value it possesses if one "understands it correctly." In order to judge properly the practical value of your method, the most important question one must answer is the following: *is everyone's subconscious prospective, such that one needs only a skilled analysis in order to discover a person's "vocation" in life, or does this quality pertain only to certain individuals?* If this prospective quality were a universal human characteristic accessible to a specific method—this method would have to be counted one of the greatest of human discoveries, something of tremendous value for both the mental patient and stable people. This is why I intended to master your method from the practical standpoint as well. You see, simply on the strength of my dream symbols I came to recognize that the long-suppressed demands of my nature had a right to exist. Obviously such a recognition does not come about without an inner struggle; I regard my new activity as a secondary occupation—I am constantly asking myself where this will lead, how much I can hope to accomplish, etc. You know that I am many-sided, you know what you told me in regard to my grasp of psychology; I heard the same message from my instructor when I was studying mathematics; and now I am hearing the same thing from my music teacher. "Too much to choose—too much to lose," since one can hope to achieve excellent training in a given area only by sacrificing other "vocations." I have made a conscious decision that psychology will be my profession. Can I be sure I am not making a mistake? What is the significance of this persisting sense of abundance or libido and of a great, even "sacred" vocation? I live so wrapped up in ideals that I can view with humor all such discomforts of real life as hunger, a temperature as low as 45°F. in my room, or insufficient sleep because of lack of time. At my last lesson both my teacher and I sat there in heavy coats and wrapped in shawls; we both laughed at the situation. Then he played Bach, and I was transported to other regions and forgot all human misery. When it comes time for him to make out a bill, neither of us knows how many hours were involved—that must be left to his wife. That is how I always was, and how I have remained. I see how different I am from "normal" people, which makes me think there "must" be some reason for it. I often wonder: what did my youthful Siegfried symbolism signify if it could not be taken literally? Thus as recently as last spring I considered the clumsy verses composed in my earliest youth still sufficiently pertinent to serve as the words for a melody: "Pastor, make the bells cease ringing, let the village silent lie, answer me the cruel question—my child, it lived—but why, oh why? Did it live that it might die? And if it broke the mother's heart—what good can life receive, please tell me, when pain rends all the world apart? But the bells just keep on ringing, and the secret goes untold. Can you explain, gray-headed wise man, are we just born to turn to mold?"

Well, another woman had the boy, and I had a girl. So all that must be viewed as mere youthful daydreaming. But was it only that? Was it nothing more than "wish fulfillment"? Why, then, all the commotion? Yesterday, too, I asked myself all these questions as I was thinking out this letter to you; and what message did I receive through a dream at night? *The dream went as follows:* Mme Bechtiereff (who lives next door) is going to Russia with her little daughter. At the last moment I get around to asking her to write a postcard to my parents once she gets to Russia. I can write a card just as well from Switzerland, but this way is surer and provides more personal contact. The woman was not especially pleasant when she spoke with me, but it is possible she will do it anyway.

Analysis: Bechtiereff is the classic Russian psychiatrist.[29] Possibly Mme Bechtiereff represents me, since recently I have been thinking intensively about whether I should go home. The association with the little daughter that occurs in the next segment of the dream confirms this assumption. I could be as useful to my country (the parents) in Switzerland as at home, but the personal contact would make a great difference. Will I be able to establish contact with my fellow countrymen (= will Mme Bechtiereff's card be delivered to my parents)? Probably Mme Bechtiereff was not so pleasant to me because I have neglected my duty, but in likelihood I will manage to restore contact after all. The crucial point is that this question, which I often consciously ask myself, is answered by my subconscious with *in likelihood—after all;* furthermore, I am depicted in the dream as an important figure in psychiatry, like Bechtiereff.

Furthermore, I often wonder whether my daughter is strong

enough to withstand the rigors of this uncomfortable journey with its numerous deprivations.

Dream—My little daughter is not strong enough, since she has a rash and besides [illegible] everywhere. I am expecting the doctor at 2 o'clock and would like to discuss it with him. But I am annoyed that someone (my cousin?) arranged for him to come so early, since I was not able to finish the housework. He does not come at 2:00. In the meantime it is no longer the doctor I am expecting but the music teacher. The table is festively set, with four flower arrangements, and the teacher has still not arrived; but I remind myself that he often comes late, that in Russia it is almost customary to arrive an hour late, and he might yet come at 3:00. Then I wake up.

Analysis: While working on my most recent music assignment I ran into technical difficulties, which put me in a gloomy mood. I am impatiently waiting to see what my teacher says and how he extricates himself from this tricky situation. The subconscious identifies the "sick" homework assignment with the sick daughter (N.B.: my daughter is not sick at all; I only fear that she might die during the difficult journey); therefore doctor = teacher. Two—the symbol of married life; four flower arrangements (= four children) point to the fact that I am thinking of my parents' marriage. The teacher does not come at 2:00, i.e., I will not have a marriage like my parents'. It also means something else. I wrote you yesterday, or meant to write it, that I began my composition lessons at least ten years too late. The dream posits 10 = 1, as my dreams often substitute 20 for 2, and says—in Russia it is almost customary to arrive an hour late. In reality my teacher told me it was characteristic of Russian composers that they all began as scholars and only later took up a musical career, after completing their academic studies. That is also how my dream portrays it. *Three* is also a symbol for genesis. Is *genesis* meant directly or symbolically here, i.e., in the form of musical creations? Here, too, the dream answers the question with *That is certainly possible. Have I analyzed the dream correctly?* The curious thing is that the subconscious gives no definitive answer to the question whether I will really accomplish something in one of the two areas. It is like a dialogue between two agencies: in response to doubts raised by the conscious, the subconscious says that one should try it, one should wait and see; it is certainly possible, in the first case even likely. How should one interpret that? Does the subconscious also doubt my talent, or are there difficulties of another sort that get in the way and might possibly prove an obstacle to productivity? *Isn't this simply a case in which a consciously critical attitude toward the world carries over into one's subconscious thought, in the course of which the subconscious seeks for and finds a source of comfort* in the recommendation that I continue working and wait for the success that will probably come? *What do you think?*

Addendum to the dream analysis: Not long ago my teacher was playing me one of his compositions, as he usually does, but this one was botched. He was very depressed about it and doubting his vocation. I responded, "What nonsense! Just let the piece sit for 4–5 weeks, or maybe only a few days—that varies from person to person—and you will immediately see what to do. One should always wait and see and not show anyone one's work in the first flush, before one has had time to acquire critical distance from the act of creation. As far as I can judge: the basic ideas are good, and you will make something of them." I believe that this dream likewise reveals an identification with the teacher through the vehicle of the botched composition, and I tell myself the same thing as, by the way, I have done in a whole series of dreams: "Whatever you do, don't give up hope! Just wait and see!"

Dream and reality: After this dream I had my composing lesson today. The teacher told me the following: "One shouldn't lose courage too quickly. The piece is good. Aside from two little mistakes, I must reproach you for devoting all your attention to one of the voices, with the result that the others serve more as an accompaniment. I would like more polyphony, and that is something you can easily change. Go ahead and work, but don't wait until you are satisfied with your piece, otherwise you will never be back; I am never satisfied with my things, either—"

So now you can examine the prospective value of subconscious thought.

Unfortunately, I have been able to test your new method only in self-analysis, and I have come to believe the following, *while freely admitting that additional experience may instruct me further:* everyone's subconscious is probably prospective to a certain extent. But this should not be understood to mean that it is always prophetic; rather, that it processes certain tendencies in us and reveals to us possibilities and likelihoods that are "in the air," i.e., very close to realization. *Yet the subconscious can also err. The subconscious is suggestible,* i.e., it can be encouraged to seek the solution to a problem in either a "higher" or a "lower" form. This is understandable, if one views the libido as a mobile quantum of sublimatable energy. Thus my subconscious *thinking* and *feeling* were influenced by you to such a degree that I thought to find a solution to the Siegfried problem in the form of a real child. The subconscious was not taken in by this putative possibility for realization and advised me to put up no resistance, since one could only regard this tendency as a "higher" one. The realization of my dream was blocked by the difficulties of everyday life. The "real" Siegfried complex therefore had to be drained of its energy and in order to keep this energy alive, it had to be channelled into another task, that of the "Siegfried" in sublimated form. What this new "Siegfried" is—I do not know. Strange to say, I no longer dream of "Siegfried," and I think this has been the case since I showed Prof. Freud my analysis of the Siegfried dream. No—that is not quite true! He appeared once more in a dream during my pregnancy, when I was in danger of losing my baby. And that is of course why my reborn daughter is called "Renate." Perhaps my many dreams with sun symbolism are—Siegfried dreams?

Possibly the misapprehension in regard to the Siegfried problem can be ascribed to conscious analysis, but I see it differently from the way you do: *in the beginning Siegfried was probably "real" for my subconscious,* which cleverly saw through your own subconscious attitude toward this problem. Later the difficulties of everyday life arose; you, as an adult, experienced person, could see all the ramifications. I was still much too young, and my first love and "vocation" were too sacred to me for me to follow your arguments and give heed to the symbols that the subconscious probably produced to warn me. I can still recall one of these warning symbols. Probably there were many of them.

So you see how I approach the problem: the subconscious can be encouraged to work through a problem in either a real or a sublimated form. Of course it can also warn one against solving the problem in a "real" form; it thereby points one toward the sublimated form. *A person's subconscious approach can, however, be completely altered by conscious processing of a problem or exposure to suggestive influences.* This is how you finally killed off the "real" Siegfried, as you explained it to me (proof that you, too, had a "real" one), i.e., sacrificed him in favor of a sublimated one. I, on the contrary, killed in my dreams the man who was supposed to become Siegfried's father, and then in reality found another man.

Although the subconscious does not reveal to us any specific fate, but only solves problems according to circumstances, or points the way, or gives us encouragement or warnings, etc.— methodological observation of these processes is tremendously valuable and interesting.—

To be continued!

Best wishes,
S. Spielrein-Scheftel

[*In the margin:*]
This letter was originally finished on January 6 and should have been sent off then.

7 January 1918

P.S. I have a certain amount of resistance to having to tell you personal things, but there is no way around it, since, as you know, one learns the most from self-analysis, and besides, I have no other form of analysis at my disposal. *Now I would be very interested to hear what you think of my comments and how you see these matters.*

16 January 1918

I have waited (*10 days!* What a coincidence! Just compare the number symbolism in the dream I analyzed!). I had no idea how many days had passed! I wanted to reread the letter after finishing my music assignment. It is all right. I succeeded with the assignment, and with two other compositions as well. What does all this signify? I am still completely flustered with amazement! Where is all this witchery leading?

[*In the margin:*]
Because of various difficulties, the P.S. was written on 7 January and then the letter lay around for ten days. I mention this because of the symbolic numerological dream. For the second P.S. I wrote 17 January instead of 16 January.[30]

19 January 1918

Dear Dr. Jung,

I shall answer at once and leave aside the whole discussion of emotion, etc., since your last letter completely baffled me. Of course I have read your monograph,[31] even twice, but you make a great mistake in believing that "your" totally new views can be grasped immediately, when some aspects of them have no forerunners in any earlier school of thought. If you believe that I will never be able to understand you—well, in that case any kind of discussion is pointless.

I, too, proceed from a pragmatic position. First I shall repeat your sentence: "Siegfried is a symbol that ceases to be a symbol the moment it is recognized as our specific heroic attitude." You say a symbol is a "bridge." Does this bridge show us anything? Do you mean that the Siegfried fantasy is an expression of my heroic attitude, so that this bridge or expression promptly vanishes when this *attitude* has found an application in real life?

If I have understood you correctly, a second question arises. My heroic attitude *toward the world* was never a secret to me, from earliest childhood on; I would have known it even without analysis. Without your instruction I would have believed, like all laymen, that I was dreaming of Siegfried, since I am always dwelling on heroic fantasies, whether in conscious expressions or in the form of a "heroic psychic attitude." I am, and most especially always was, somewhat mystical in my leanings; I violently resisted the interpretation of Siegfried as a real child, *and on the basis of my mystical tendencies* I would have simply thought that a great and heroic destiny awaited me, that I had to sacrifice myself for the creation of something great. How else could I interpret those dreams in which my father or grandfather blessed me and said, "A great destiny awaits you, my child"?

Something else that is quite important. Does the subconscious give any indication of the arena in which one should live out the "heroic attitude" represented by the symbol?

According to Freud, the Siegfried fantasy is *merely* wish fulfillment. I have always objected to this *merely*. I told myself I was slated for something great, I had to perform a heroic deed: if analysis now reveals that my love for X was not perfectly platonic, as I was convinced it was and wanted it to be—why should I resist and not view it as my heroic deed to sacrifice myself after all for this sacred love and create a hero?

Do you feel that I am guilty of inconsistency because the subconscious showed me another path, using the "bridge" (symbol of the heroic attitude), a path which I mistook, or does my error consist simply in my being too young, too inexperienced, too idealistic, and therefore choosing a form of realization for my "heroic attitude" that was unacceptable in sober, everyday life? *The solution to this problem is extraordinarily important to me, for:* if I had not mistaken my psychic problems and sought a wrong application, simply as a result of my lack of experience with prosaic reality— then the way out I found is the correct one: I realized the "heroic attitude" in two directions, (1) by replacing X by J and (2) in music. I personally believe that I represent the "heroic attitude" in music and the "religious feeling" in science. (By the way, the two flow into each other, so that I am not so sure.)

But if I discover that I missed the path indicated to me by the symbol, I am terribly eager to learn where the right path lies.

You assume that music is only a bridge for me, a mode of expression for great feeling per se. Is my work as a doctor merely a bridge? If not—why is music merely a bridge for me? Your reason for thinking that cannot be simply that I am already "trained" as a doctor and not yet in music? I might have made a mistake in my choice of a profession, and in a few years' time I would also have enough musical training. After all, you are not expert in music, and yet I am convinced you would notice what a tremendous difference in quality there is between the things I used to compose and what I am doing at present. Even now I cannot play my own pieces, but I can transcribe them (approximately, of course), whereas earlier I messed up everything and instinctively created a kind of notation that in effect resembled the notation used in Gregorian times and even earlier. Yesterday I played one of my chorales to a lady with musical training, a singer, without telling her the composer's name. She found the piece very lovely, likewise my counterpoint assignment, which, to be sure, satisfies me less than the chorale, which I, too, like. Where can one find a criterion? Of course I will not become a great composer like Bach, Beethoven, and the like. That I shall leave to those who come after me. My daughter, for instance, is composing constantly, with and without words, melodies which I transcribe and which perfectly echo the style of the old prayers (which she has of course never heard). But will I become a "great figure" in psychology? In dealing with psychological problems, I always have resistance to overcome, stemming from infantile times; with music I experience no such resistance and can give myself to it completely. *Continuation of the dream of the Gothic cathedral. I no longer dream of prison, but of new houses, airy and spacious, surrounded by many green meadows. Once I dreamed that the Gazette de Lausanne* contained the following cartoon in color: in the foreground a German general, forceful, furiously determined, energetic, and behind him the Russian (Kerensky?)[32] with his army, just like Christ, full of idealism and goodness. The Russian soldiers are listening to him, but not one of them stirs. The caption read: *"Why the Russians lost."* I woke up laughing, because the cartoon was really most telling, and said to myself, "Do you know why the Russians lost? Because they believed too much in human goodness and other ideals and therefore dreamed instead of acting."

What is this delightful dream aiming at? Should I try to act rather than dream in my music, or in my work as a doctor? All right. I am ready to become active as a psychotherapist, but where am I to find patients? Would you recommend me if I went to Germany? — Probably not, although you consider me intelligent and also detect a "heroic attitude" and "religious feelings" in me, and thus also consider me a good human being. That's just the way the world is, I guess, and that is why it is so difficult to find a practical path that will lead one out of one's daydreams, other than in musical creations.

What do you say to this?

Best wishes!
S.S.

P.S. I am pleased that I am almost finished with checking over the translations of your works that were sent to me. I would be completely finished if this letter had not held me up.

[Probably written 27–28 January 1918]

Dear Dr. Jung:

It is not only the Jewish people who murdered their prophet; indeed, it seems to be the fate of prophets that they are never recognized in their own country during their lifetime. Now, the whole business of messianism (or Christianity) is quite interesting. If one sees this religion the way it is presented to us in school, it is of course nonsense, and rather harmful nonsense at that. But if we penetrate deeper into the nature of the Christ legend—the question arises: has the Saviour already been on earth, or will he only come at the end of the world, as the "unbelieving" Jews assert, and with perfect justification. Christ is the symbol for the unification of the heavenly with the terrestrial, the transitional stage between man and God, the most complete image of the sublimation process, since we shall achieve the "higher life," "spiritual" salvation, after overcoming all animal and selfish urges in ourselves.

For *humanity* Christ has not yet come, for if all human beings perfectly realized the Christian ideal of complete self-negation (i.e., negation of all animal and selfish drives), it would lead to the extinction of the world. This would be conceivable only as a reaction to some terrible bestiality on earth, and that explains the Jews' prophecy that the Messiah will come after a terrible war, in which the passions are unleashed to such an extent that one cannot continue; only then will a general impetus toward the Divine become possible.

Even if Christ has not yet come in this completely realistic sense, he does live in each of us as a tendency and as a reaction to the base elements inside us. In this respect the Christians are certainly right when they assert that the Messiah awaited by the Jews is already at hand. And thus it is also understandable that everyone who believes in Christ finds salvation once he overcomes his own self and his baser urges.

"The more valuable a person is—the more he can sublimate"; thus you quoted Freud's words to me. In connection with the story of little Anna, you explain that although the little one knows the great secret of how people are made, she prefers to give fanciful explanations which do not correspond to reality. Does this disprove Freud's assertion that all our "higher" intellectual and spiritual urges arise at the cost of suppressed instinctive urges? (a process *Freud calls sublimation*). My little daughter, too, recently arrived at the correct solution to the genesis problem. Here also the result was a colossal increase in her general interest and fantasy life; here also artistic creations, first in the form of the enclosed little dolls and animals, which she cuts out quite on her own, without anyone's showing her how. Why could one not explain this is the Freudian manner: a result of the child's initiation, part of the energy attached to her instincts was stimulated, and since one has a natural resistance to confronting sexual issues—one "sublimates" this newfound energy, i.e., one turns to art and science.

You reproach us Jews, excluding Freud, with viewing our most profound spiritual life as infantile wish fulfillment.

1. In response to that I must first counter that there is hardly another people as prone to seeing mystical and prophetic import everywhere as the Jewish people. Freud's clear analytical and empirical spirit contrasts with that inclination. One person cannot delve into all the problems of the world. It was Freud's accomplishment that he traced the manifestations of instinctive life back into earliest childhood; Freud also showed us how our entire future development depends on these first experiences of childish in-

stinct. Starting with these observations and even his explanations, one can go further and say that instinct is not the primary thing, but sometimes an expression, sometimes a means by which something else is communicated to us via various combinations of the psychic elements in us, etc., etc. The value of every insight is relative; you see that even the Darwinian theories are only relatively important now that we also have access to Mendel's findings.[33]

I do not see why Freud should be thought to denigrate man's higher accomplishments simply because he sees their roots, i.e., the driving force behind them, in suppressed instinctive urgings going back to earliest childhood.

2. And this I consider crucially important: Freud views every pathological symptom and every product of the "unconscious" as a *compromise. According to Freud, it is an attempt at adaptation or cure, i.e., the wish is gratified, but in a form permitted by internal censorship, by means of which the patient, with his otherwise intolerable desires, adjusts to the world's requirements.*

3. You see neurosis *chiefly* as a process of regression. *Freud* sees *chiefly* inhibited development. If one chooses such a general definition, both are clearly right. You say that an unfulfilled life goal leads to neuroses, i.e., to regression. Freud says that as a result of inhibited development a person does not find his mission in life, i.e., *cannot sublimate sufficiently.* Where do you see a contradiction here? Freud also asserts that external circumstances matter a good deal in determining whether an individual becomes healthy and capable of work or is forced back into infantile ways, so to speak.

4. You are now devoting all your attention to the individual's "vocation," which finds expression in subliminal symbols (you call them "semiotic signs"—what does that mean?). Freud does not pay any attention to this, because he believes that it is sufficient to present a patient with the instinct fixations that are making him ill and to submit them to his conscious for processing; this is supposed to call forth a healthy reaction, so that he will now consciously find his life goal. Therefore subliminal symbolism has interest for Freud only as a disguise for instinctive desires: he prefers the patient to complete the process of adjustment by con-

sciously working through the infantile patterns that are making him ill. By contrast, you say that the patient must come to know the subconscious pathways; he must realize that the noblest urges within us choose the language of symbols and seek to reshape the pathological elements in us to serve the higher life goal.

5. *Freud* would never, never argue that the transference to the doctor is not simultaneously an attempt at adjustment. Why should he? Even if the patient transfers all his infantile attitudes (wishes) to the doctor, it is simply obvious that he learns in the process to adjust his infantile attitude to reality. I see absolutely no difference between transference to the doctor and every other sort of transference: in giving one's own personality, one takes on the personality of the Other, whom one loves. Now, then, you are so extraordinarily valuable in my eyes that I should not like to see you become narrowly partisan. It is very possible that Freud will never understand you when you propose innovative theories. In his lifetime Freud has accomplished such extraordinary things, and he has enough to keep him occupied for the rest of his days, simply working out the details of his vast edifice. You, on the other hand, are still capable of growth. You can understand Freud perfectly well if you wish to, i.e., if your personal affect does not get in the way. The Freudian theories were, are, and will remain extraordinarily fruitful. To reproach Freud with one-sidedness seems very unfair to me, since each of us, and particularly one who constructs a mighty world-edifice, at first appears a king; then, when people have had enough and want to free themselves from his sphere of influence, he is denounced as one-sided and distasteful. You should have the courage to recognize Freud in all his grandeur, even if you do not agree with him on every point, even if in the process you might have to credit Freud with many of your own accomplishments. Only then will you be completely free, and only then will you be the greater one. You will be amazed to see how markedly your entire personality and your new theory will gain in objectivity through this process.

As far as I am concerned—I believe wholeheartedly in the prospective and prophetic significance of our subconscious. Yet there is some question as to how far we can function with it, i.e.:

1. Is every person's subconscious prospective? Probably yes. Is it

prospective in everyone to the same degree? That is, is it like a divine formula, let us say, which everyone can read within himself if he only wishes to? Or is it a capacity, like intelligence, for instance, which manifests itself with different force in different people? What do you think?

2. Have we already advanced to the point that we can systematically explore the subconscious in regard to its prospective significance? I will not deny this, just as I readily acknowledge that you have laid a groundwork for this venture whose value cannot yet be measured.

3. At the point to which you have carried our knowledge, can one already determine, in my case, for example, how one should act in a specific situation, or will act—*or is the subconscious to be viewed only as an extension of consciousness, where problems initiated in one's conscious thoughts and emotions are processed further, not with perfect clarity and consistency, but in the usual incomplete human way we are already familiar with from conscious thought?* How do you view this matter?

4. Your idea that a symbol is *always* bipolar—is new and very interesting to me.

5. Now, if a symbol is always bipolar—where does one find a clue as to which side of it points us toward our "vocation"? Sometimes, of course, that is quite easy, since one instantly distinguishes the "common" from the "more elevated." But a sexual problem can often also be a "more elevated" one, since it also forms part of the life goal imposed by God. How should one decide in such a case where the right path lies? My Siegfried problem, for instance, might just as well yield a real child as a symbolic Aryan-Semitic child—for instance, a child that resulted from the union of your and Freud's theories. Do not forget that until I had gone through many, many analyses I never dreamed of [illegible—perhaps "Siegfried"] directly. It was sometimes a candle (light) which you gave me, sometimes a book which grew with colossal speed, sometimes there were dreams containing elements of Wagner's *Siegfried*, sometimes music, sometimes prophetic dreams and prophecies which only yielded "Siegfried" as a real child upon being subjected to analysis. Not until I was in Vienna did I begin to dream of the child directly, and even then not quite directly, since

it was not a child born to us; rather, sometimes I was Siegfried in disguise, sometimes it was an Aryan-Semitic minstrel, Aoles;[34] sometimes a song implied that it was a child born out of wedlock and deserted by its father, whom it resembled down to the slightest feature. Life arranged things in such a way that Siegfried was lived out in another way. *But where, in the course of analysis, does one find support for the assumption that Siegfried is supposed to be not a real but an ideal child? I struggled with this question for years until I succeeded in no longer regarding the symbols of the subconscious from the prospective point of view and attributing to them only the meaning of infantile desires.* The struggle was very difficult for me, and the guilt resulting from my missing my life goal so great that Siegfried almost took my baby daughter's life. *What contradiction exists between Siegfried and my little Renate that the two components found themselves locked in such a bitter struggle within me when little Renate was to be born?*

As you know, I have already written to you that during my pregnancy I almost lost my daughter, simultaneously with or as a result of the appearance of a powerful Siegfried dream. Finally my child proved victorious in reality, and I called her Renate, as another dream instructed me. Siegfried was vanquished. But is he dead? Now hear how it continued. I was working in the surgical clinic, since I had simply had enough of psychoanalysis and wanted to do something useful, even at the cost of my individuality. After I had subjected myself to this discipline for a while—my real nature broke through, and in obedience to a dream I composed my songs. I took them to the conservatory to get my mistakes corrected; on the way I took a wrong turn and unknowingly ended up in another music building, where I first met my future teacher. For many months I was convinced I had been at the conservatory, to such an extent had I shut myself off from the world. Everything went along peacefully until the day I sent you the Pangasian verses to hear what you thought of them. I still knew nothing, but it came about thus: the teacher selected these verses at random from my book, to have me set them to music. I knew that in such matters there was no such thing as chance and that they must have had some connection with him and probably also with me. And the next time I saw him this was confirmed by a slip he made: he read *mon cour-*

age instead of *son courage* (*"Je sais de quels remords son courage est attaint: le lâche craint la mort et c'est tout ce qu'il craint"*). I felt the application to myself and also to you, for I thought that one has never lived an experience in vain and that one has a sort of underlying concept in one's life which in a certain sense always causes one to find analogous elements. I wanted to see whether the subconscious proved more clairvoyant in this respect than the conscious mind, and since I was acquainted with the sensitivity of your subconscious, I sent the verses to you. But the attempt failed, since you put up a certain resistance—probably unbeknownst to yourself. What followed revealed the secret to me in an utterly amazing fashion and showed me how profoundly things in this world are interconnected. . . .

28 January

What happened was too profound and shattering; I cannot yet speak of it. For a long time after the realization I remained as if paralyzed; the realization was that one cannot eliminate a psychic element by killing it. Perhaps I shall tell you someday what I experienced, since it is really amazing, but as yet I cannot do that. I can say no more than that, after long amazement, which completely paralyzed me, I awakened as from a dream with the words "So he is alive after all, her Siegfried!" What is this, and what does it want of me? Thereupon I wrote you, to obtain clarification as to how this "symbol" should be interpreted. Now I am anxious to know the following: since I consider it a "higher achievement" of equal merit to create "Siegfried" as either a physical or a spiritual child, and since as a result of various considerations and decisions he is now becoming a spiritual child—I should like to know whether indications can be found that I view Siegfried as a spiritual child? Does our subconscious give us any clues as to which of two noble contents we should choose, or does it say, for instance, *"It is your lot to create a great Aryan-Semitic hero"* and then leave it to me whether I fulfill this high religious vocation by realizing this great poet, musician, and world savior in the form of a child or in the form of an artistic or a scientific work?

In addition to these two possibilities a third presents itself; perhaps my belief in this vocation to create Siegfried in a real or sublimated form is simply a pathological attempt at self-aggrandizement, a megalomania which permeates all my dreams and fantasies? *Perhaps my subconscious is announcing that I will create Siegfried or must create him merely because I consciously wanted to have him and created these dreams by autosuggestion?* Even if I intellectually accepted this third explanation, my whole being resists it, for reality would be much too barren for me without belief in Siegfried. Could it really be merely "wish fulfillment," my former dream that my grandfather or father blessed me by laying on his hands and pronouncing, "A great fate awaits you, my child"? Siegfried for me = Christ, and yet it is not exactly the same. He arose from the life I shared for years with a German (Aryan). That is why he is correspondingly transformed, and that is also the source of his name, "Siegfried": = Aoles = Balder, etc.[35]

And now one other point: you have frequently seen that I took my musical "inspirations" seriously. The more I work on my musical compositions—the more I am drawn into them, in spite of all opposition and criticism. I am unequivocally making rapid progress, but I have no criterion by which I can properly evaluate my achievements, particularly in relation to how far I will eventually go. How should I behave in this curious situation? Freud would probably say that I am identifying with my child, who was supposed to become a musician—according to this interpretation it would be wish fulfillment. Of course one can also proceed from another position and ask: *why should Siegfried become specifically a poet and a musician?* I could of course interpret "music" symbolically, but what basis would I have for that? For me music is a most intimate and unmediated spiritual need, also an intellectual need, since now that I understand more and more about it, it also gives me high intellectual pleasure. I would say that I always conceived of Siegfried as a musician because this extraordinarily important disposition of mine was the one that was the least lived out. All right: now I am living it out—but is it reasonable? Is it really possible to live out one's different dispositions and life goals unless one does so through 12 children? Thus reason tells me that I should renounce my musical "calling" because I will accomplish more in

my scientific profession. But emotionally I cannot do it; giving up
music would be like ripping out part of my soul, and the wound
would never heal. Is this neurosis? — If yes, why? Or is it not
neurosis? — If not, why not? Why cannot one assume, with Freud,
that I am a "savior or sacrifice" type, one who depicts her desires
in symbols that express complete dissolution of the personality,
like, for instance, all the great heroes who die for their ideals, like
the sun-god Siegfried, like music in particular among all the arts,
which likewise demands total self-surrender?

What do you think of all this?

Many other questions cry out for answers, but that is enough for
now. *Please be so kind as to return the letter to me, since it is one
of the building blocks for my future development and I shall need
it again.*

With best wishes,
S. Spielrein-Scheftel

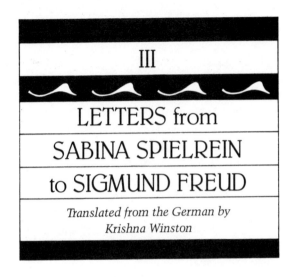

III

LETTERS from
SABINA SPIELREIN
to SIGMUND FREUD

Translated from the German by
Krishna Winston

30 May 1909

Dear Professor Freud:

I would be most grateful to you if you would grant me a brief audience! It has to do with something of greatest importance to me which you would probably be interested to hear about.

If it were possible, I should like to ask that you inform me of a convenient time somewhat in advance, since I am an intern at the hospital here and therefore would have to arrange for someone to substitute for me during my absence.

Perhaps you expect me to be a brazen seeker after fame who plans to bring you some wretched "earth-shaking" scholarly paper or something of the sort.

No, that is not what leads me to you. You, too, have made me feel awkward.

With expressions of my esteem,
Looking forward to your kind reply,
S. Spielrein

Pension Hohenstein, Plattenstrasse 33, Zurich

10 June 1909

Dear Professor Freud:

Please forgive me for disturbing you again: "3 happens to be the divine number."[1] You imagine that I have turned to you so that you may mediate between Dr. Jung and myself? Yes, but there was no quarrel between us! *My dearest wish is that I may part from him in love.* I am analytical enough, know myself well enough, and am sure that for me infatuation *à distance* would be best. Suppressing an emotion will not work for me, for if I do it with Dr. Jung, I will never be able to love anyone else; but on the other hand, if I leave the door open just a crack, a young man will certainly turn up who seems more or less appealing, in whom I might find similarities to my beloved and whom I will finally come to love. I am hesitant to cite a historical example to "Freud," because I may well be prattling nonsense; but I constantly find myself thinking of the relationship between Berne[2] and his beloved. She, after all, was able to love and marry another, and yet she remained tied to Berne all her life, indeed was always with him in spirit. I, on the contrary, would like to part from Dr. Jung completely and go my own way. But I can do that only to the extent that I am free to love him: if I either forgive him everything or murder him. One sentence rings constantly in my ears: "Judith loved Holofernes and had to murder him." Far be it from me, Professor Freud, to bring accusations against Dr. Jung before you! On the contrary: I would be happy if someone could demonstrate to me that he is worthy of love, that he is no scoundrel. For over three months I have analyzed everything, I withdrew into nature to try to save myself and my ideal; finally I spoke with a colleague of mine, or, rather, showed her all the letters, with the result that I felt much lonelier than before, for my beloved could not be saved, and the thought that he might be a complete no-good, that he was using me for his first experiment, etc., etc., drove me absolutely wild; this suspicion sneaks into all my thoughts, it weighs on me like a heavy lid on my head, and if I am on the verge of feeling hopeful about something, I have only to recall a phrase like "wretched no-good," "Let Siegfried fall," or, if you would like to hear more, "A kiss without consequences costs 10 francs,"[3] etc., etc., and my fire is immediately extinguished: "Don't get so heated up! It's no better than all the other filth in this world, even if it sounds so lovely from a distance," "Don't trust Friedel," etc., ad infinitum. So my last hope of salvation was to speak with a person who deeply loves and respects him, who possesses a profound knowledge of human nature, and when I received your last letter, unfavorable though it was to me, tears came to my eyes: "He loves him! What if he could understand all this!" The next-to-last time I went to Dr. Jung's lecture, my friend noticed that Dr. Jung suddenly turned pale. She looked around and saw me standing there, completely white in the face, by the coat rack. I left, since I felt that my "ambitia" might lead me to commit some folly. The next time I sat down opposite him and watched him carefully, to the extent the complex permitted; everything within me was in an uproar. To suffer this disdain at the hands of a person whom one loved more than anything in the world for four, five years, to whom one gave the most beautiful part of one's soul, to whom one sacrificed one's maidenly pride, allowing oneself to be kissed, etc., for the first and perhaps the last time in my life, because when he began my treatment I was nothing but a naïve child . . . I told him no one dared do such a thing to me, etc.

Enough for today, dear Professor Freud, since my duties will summon me at 5:00 tomorrow morning.

11 June

I knew I would be unable to sleep. Now, Wanderer, the moment comes, "you must stay cool and clear." Well: I cannot help complaining of a faithless lover. Hardly anyone in the world believes in faithfulness; instead of the love of one young man, they say, one can win the love of another, or transform the feeling some other way. Four and a half years ago Dr. Jung was my doctor, then he became my friend and finally my "poet," i.e., my beloved. Eventually he came to me and things went as they usually do with "poetry." He preached polygamy; his wife was supposed to have no objection, etc., etc. Now my mother receives an anonymous letter that minces no words, saying she should rescue her daughter, since otherwise she would be ruined by Dr. Jung. The letter could not have been written by one of my friends, since I kept absolutely mum and always lived far away from all the other students. There is reason to suspect his wife. (?) To make a long story short, my mother writes him a moving letter, saying he had saved her daughter and should not undo her now, and begging him not to exceed the bounds of friendship. Thereupon his reply: etc., etc. "I moved from being her doctor to being her friend when I ceased to push my own feelings into the background. I could drop my role as doctor the more easily because I did not feel professionally obligated, for I never charged a fee. This latter clearly establishes the limits imposed upon a doctor. You do understand, of course, that a man and a girl cannot possibly continue indefinitely to have friendly dealings with one another without the likelihood that something more may enter the relationship. For what would restrain the two from drawing the consequences of their love? A *doctor* and his *patient*, on the other hand, can talk of the most intimate matters for as long as they like, and the patient may expect her doctor to give her all the love and concern she requires. But the doctor knows his limits and will never cross them, for he is *paid* for his trouble. That imposes the necessary restraints on him.

"Therefore I would suggest that if you wish me to adhere strictly to my role as doctor, you should pay me a fee as suitable recompense for my trouble. In that way you may be *absolutely certain* that I will respect my duty as a doctor *under all circumstances.*

"As a friend of your daughter, on the other hand, one would have to leave matters to Fate. For no one can prevent two friends from doing as they wish. I hope, my dear and esteemed Madame, that you understand me and realize that these remarks conceal no baseness but only experience and self-knowledge. My fee is 10 francs per consultation.

"I advise you to choose the prosaic solution, since that is the more prudent one and creates no obligations for the future.

"With friendly good wishes,
etc."

How terribly insulting that must have been for my mother, for my parents never in their lives accepted presents, and though my mother did not know that Dr. Jung had the right to accept private patients, she did give him gifts in lieu of money, which were also supposed to express her friendly disposition toward him. Of course the entire matter has become complicated lately (precisely because he has ceased to figure as a doctor in my life).

12 June 1909

Now comes letter No. 2:

etc. . . . "I have always told your daughter that a sexual relationship was out of the question and that my actions were intended to express my feelings of friendship. When this occurred, I happened to be in a very gentle and compassionate mood, and I wanted to give your daughter convincing proof of my trust, my friendship, in order to liberate her inwardly. That turned out to be a grave mistake, which I greatly regret. . . .

"The headaches from which she suffers occur only periodically and are the result of unfulfilled desires which unfortunately cannot be fulfilled by me." etc.—

I cannot bring myself to paraphrase No. 3; I could only show it to you; it is even more insulting *to me* than No. 2, and it contains as a postscript:

"I would ask you to inform *Herr Spielrein*, who also knows me personally, of the contents of this letter."

I still knew nothing of this correspondence, only about the 1st letter, and with a different interpretation. Now suddenly my friend's behavior alters abruptly. First he does not want to come to me, as is certainly proper out of consideration for himself, because his soul is constantly torn between two women, and in the end he would have to flee. "To America?"—"Perhaps also to Africa!" (he called me the Egyptian), and so he allotted me 1 hour per week like all of his female patients. One can imagine how my "ambitia" suffered! Oh, well, no need to go into that. After three times, I think, I went to him. When one thinks that this same person once wrote to me, "Your letter came like a ray of sun amid the clouds," or "How happy I am to know a person with a magnificent spirit," etc., that he gave me his diary to read (I do not wish to dredge up "touching" details), asserting that no one could understand him as I could, that only a short time ago we could sit in speechless ecstasy for hours, that he wept in my presence, etc., etc., and all this had been going on until recently. And now—I arrive in a mood of deep depression, since I have just learned of a tragedy that occurred with a woman patient whom he first led on, then rebuffed; then people talked about other such "feats," and thus it was only natural that I should think he had been toying with me until he received the letter from my mother and took fright. There was not a single person who had anything good to say about him except me, who at that time could have asserted just the opposite. I admitted these thoughts to him. All thoughts vanished. I know only that he gave me a long sermon about all he had done for me and was still doing, that . . . well, what it all added up to is that he is just my doctor again. Yes! He said he thought he had committed a folly; it had not done me good; I want too much now because he was too good to me, etc. Anyone with the slightest insight into another person's soul will have guessed that I completely took leave of my senses. That he should say such a thing to me, who had always been so proud, who had defended myself in letters against every impertinence (one even ran to 40 pages), who had finally simply been forced as a patient to confess my love for him and had warned him countless times against too thorough an analysis, lest the monster get in, since my conscious desires are much too compelling and demand fulfillment. I begged him ever so many times not to provoke my "ambitia" with various probings, because otherwise I would be forced to discover similar complexes in him. Finally, when the inescapable had happened, and when at the very outset I observed anxiety and deep depression in him, I renounced everything; he knows that. His profoundly sensitive soul was more important to me than anything else; from then on I always refused the "consequences." My love for him transcended our affinity, until he could stand it no longer and wanted "poetry." For many reasons I could not and did not want to resist. But when he asked me how I pictured what would happen next (because of the "consequences"), I said that first love has no desires, that I had nothing in mind and did not want to go beyond a kiss, which I could also do without, if need be. And now he claims he was too kind to me, that I want sexual involvement with him because of that, something he, of course, never wanted, etc. You can form a picture. My ideal personage was completely destroyed; I was done for; I thought I wanted to kiss him and had no will to resist, since I no longer respected either him or myself. I stood there with a knife in my left hand and do not know what I intended to do with it; he grabbed my hand, I resisted; I have no idea what happened then. Suddenly he went very pale and clapped his hand to his left temple: "You struck me!" I had no notion of what I had done, found myself sitting in the trolley with my hands over my face and weeping in torrents. I did wonder why people asked me if I were injured, etc. I rushed over to a cluster of my women colleagues, and the first thing I heard was, "Look, you're bleeding!" And sure enough . . . my left hand and forearm were covered with blood. "That's not my blood, that's his: I murdered him!" I babbled, and other such rubbish. After my hand was washed off, I noticed a curious impression of fingernails. I wanted to go to the hospital to Dr. Z.,[4] in order to throw myself at him, since I thought I was hopelessly lost and had only scorn for myself. And I did commit various follies! At night I had severe pains, particularly in my right shoulder joint, and thought for a long while that I was having an attack of rheumatism, until it occurred to me that they might come from the business the day before with Dr. Jung, whom I must have boxed on the ears. Oh, Lord, what a mess! For two days I raged and wept; in between I wrote a letter to Dr. Jung, which he has not yet received, in which I described my state to him. I also realized that we must separate, and could not bear the thought that this had to happen after such a horrible scene. At that time Prof. Freud first appeared to me as an angel of deliverance. I wrote a poem to you.

12 June

"Turrrible headache!" as the Switzis say. Should I continue? At first the letter to you was supposed to be anonymous: "Take heed . . ." etc. That did not work. I left for the lovely Orselina region, to try to get over it with the help of nature. To my surprise, I receive two brief, dry letters from Dr. Jung. In one of them he writes that on Friday (the day of our usual rendezvous) he is leaving town, because

he considers it better for us not to see each other this particular
Friday. "Thus the whole painful business will be more easily laid
to rest." In the intoxicatingly beautiful natural setting the storm in
me soon calmed, so I wrote to Dr. Jung. " 'Ambitia' ? Love occupies
a loftier position! I forgive you, because in spite of everything I love
you. It offers one's 'ambitia' great satisfaction, too, when one can
forgive. Go, enjoy life where you wish, as you wish," etc. etc. As a
precaution I did not mail the letter, since I learned that my mother
was coming soon, and I hoped to find out various things from her.
Unfortunately I must interrupt myself here, in order to go first to
my supervisor and then to Dr. Jung's lecture. Let my love be spread
abroad to all the world. Well. In a frenzy again. I shall send you the
entire original of the famous 3rd letter because I cannot stand to
look it over again. Now my mother comes to call on Dr. Jung,
because he had invited her, as you can see from the letter. (Yes!
Forgotten! The expressions: "She still pours out her disdain for my
character and my views," etc., suggest that the letter was written
on the very day my friend received the box on the ears from me; I
must remark here that I answered it immediately, beginning with
"It is not true, I did not do that," and continuing with "I did not
want that," because, after all, I was completely unaware of it and
was most amazed to hear from him that I had done any such thing.)
My mother wanted to see me first and could not locate me, since I
had intentionally not left behind a precise address in Zurich, and
she was already on her way by the time the telegram with my
address arrived. Now she writes an anxious letter to Dr. Jung and
in reply receives letter No. 4, in which I have underlined a "classic"
passage with blue pencil. Thereupon—my mother writes that she
planned to turn to Prof. Bleuler, but wanted to speak with Dr. Jung
first, and since she has already travelled this far, she can come to
see him if he is anywhere nearby. Then comes the letter I am
sending you numbered 5. I feel one need not be a psychiatrist to
understand why my mother felt deeply offended and wrote that she
did not want to compromise her daughter by coming to see Dr.
Jung during his office hours at Burghölzli. She would like to meet
Dr. Jung at a hotel, like the Baur au Lac. Didn't she have the right
to make such a request? If Dr. Jung did not want to see her, there
had been no need for him to write to her, the mother (!), saying he

wanted to tell her something important about her child, and any decent person should be able to show enough consideration toward a lady, the mother of his friend, to agree to see her. *He answered not a single word!* Noble? After a short while I saw my mother. At first she wanted to conceal the entire correspondence from me, but I remained amazingly calm and asked her about everything. I did not utter a word of reproach toward my mother, because although I viewed her actions as most ill-advised, I found them absolutely understandable from the standpoint of an anxious mother who sees her child in mortal peril.

Interruption. Have to go to the hospital.

13 June

Lamento! I feel so languid and sleepy when I sit down to write, and so happy when it is all done. Yesterday I was able to work better than I have for a long, long time. So . . .

Was reading letters. Yes! I cannot get a single word out, but from all sides all sorts of poems thrust themselves upon me. "Turrrible headache" again. Ah, well. I am really lucky that my parents have reacted so reasonably to these events. I described the manner of our parting to my mother, and she passed it along to my father, who said only, "People have made a god out of him, and he is nothing but an ordinary human being. I am so glad she boxed his ears! I would have done it myself. Just let her do what she thinks necessary: she can take care of herself." I know that even if it had come to consequences my parents would not say anything to me, because the way I choose to live is my own personal affair. I was not ashamed of myself, but now I cannot possibly face my father, because I would find myself thinking: the person I loved so deeply and praised so highly behaves thus and so. He has no compunctions about speaking in such a disgusting fashion about something he only recently called sacred, or about dragging his best friend through the mire before his own eyes and those of her parents. Why? — Out of cowardice, out of self-indulgence. Ugh, how despicable such a personage must seem to anyone else. Just think, Professor Freud, he did give me his entire soul! When he handed me his diary, he said hoarsely, "Only my wife has read this . . . and you!" And Dr. Jung is no hermit; he sees many other women besides me. I stress this point to make it clear I am not one of those women who merely want to have a little affair, with or without "consequences"! For a long time our souls were profoundly akin; for instance, we never discussed Wagner, and then one day I come to him and say that what distinguishes Wagner from previous composers is that his music is profoundly psychological: the moment a certain emotive note occurs, its matching melody appears, and just as the emotive note at first rumbles dimly in the depths when the appropriate situation is evoked, so, too, in Wagner the melody first appears almost unrecognizably among the others, then emerges in full clarity, only to blend and merge with the others later on, etc. Wagner's music is "plastic music." I liked *Das Rheingold* best, I say. Dr. Jung's eyes fill with tears. "I will show you, I am just writing the very same thing." Now he tells me how Freud sometimes moved him to tears when they thought along the same lines this way. He found your face enormously likable, particularly around the ears, etc. That was 1½ or 2 years ago, when there was still no question of a closer erotic relationship between us. He, too, always liked *Rheingold* best.

Such an infinitude of thoughts rushes in on me that I can barely make any headway. Perhaps that will come later. How dreadful it will be for me if my mother intervenes now, takes her little child under her wing, and my friend flees like a wretched coward and pollutes something that was so noble, so clear, and so pure. If only he had come to me, had said that our friendship meant more to him than any stupid gossip, that we should separate until coarse sexual feelings no longer occupied the foreground for him, but that later he would come to see me, that if I wished, he would even come now, that he would have the courage to acknowledge me as his dearest friend, not just in hidden corners and with various subterfuges. What would I do then? I would say he is a person whom I revere like a divinity, from whom I wish to separate in deepest love, lest a moment come that might make a mockery of this impression. Do you suppose I want to warm myself in the glow of Dr. Jung's fame by having him declare me his friend? If so, you would sorely mistake me. During the first period, before I knew how people regard the "insane," I made no secret of the fact that I was a patient at Burghölzli.[5] But I did not tell anyone that I knew Dr. Jung, that I impressed him thus and so; I wanted to love him selflessly. And if I wanted to make such a claim, I could prove it as well, for I possess a letter written on 25 November 1905[6] to Prof. Freud in which Dr. Jung describes me as a "highly intelligent and gifted person of greatest sensitivity." I was still a baby of 19 then, and ran around in very simple dresses and with a long, dangling braid, since I wanted to elevate my soul above my body. That explains why Jung went on, "Her character has a decidedly relentless and unreasonable aspect, and she also lacks any sense of appropriateness and external manners, most of which must, of course, be attributed to Russian peculiarities." How else should the good man have spoken, when I wanted to see him poor rather than rich, since wealth destroys the soul; when I wanted to view everyone as a fine person and of course soon had to recognize that "it's all a swindle, all a comedy, people are all stupid and false," etc. Ability to view the world as an artist would come only with age, with the awakening of the sexual component. Then unreasonableness makes way for "maidenliness." But at that time Dr. Jung also failed to understand a number of things; before my very eyes he has undergone such great intellectual growth; I was in a position to follow his development step by step, and I learned a great deal not only from him but also from observing him. He gave me some work to do on his first paper, "The Reaction-Time Ratio in the Association Experiment." We had numerous discussions about it, and he said, "Minds such as yours help advance science. You must become a psychiatrist." I stress these things again and again so that you may see it was not just the usual doctor-patient relationship that brought us so close together. He was writing the paper while I was still in the mental hospital. At that period I told him once I had dreamed about his wife, who complained to me about him, saying he was so terribly dictatorial and that life with him was difficult. Even then he did not respond to this like a doctor, but sighed and said he had realized earlier that living together was difficult, etc. I spoke of the equality or intellectual independence of woman, whereupon he replied that I was an exception, but his wife was an ordinary woman and accordingly only interested in what interested her husband.

My head—heavy as lead. Two most powerful components are battling within me: on the one hand, my hurt pride demands that I demonstrate to you what I meant to this man—I have many, many letters from him which are clear enough; on the other hand, you see that up to now I have been unable to bring myself to quote you a single letter in which he calls me anything but a friend or says anything sentimental to me. That is too valuable to reveal. "No ashes, no coals / can have such a glow / As a secretive love / of which no one must know."[7] But now I really must quote a passage, since you say you want to hear *altera pars*, too.[8] "Therefore, if one is already married, it is better to engage in this lie only once and do penance for it immediately than to repeat the experiment again and again, lying again and again, disappointing someone." I think that is plain enough—or how about the preceding passage? "When love for a woman awakens within me, the first thing I feel is regret, pity for the poor woman who dreams of eternal faithfulness and other impossibilities and is slated for a rude awakening." You can find his associations in the study by Dr. Binswanger[9] (I immediately recognize the assoc. as his, and of course he did not deny it): child—care—take it. In another place, faithfulness—ruefulness. He told me we had to take care (because of me and himself). Perhaps something else will come along later; for the time being I feel too idiotic and want to get to the end as quickly as possible. My state after learning of the entire correspondence can well be imagined. I told my mother that it definitely went too far, and especially that I cannot tolerate such disrespect for my mother; on the other hand, I could not stand it when first my mother, then my girl friend reviled him, and also could not bear for him to see me so humiliated. I wanted to write to Prof. Freud again, but I was warned against that by a dream in which I portrayed you as willing to listen only to your brother (that is how Dr. Jung is usually symbolized), not to me. I thought of all sorts of revenge, but every time love intervened, saying that he could not be saved by being publicly disgraced, that is, he would be incapable of realizing what he had done, and if until now he has behaved disgustingly only out of cowardice, he would come to suspect all finer feelings and would turn into a scoundrel out of conviction. And so I decided to hold out as long as possible and to appear at his lectures, so that my presence might induce him to think the whole matter over. Not long afterward I learned through acquaintances that Dr. Jung was telling people he had treated a patient for a long time without pay; but now he had been forced to write her mother that she should pay him for his services because this patient was making certain demands on him. An acquaintance of his then asked whether there wasn't a student in the colony claiming to be involved in some sort of affair with Dr. Jung; that was nonsense, Jung said, since she was only his patient; he supposed a doctor really should be cautious about treating patients gratis. He said people talked about his having eight mistresses, etc., while he was really a perfectly harmless person. Now: it is absolutely certain that I told no one anything about Dr. Jung except my girl friend [. . .]

[. . .] For instance, and even if I said something, he could not deny any of it! I am prepared to show you everything I possess in the way of documentation. The person to whom Dr. Jung made his admission (someone else tells me) smiled, of course, saying that Dr. Jung wanted to paint himself as lily white for his wife's benefit; this person saw nothing wrong with sharing the story with his friends and acquaintances, among whom I also number, something Dr. Jung could not have known. And of course I recognized our story at once. Noble?

14 June

"All's well that ends well." A conversation *à distance* is difficult, and since I am dealing with "Freud" [. . .]

20 June

Dear Professor Freud:

Do you see how long I must turn things over in my mind before I resolve to write to you! Yesterday afternoon (this should be part of the anamnesis) I spoke to the "miscreant" himself between 4:30 and 6:00. Yes! If he had more enemies like me, all would be well with him in the world! Two exclamation points should be enough. He promised to write you an honest account of everything. If he were really capable of doing that, if he were capable of being honest with himself, how happy I should be! (3) Ah, but you are a sly one, too, Professor Freud: *"audiatur et altera pars."*[10] The first logical conclusion was that you should have agreed to see me without putting up the slightest resistance. But one likes to spare oneself unpleasant moments. Right? Even the great "Freud" cannot always ignore his own weaknesses. — Well, the necessary corrections and explanations of his and my behavior will be provided for you by *Dr. Jung.* You have, of course, every right to show him my entire correspondence with you. I should only like to add something I forgot to discuss with Dr. Jung. He admitted that he had excused his passion for me by speaking to you of the matter in terms of love for your daughter; I wish to emphasize most strongly that I do not believe Dr. Jung was aware at the time of any evil intention on his own part—that would be too revolting! I incline, rather, to think that he had betrayed himself, that he was looking to you for support, that he wanted your love and therefore in his own defense grasped at the first plausible thing that entered his conscious mind upon hasty reflection, and which also appeared suitable to him in that particular situation because it would be pleasing to you. And now I want my beloved to have the courage to admit that although he did find Frl. Freud attractive, the roots of his love for me must be sought somewhere else entirely. It seems to me that such an admission can only raise him in the estimation of his friend.

My project is coming to an end, and deep depression is taking hold of me. Who is this Prof. Freud to whom I am writing? Can he grasp what it means to a proud soul to be ridiculed this way by her best friend? Who knows what he meant when he said he had transferred his libido from Frl. Freud to me? Perhaps he felt that your daughter occupied a lofty moral position in any case, and I happened to be the first girl with whom he came into closer contact, that in appearance I somewhat resembled this dear girl, etc. One might think I was jealous, but then I would have to be jealous of Frl. S.W.![11] After all, love is always transferred from one object to another, and I can take comfort in thinking that the love for me went deeper. So he ingratiates himself with my beloved Prof. *Freud*, completely forgetting everything, yes, everything there was between us, maybe even now laughing at me because I went to see him and deprived myself of my only weapon by abjuring any desire to harm him and leaving it up to him to speak with you? No, Prof. Freud! No! I will not say it, because it is too emotional. It is important that you realize that I was hostile only toward you, and long before I heard anything about your daughter. In conversation and also in a letter Dr. Jung identifies me with his mother, and I him— with my brother and father (N.B.: two people!). In the course of an analysis it turned out that so-and-so many years ago Dr. Jung had been fond of a dark-haired hysterical girl called S.W., who always described herself as Jewish (but in reality was not). At that time Dr. Jung was not yet married. Now just listen, Prof. Freud, and tell me if this is not interesting: Dr. Jung and I were very good at reading each other's minds. But suddenly he gets terribly worked up, gives me his diary, and says mockingly that I should open it at random, since I am so wise and know how to find my fortune. I open it— and lo and behold! it was the very passage where S.W. appeared to Dr. Jung one night in a white garment. I believe it is the only place in the entire book where he mentions this girl. For revenge he then described this girl in his dissertation; she was supposed to be very pretty and intelligent. This girl was deeply rooted in him, and she was my prototype. It is also significant that right at the beginning of my therapy Dr. Jung let me read his dissertation, in which he described this S.W. Later on he would sometimes turn reflective when I said something to him; such and such a woman had spoken in just this way, etc. And it was always this girl! Now in his fear he has forgotten everything about that; he comes to Freud and looks for an excuse and help. He recalls that Freud's daughter[12] once appealed to him so much, and now the easiest way to obtain the father's favor is to explain the matter as a transference of the affinity with your daughter. You will certainly understand, Professor Freud, that it is completely irrelevant to me whether his love for me is a transference from Frl. S.W. or X. Freud; the latter transference would even be more to my liking, for—flattery is not my sort of thing, and fortunately I cannot very well practice it in this situation anyway, since I do not know your daughter—but it might well be that Prof. Freud's daughter would be the more significant personality, one whom I could replace *psychosexually*, for I believe the letter gives you sufficient evidence of a deep psychic kinship between us; and besides, of course, your daughter is said to be very pretty, which would be especially flattering to me, since I cannot be so bold as to consider myself pretty. And yet I suspect that this interpretation rests on an unconscious nastiness. Why? At the time Dr. Jung met your daughter, we were already such good friends that Dr. Jung could admit to me without further ado that he had met your daughter, who had impressed him as a very pretty and intel-ligent girl. With my acute sense for such things, Frl. Freud did not cause me the slightest jealousy: I was aware that Dr. Jung knew quite a number of intelligent women and would meet others, and I could clearly perceive her psychic kinship with me. The person who stood in my way was Prof. Freud himself. He displayed certain peculiarities of character which I recognized at once, because they are also present in me, completely suppressed, and so I thought that Dr. Jung must be repelled by you, and if you become disgusting to him, I will, too. I even prophesied [. . .] Let him love whom he wishes; I am perhaps most willing to let him have your daughter, since I do not know her and I can imagine her as worthy of his love. But he can never deny that for years a profound psychic affin-ity existed between us, that he was forever exclaiming, "What intelligence!" or other things I do not like to mention, although I would be so happy if I knew he had told you about many of these matters; he cannot deny that he viewed me and his love for me as something sacred; he cannot deny that he assured me many times over that no one could understand him the way I could. . . . I re-ceived a great deal from him, and he from me, so he should not hesitate to acknowledge me as his deeply esteemed friend and ad-mit that in order to obtain the favor of Prof. Freud he portrayed the transference as one from Frl. Freud, when actually it did not origi-nate with her but with Frl. S.W. He should confess honestly that his beloved was always large-spirited and self-respecting in her love (up until the last three weeks, when she suddenly lost her belief in everything noble in the world). After all, didn't Dr. Jung sigh, "I love you for the magnificence of your passion"? (If she had wanted to accept the consequences at the beginning.) Yes, yes, I'll tell you why! After all, my friend has told you a number of things in a distorted light! It was Wagner who planted the demon in my soul with such terrifying clarity. I shall omit the metaphors, since you might laugh at the extravagance of my emotion. The whole world became a melody for me: the earth sang, the lake sang, the trees sang, and every twig on every tree. I feel as if [. . .]

[Around 1909]

[. . .] result was that I wept with awe, that I could not do anything any more, and went into my examination thinking only of my "vocation." I was vanquished and no longer dared to resist. A week ago I went to see Dr. Jung. He receives me with great coolness. It comes out finally that his "ambitia" was hurt because I had taken ages to answer his letter, since I did not want to give him my new address, so as not to be disturbed in my work by emotional upheavals. I told him how my exams had gone, but was deeply depressed that he displayed no pleasure at hearing I was capable of doing good work after all and was now an official candidate for the medical degree. I was ashamed of having believed in any prophecies and told myself: not only does he not love me, I am not even a good acquaintance, whose welfare matters to him. He wanted to show me we were complete strangers to each other, and it is humiliating if I now go to see him. But I decided to go the following Friday, but to act completely professional. The devil whispered other things to me, but I no longer believed them. I sat there waiting in deep depression. Now he arrives, beaming with pleasure, and tells me with strong emotion about Gross,[13] about the great insight he has just received (i.e., about polygamy); he no longer wants to suppress his feeling for me, he admitted that I was his first, dearest woman friend, etc., etc. (his wife of course excepted), and that he wanted to tell me everything about himself. So once more this most curious coincidence that the devil so unexpectedly turned out to be right. Should one praise him or damn him? This immortal saying: "Part of a power that would / Alone work evil, but engenders good."[14] This demonic force, whose very essence is destruction (evil) and at the same time is the creative force, since out of the destruction (of two individuals) a new one arises. That is in fact the sexual drive, which is by nature a destructive drive, an exterminating drive for the individual, and for that reason, in my opinion, must overcome such great resistance in everyone; but to prove this here would take too much of your time.

Time for bed!

*[Fragment of a letter
written around 1909]*

[. . .] may end.

> "Oh, once there was a dream so wondrous strange
> One fine, cool night the Rhine sang long ago
> . . . .
> . . . .
> It sang of a poet
> Black eyes, golden hair . . ."
> etc., etc.

Thus Siegfried came into being; he was supposed to become the greatest genius, because Dr. Jung's image as a descendant of the gods floated before me, and from childhood on I had had a premonition that I was not destined for a mundane life. I felt flooded with energy, all nature spoke directly to me, one song after another took shape in me, one fairy tale after another. Just wait, Professor Freud! When I confessed this complex to Dr. Jung for the first time, he treated me with tenderest friendship, like a father, if you will. He admitted to me that from time to time he, too, had to consider such matters in connection with me (i.e., his affinity with me and the possible consequences), that such wishes are not alien to him, but the world happens to be arranged in such a way, etc., etc. This talk calmed me completely, since my ambitia was not wounded and the thought of his great love made me want to keep him perfectly "pure." You understand what I mean. One time I go to bed with Rauber's *Anatomy*[15] and first quickly write a letter to Dr. Jung; I do not want anything that might deprive me of him as my deeply respected friend, doctor, beloved; I want to be his absolutely unselfish friend, etc. Now I place the letter in Rauber's book and tell myself indignantly, "I don't want to be the robber!"[16] "No," my other component replies, "you won't be the robber, he will!" The next time I go to see Dr. Jung, I am full of the most lovely feelings of friendship, but he is markedly cold and has to leave soon. I feel completely blocked and *for the first time* in years I wait by the meadow, knowing that he will soon pass that way. He did not speak to me, and likewise for the first time I asked him where he was going; usually I had kept myself on such a tight rein in his presence. No, pardon me, I must make a correction. One time I did say to him that I had abreacted everything with him and now I wanted to hear more about him; he admitted to me that he was afraid of that (all this was more than two years ago) because among other things I was lurking in his subconscious, and his affinity with me was to that extent un[. . .][17]

[. . .] is certain insofar as she might easily cross the threshold, something he as a married man cannot very well permit; but one is most constricted when one is speaking of one's own complexes. I respected this honesty on his part so much that I did not question him about anything else that concerned him directly, not even the most minor details!

He told me he was going to the theater, and once more something made me ask what play was being performed. He laughed: "A silly story: *The Rape of the Sabine Women*" (My name is Sabina.) Naturally I was taken aback, and he continued, "The director did not realize there was a people by that name, and in order to make the play sound more appealing, he called it *The Rape of the Sabinettes.*"[18] What a strange coincidence, and that was not the only one. I was able to read Dr. Jung's thoughts both when he was nearby and *à distance*, and he could do the same with me. But I could also do it with my girl friend. One fine day something happened to her that I could not possibly have anticipated, because it was too strange. She calls me up and asks me what I dreamed the night before. I say, "Oh, it was such nonsense that I can't very well tell you," etc. Then she insisted; I told her, and you can picture the impact it had.

Soon I had had enough of these dreams and took a trip to Lake

Maggiore to prepare for my examinations. I finally managed to work, but for many reasons not as well as I had hoped, so I decided to go with my woman colleague to the physiology professor and ask him to register us in the group that would be examined two weeks later. We were supposed to have our examination on 1 May 1908; so the next date would be the 8th and the following one the 16th. Now I dream that we appear before the professor, who of his own accord sets my examination for the 6th and refuses to make any change; what happens with my colleague is unclear. We get back to Zurich. The first familiar face I see is the attendant from the physiology department (N.B.: I did not go to the physiology building; I quite simply met him on the street.) "When is the exam?"—One is on 30 April, I think, the other on 6 May, etc. To be sure, we all considered the rumor false, but basically we were rather afraid that we would in fact be called on 30 April. My woman colleague teased me a little for being a prophet yet again, and I explained cautiously that all the dreams that had appeared to me with such clarity had up to now come true. So we go to the prof. [. . .][19]

[. . .] that I am to be examined on 6 May. How my colleague fared I unfortunately no longer remember exactly. I only know that she was in another group, I believe . . . no, I don't know! I was so deeply shaken by this curious coincidence that at first I did not dare say anything. Then I grew calmer and decided to postpone the examination after all; I was already at his door when I learned that the examination could not be postponed because no date had yet been set for the anatomy exam. Well, if this demonic force in me is right, my final anatomy exam will have to fall on Friday, the 8th, because this day of the week was always significant in our family: Mother was engaged on a Friday, married on a Friday; I was born—on a Friday; my brother was engaged on a Friday; the only time I had free for going to see Dr. Jung was on Friday. I thought further that as a sign that my boy child would become a great musician I should go into the exam and be assigned the cerebellum, which possibly contains the rhythmic center. The exam was set for 8 May. Now I ask a gentleman, "What shall I have to analyze?" He thinks for a bit—"The brain." Then he looks at me and adds, "Cerebellum."

We get to the examination and ask the attendant what specimens have been set up; he mentions several, among them the cerebellum. Now I was absolutely certain that would be my assignment, and told the others. Then we had to draw lots. I draw No. 6, and since I am sure that it will be the cerebellum, I tell the professor, when he asks what number I have, "It might also be a 9." But he replied that it was a 6, since the dot was down below. I go to my position. Right! Cerebellum! The examination went well, except that negativism continued to assert itself in a curious way. So, for instance, I described quite correctly the path of the *Arteria vertebralis*, but I insisted on calling the 7th vertebra the 1st, and so for a long while could not understand why the prof. looked so puzzled; finally he found the key and of course had to laugh. I am not certain, but as I recall, I stubbornly resisted recognizing the *Arteria andortiva* among the innumerable branchings. Odd things happened in the part of the exam in which I had to use the microscope, too, but I do not wish to trouble you further with them. I am telling you all this in such detail because it seems so unbelievable, and yet you can ask Dr. Jung whether I have not recounted things that actually existed. My colleagues were witnesses to everything. The impact these miracles had on me [. . .]

[. . .] we left the hospital. The two who were waiting outside for us followed us, laughing loudly. So I was saved! But what the attendant and Dr. Lutz[20] thought of the matter may be known only to posterity. Now my first thought was: this matter must be put to rest; and the next morning Dr. Lutz received the following letter from me: "Dear Dr. Lutz: I am sorry not to have seen you yesterday evening. I had something urgent to tell you, and some *Gugeli*[21] to give you; the attendant was looking at me so suspiciously that I felt uneasy and left in a hurry, but I could not resist and ate up your *Gugeli*. Now I am sending you the small portion that was left over. With cordial greetings, Your Hanna Wrut*
P.S. Unfortunately I also had to eat up the rest."
(or something like that)

*"Wrut" means in Russian—"They are lying"—

Today I had to have my card checked by Dr. Lutz. I was the last one of a small group. He reads off my name, which is written clearly enough as Spielrein, and he asks me twice, "Are you called Spiele-rein or Spielerei?" Whether it was a coincidence or an allusion—I do not know. With the straightest face in the world I replied, "Spie-lerein,"[22] and truly I said it without the slightest evil intent, but quite involuntarily, because my attention was blurred by the colos-sal effort I had to make to keep from bursting out laughing. Not until [. . .]

1914[23]

[. . .] Otherwise I do not despise him at all, but I deplored his behavior toward you, Professer Freud, and his attitude toward the Society—yes, if you will, resented them. I could forgive J.'s attitude toward our Society even less than that business with me. I saw him only once after my marriage, but, then, I am not the father but the sister. In spite of all his wavering, I like J. and would like to lead him back into our fold. You, Professor Freud, and he have not the faintest idea that you belong together far more than anyone might suspect. This pious hope is certainly no treachery to our Society! Everyone knows that I declare myself an adherent to the Freudian Society, and J. cannot forgive me for this. Nothing to be done!

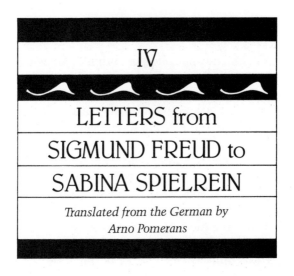

IV

LETTERS from
SIGMUND FREUD to
SABINA SPIELREIN

Translated from the German by
Arno Pomerans

4 June 1909,
Vienna, IX. Berggasse 19.

Dear colleague,[1]

You have put me in a predicament. I cannot possibly ask you to travel to Vienna on a matter that, as you put it in your letter, concerns me very personally.

Indeed, I cannot even guess what this matter may be, and how you were led into offering to make this sacrifice. For the present, I would therefore ask you to let me know in writing what it is all about, so that I may form my own opinion of the expediency of your journey, and possibly reflect a little on the matter beforehand.

Yours faithfully,
Freud.

8 June 1909,
Vienna, IX. Berggasse 19.

Dear colleague,

Your remarks make it clear that I had completely misunderstood your letter. All the same, I am glad that I asked you for a preliminary intimation of what was bringing you to Vienna, for now I can

113

tell you unhesitatingly what my attitude would be to the subject that so concerns you.

Dr. Jung is my friend and colleague; I think I know him in other respects as well, and have reason to believe that he is incapable of frivolous or ignoble behavior. I am reluctant to set myself up as judge in matters that affect him intimately; I do not feel competent to do so, and if I were compelled, I should not be able to ignore the old legal dictum: *audiatur et altera pars.*

Nor do I think that you would wish me to act less judiciously. From the enclosures you sent with your letter, I rather gather that you used to be close friends, and it is not difficult to infer from the present situation that this is no longer so. Did that friendship perhaps arise from some medical consultation, and did his readiness to help a person in mental distress perhaps kindle your sympathy? I am tempted to think so, for I know of many similar instances. But I know nothing of how and through whose fault it came to grief, and do not want to pass judgment on that. Still, if on the basis of the above assumptions I might be permitted to address a word to you, then I would urge you to ask yourself whether the feelings that have outlived this close relationship are not best suppressed and eradicated, from your own psyche I mean, and without external intervention and the involvement of third persons.[2]

Should these remarks be inappropriate, then I would beg you not to take them amiss.

Yours faithfully,
Freud.

P.S. I am returning the indiscreet enclosure and can only say that I do not hold the somewhat gushing effusion against the young man, although as his senior I have to smile at such appraisals.

24 June 1909,
Vienna, IX. Berggasse 19.

Dear colleague,

I have today learned something from Dr. Jung[3] himself about the subject of your proposed visit to me, and now see that I had divined some matters correctly but that I had construed others wrongly and to your disadvantage. I must ask your forgiveness on this latter count. However, the fact that I was wrong and that the lapse has to be blamed on the man and not the woman, as my young friend himself admits, satisfies my need to hold women in high regard. Please accept this expression of my entire sympathy for the dignified way in which you have resolved the conflict.

Yours faithfully,
Freud.

27 October 1911,
Vienna, IX. Berggasse 19.

Dear Frau Doktor,

As a woman you have the prerogative of observing things more accurately and of assessing emotions more closely than others.

It is therefore most pleasant that you should wish to smooth out wrinkles and folds with a soft hand, as it were. True, I am often hurt by my inability to raise the level of personal conduct and mutual understanding among our members to that which I would like to foster among psychoanalysts. Our last evening was not exactly a glorious one.[4] But I am not always as humorless as I must have appeared on that particular occasion. For the rest, I fully approve your attitude and look confidently to the future. I have been doing that, after all, for many years and under much more difficult circumstances.

I am grateful for your friendly words and hope that you will feel quite at home in our circle.

With cordial greetings,
Freud.

14 June 1912,
Vienna, IX. Berggasse 19.

Dear Frau Doktor,

Your blonde patient called on me the day before yesterday to assure me of your well-being and to thank me for recommending a doctor. I, too, was very gratified.

I shall be in Vienna until 13 July, but will then be taking a break until 1 October. If all your compatriot wants is a consultation with me and referral elsewhere for treatment she is welcome to call. But, as you know, at the age of 51 it is no longer possible to master a long-standing compulsive neurosis. Some amelioration is the most that can be expected. Hence I would not hold this case up before your compatriots as a test of the powers of psychoanalysis.

Everything you write about yourself is of interest to me, even if some of it is not new. Since our conversation on the subject I have come to share your views of the priority problem. The germ of this idea may certainly be found in our earlier work. Indeed, if one wants to be precise, the clear expression of the same idea may be found in Abraham's[5] "Dream and Myth,"[6] p. 70. Jung must have forgotten this passage when he dictated the words in question to you, and so did I when I wrote that note in *Imago*. Elsewhere, I shall have to amend my praises of Jung in your and A's favor. On the whole, however, this priority question is not very important.

I look forward as October approaches to receiving your decision about coming to Vienna in order to break your dependence on Jung. I am most grateful for your clever words to Jung; there is no lack of others who are at pains to widen these chinks into a breach.

With cordial greetings and best wishes for your work,

Yours sincerely,
Freud.

Karersee, 20,
August 1912

Dear Frau Doktor,

Your letter would have been a great surprise had I not spoken to Dr. Jekels a few days before leaving Karlsbad, and been told the great news.[7] So you are a married woman now, and as far as I am concerned that means that you are half cured of your neurotic dependence on Jung. Otherwise you would not have decided to get married. The other half still remains; the question is what is to be done about that.

My wish is for you to be cured completely. I must confess, after the event, that your fantasy about the birth of the Saviour to a mixed union did not appeal to me at all. The Lord, in that anti-Semitic period, had him born from the superior Jewish race. But I know these are my prejudices.

We had agreed that you would let me know before 1 Oct. whether you still intend to drive out the tyrant by psychoanalysis with me. Today I would like to put in a word or two about that decision. I imagine that the man of whom you say so many nice things has rights as well. These would be badly prejudiced by treatment so soon after your marriage. Let him first try to see how far he can tie you to himself and make you forget the old dreams. Only what remnant he fails to clear up belongs properly to psychoanalysis. Meanwhile, it might happen that someone else will turn up who will have more rights than both the old and the new man put together. At this stage, it is best for analysis to take a back seat.

I shall always take the keenest interest in your life and your plans. Practical advice, of the kind you seem to want, I do not have at the moment. One day, though, I may be able to suggest a suitable person for your proposed institute.

I am confident that you will not forsake our cause, but will make a valuable addition to it.

I cordially greet you and the partner of your days.

Yours sincerely,
Freud.

*13 October 1912,
Vienna, IX. Berggasse 19.*

Dear Frau Doktor,

The enclosed is what you asked for. I cannot tell whether it meets your requirements, but you will no doubt let me know. I may well be referring patients to you. The supply from abroad, though fitful, is quite enough for me. It would please me very much if you were to associate yourself more closely with Abraham. There is much to be learned from him, and his sober manner is a good counterweight to the many temptations to which you are exposed in your work. Why you isolate yourself so much I do not know; there is also too little in your letters about your husband.

I shall forward the dream you enclosed to Stekel for the *Zentral-*

blatt.[8] It is clear enough. The foot is also a favorite substitute for what is otherwise a more autoerotic object.

Cordial greetings,
Yours sincerely,
Freud.

20 January 1913,
Vienna, IX. Berggasse 19.

Dear Frau Doktor,

What made you go to a sanatorium? Why have you had an operation? You write nothing about it all and I must content myself with the fact that you are well.

The decision concerning your friend is very simple. If she needs analysis—and this seems to be obvious from your letter—then she does not have to come to Vienna for a consultation. She can decide beforehand whether she wants to go to Abraham or to me (a male physician seems eminently suited to her case). There is nothing more in my favor than the higher fee and the fact that I would make the better father figure. However, if she chooses me she may have to wait a few weeks. Her turn would doubtless come in February. I could let you know by telegram when I have an hour free. Since the pat[ient] is no mistress of resolve you must make the decision, which has to be binding on her.

The first issue of the *Zeitschrift,* a fair proof of which lies before me already, carries a review of your last great contribution.[9] We have taken the liberty of criticizing it freely, because the Zurich people have asked us expressly to do so. Don't be angry, and read it through with indulgence.

My personal relationship with your Germanic hero has definitely been shattered. His behavior was too bad. Since I received that first letter from you, my opinion of him has greatly altered. Scientific cooperation, however, will presumably be maintained.

I send you my cordial greetings and hope to hear from you.

Yours sincerely,
Freud.

P.S. If you keep sending us regular contributions, your name will soon be put on the masthead of our journal.

INTERNATIONALE ZEITSCHRIFT FÜR ÄRZTLICHE PSYCHOANALYSE

Vienna,
9 February 1913

Dear Frau Doktor,

You have sent me another very good dream. Perhaps you could add a few more words to draw particular attention to the typical features of this transposition. How easily the patient succeeds in wresting her destiny from the father who has rejected her. All done with the simplest of means.

Your news about Kraus[10] is also welcome, for it is the most recent sign of his slowly approaching lucidity. His approach could have important repercussions for Germany if only he gave it more publicity. But that is exactly what he does not want to do.

You have the right to take a rest now yourself. You have done a great deal of serious and important work and are fully entitled to take a break for a while and collect your thoughts.

Cordial greetings,
Freud.

INTERNATIONALE ZEITSCHRIFT FÜR ÄRZTLICHE PSYCHOANALYSE

Vienna,
8 May 1913

Dear Frau Doktor,

I am sorry to hear that you are consumed with longing for J., and this at a time when I am on such bad terms with him, having almost reached the conclusion that he is unworthy of all the interested concern I have bestowed on him. I feel that he is about to destroy the work that we have built up so laboriously, and achieve nothing better himself. Quite apart from our scientific differences, his personal behavior merits severe criticism. But no doubt it is fruitless to complain about him to you. Let me therefore, rather, stress the one thing that is quite clear to me and more welcome. I gather that you are composing your thoughts, which is bound to benefit the child.[11] That is the right course. I hope that this commitment of your libido will prove happier for you than the earlier one. You will also find it easier now to be content with being restricted to just one man. I imagine that you love Dr. J. so deeply still because you have not brought to light the hatred he merits. When I had to take sides at the beginning of our correspondence, it looked as if it would work out. I am glad that I am now as little responsible for his personal achievements as I am for his scientific ones.

Please let me know when the child is due so that I can send you my heartiest congratulations.

Yours very sincerely,
Freud.

INTERNATIONALE ZEITSCHRIFT FÜR ÄRZTLICHE PSYCHOANALYSE

San Martino,
28 August 1913

Dear Frau Doktor,

I am glad to hear that you are quite rightly beginning to use your spare time in order to come to terms with the present and with life. Let us hope that this bad period will save you an analysis. I can hardly bear to listen when you continue to enthuse about your old love and past dreams, and count on an ally in the marvelous little stranger.

I am, as you know, cured of the last shred of my predilection for the Aryan cause, and would like to take it that if the child turns out to be a boy he will develop into a stalwart Zionist.

He or it must be dark in any case, no more towheads. Let us banish all these will-o'-the-wisps!

I shall not present my compliments to Jung in Munich, as you know perfectly well.[12] To you, however, I wish all the best, a surfeit of gentleness, humor and understanding, so that much of it may be passed on to the small young life.

We are and remain Jews. The others will only exploit us and will never understand or appreciate us.

> With many cordial regards,
> Yours,
> Freud.

> *29 September 1913,*
> *Vienna, IX. Berggasse 19.*

Dear Frau Doktor,

Well, now, my heartiest congratulations! It is far better that the child should be a "she".[13] Now we can think again about the blond Siegfried and perhaps smash that idol before his time comes.

For the rest, the small She will speak for herself. May she fare well, if wishes still have a vestige of omnipotence!

> Yours,
> Freud.

P.S. I was in your city for a few hours on the 25th.

> *15 May 1914,*
> *Vienna, IX. Berggasse 19.*

Dear Frau Doktor,

Now you are going crazy yourself, and, what is more, with the same symptoms as your predecessor! One day I, all unsuspecting, received a letter from Frau Jung saying that her husband was convinced I had something against him.[14] That was the beginning; you know the ending.

And your argument that I have not yet sent you any patients? Exactly the same thing happened with Adler, who pronounced himself persecuted because I had sent him no patients. Do you not recognize the well-known mechanism of unduly magnifying a man in order to hold him responsible?[15] I have not seen a patient from Berlin for at least six months, or anyone else I could have sent on to you. As it is, I have the greatest difficulty in providing for my young people in Vienna. Half the analysts and all those outside our camp take pleasure in abusing me, and then you are surprised that all nervous patients do not flock to me for referral to doctors. I do not know whether Abraham is able to hand over many patients, but I am sure he will take your wishes into account unless you distance yourself from the work of the Association.

What in the world could I possibly have against you after the relationship we have had up till now? Isn't it nothing more than your own bad conscience due to your failure to free yourself from your idol? Think about it again, and write to me about it.

Cordial greetings,
Freud.

12 June 1914,
Vienna, IX. Berggasse 19.

Dear Frau Doktor,

Thank you for giving me the chance of sending you these few words. I want to tie together what I have to say into one knot, as it were. Please let me know if you want to appear on the masthead of our journal.[16] If so, then it will be done in the next issue. But think it over! We shall shortly be removing all Zurich names and addresses. It would be the clearest sort of partisanship if your name was placed on it now. And this at a time when you are still in love with Jung, when you cannot be really angry with him, see in him still the hero hounded by the mob, write to me in the terms of his libido theory, blame Abraham for telling the plain truth! You, too, must be wanting to make a clear decision; irresolution will serve you no better than it did the good Pfister,[17] who suddenly finds himself between two stools. Don't stand on ceremony, but whatever you decide to do, do it unreservedly.

Of course I want you to succeed in casting aside as so much trash your infantile dreams of the Germanic champion and hero, on which hinges your whole opposition to your environment and to your origins; you should not demand from this phantom the child you must once have craved from your father. Your pedagogic efforts are certainly in the right direction. Warm your life's intentions with your inner fire instead of burning yourself up with it. Nothing is stronger than controlled and sublimated passion.

You can achieve nothing while you are at loggerheads with yourself.

There will be a warm welcome for you if you stay with us here, but then you will have to recognize the enemy over there.

> With best wishes,
> Yours,
> Freud.

> 20 April 1915,
> Vienna, IX. Berggasse 19.

Dear Frau Doktor,

Many thanks for your half-yearly membership fee, which I shall hand over at our next meeting. I fully agree with your treatment, but don't let's talk too much of Jung; you will always find one or more excuses for him. Your reports from Z. have been supplemented recently by Dr. Pfister, who spent several hours with me and who was my guest one evening along with Rank[18] and Sachs.[19] My impression is that those people are more stupid than we ever dared think.

I readily accept that you only seem unproductive on the surface, and that changes are taking place within you to meet the new circumstances. I should very much like to know what your father is doing, a man I found so interesting, albeit inflexible, too. I wonder whether the war has not hit him particularly hard.

Dr. Rank is free, which makes it possible for both journals to continue, though admittedly in the slow tempo that circumstances have forced upon us. In any case the first issue of the *Zeitschrift*[20] has come out, and *Imago*[21] is at the printers. There are contributions by me in both, because I have more time than I would like, or even than I can use productively.

Dr. Tausk,[22] about whom you inquire, is attached to the local general hospital. The meetings of the Association are lively and reflect a good spirit. Stekel's *Zentralblatt* has ceased publication.[23] Once the flood has receded we hope to refloat our little ship. Unfortunately no dove with an olive branch is yet in sight.

> Cordial greetings,
> Yours sincerely,
> Freud.

18 November 1917,
Vienna, IX. Berggasse 19.

Dear Frau Doktor,

I was glad, as a sign of life, to receive a token of your interest. You are right: times are hard and not favorable to scientific work. We are trying, here in Vienna, to fill the time as actively as possible. The Association carries on, the journals continue to appear, hope remains firm that our cause will withstand the storm.

With cordial greetings,
Yours,
Freud.

Badgastein,
2 August 1919

Dear Frau Doktor,

I, too, was glad to hear news of you, thanks to your brother's visit,[24] but then could only regret that this time of war has brought nothing but harm to you as well. I can answer your question by saying that you may remain our member and our debtor for as long as you wish. I shall give instructions that the *Zeitschrift* be sent to you regularly. Please contact our editorial director, Dr. Otto Rank, Vienna I, Grünangerg. 3–5, about this matter.

I cannot fit the proposed discussions in the Zurich psychoanalytic group you mention into any chronological order. It must all have been brewing for quite some time. Moreover, to the best of my knowledge Jung's society has not been known by that name for some years. I also feel that I have no right to dissuade you from participating in the translation of Jung's writing, the less so since you write that you enjoy doing it, and since it helps you to earn a living. I would only remark that the explanation you offer for your personal involvement is most unusual. People generally do that sort of thing only if it is in keeping with their own principles. It is sad indeed if circumstances have forced you to undertake it without such conviction.

I would naturally like very much to have you as translator of my own psychoanalytic books. But you are right, now is not the time for that. Moreover, most of it has long since been translated into

Russian by an unauthorized party, and I have the books in my possession. *Everyday Life* and *5 Lectures*[25] were, if I am not mistaken, even authorized by me (Dr. Medem[26] and Dr. Ossipoff[27]).

Please send your promised contributions[28] direct to the publisher (Rank) since I want to pursue a nomadic life in Aug. and probably Sept. as well. Dr. Tausk put an end to his unfortunate life on 3 July.

In the hope of hearing happier news from you, too, in the near future, I send you my cordial greetings.

Yours,
Freud.

3 January 1921,
Vienna, IX. Berggasse 19.

Dear Frau Doktor,

I am very interested to hear your news and about your experiences, but I am sure that you do not really believe that advice on acute cases can be given at such a distance.

There has been an error on your part as regards Claparède.[29] I praised his translation unreservedly, saying that it sounds better than the original German text. Perhaps he took exception to a critical remark about his introductory paper in the *Revue de Genève* ("Fr. et la Psychanalyse"), but I could not spare him that because he presented the libido theory to his readers in an entirely erroneous form.[30]

With best wishes for good health and for your work in the New Year.

Yours,
Freud.

12 June 1922,
Vienna, IX. Berggasse 19.

Dear Frau Doktor,

I have left your last few letters, which I have read with a great deal of interest and with appreciation for your achievements, unanswered for the most part, but only because they did not seem to demand a reply and because I am overburdened with correspondence. Your letter of today, however, calls for an immediate answer.

I gather from you that the matter is a burning one, and that you have an urgent need for "active therapy." I do not agree with either point and, in particular, consider your first choice, my intervention, to be highly questionable.

The people of Geneva are each and every one of them dilettantes to whom you must gradually transmit something of your analytical training. Claparède himself is no exception. Saussure,[31] when he returns from Cery, will probably be the only expert apart from you. The same people are also so exclusively jealous of their independence, and so insusceptible to advice from afar, that to this day they have not even joined the psychoanalytic organization. Thus, on the one hand, we do not have to answer for their doings, mistaken and pernicious as they are, but on the other hand, we have no right to advise or dissuade them without being asked. If I did what you suggested, I should produce nothing but national-patriotic resentment against the old leader who feels entitled to play the psychoanalytic pope.

These people, it so happens, carry their political point of view over into science, and use it to conceal their total or partial ignorance. Those in Zurich are not really any different, and there is nothing we can do about it until they are joined by members who are trained in keeping with our ideas.

Just imagine if one of our groups did something as absurd with psychoanalysis. We could do nothing except persuade them to leave the international movement, and those from Geneva are not even in it!

Something else now. In order to judge Coué-ism[32] one would have to have studied B's book as well as others.[33] That might not be enough, either. In practice, one ought to have a look at things for oneself. And I have neither the time, the inclination, nor the strength for that. Besides, it is quite possible that behind all the commotion there lies a piece of useful ego psychology, much as with Adler. The enthusiasts want to make use of this little piece to oust the whole of psychoanalysis. Let them try and let them continue as heretofore to accentuate the differences strongly.

With cordial greetings,
Yours,
Freud.

9 *February 1923,*
Vienna, IX. Berggasse 19.

Dear Frau Doktor,

I am in receipt of your letter and really believe that you are right. Your plan to go to Russia seems to me much better than my advice to try out Berlin. In Moscow you will be able to accomplish important work at the side of Wulff[34] and Ermakoro.[35] Lastly, you will be on home ground. These are difficult times for us all.

I hope to hear from you soon, but would earnestly request that you write your address on the inside of your letter, which so few women are wont to do.

Cordially yours,
Freud.

Frau Dr. Spielrein[36]
IX Alserstrasse
Pension Cosmopolite

Please examine this lady and if, as is likely, she has a neurotic history, perhaps start treatment.

With sincere greetings,
Freud.

PART TWO

The STORY of SABINA SPIELREIN

ALDO CAROTENUTO

Translated from the Italian by

John Shepley

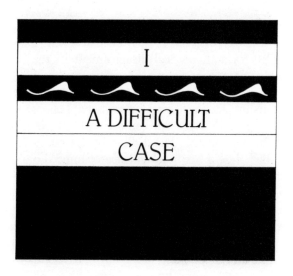

I

A DIFFICULT
CASE

THE FRIENDSHIP between Freud and Jung was fraught with bitterness. When two great men who have a high opinion of themselves are insufficiently aware of the undercurrent of rivalry in their relationship, even a slight disagreement may become the pretext for one to impose his supremacy on the other. An understanding of human failings makes us indulgent in our judgment, but we are especially surprised to find this mechanism at work in two men whose names are linked with the study of the deep motivations of human behavior. The facts of the quarrel are well known. After a period of intense professional collaboration, documented by their correspondence, Freud and Jung decided to break off their relationship and go their separate ways. Two explanations have been given for this rupture: on one side it has been maintained that the split occurred primarily for scientific reasons; on the other, the idea has been put forward that the motives were entirely psychological.

Naturally the two theses presuppose an underlying discourse. Those who uphold the scientific explanation point to the complete incompatibility of the two men's theories; once one has ascertained the validity, for example, of the Freudian doctrine, one arrives at the absolute rejection of Jungian ideas, which appear false and reductive vis-à-vis those of Freud. The overwhelming majority of Freudian psychologists have subscribed to this version of the facts. The other hypothesis, the psychological one, instead places the possibility of a theoretical disagreement in the background, while pointing out a fundamental emotional problem in which the two men were entangled, perhaps from the opening exchange in their relationship. As I have stated elsewhere,[1] I choose this second hypothesis, especially since one can see that Jung, from the beginning, even before meeting Freud directly and becoming involved with him, had shown his independence of mind. Both recognized the importance of the unconscious, but they differed on the etiology of its mechanisms. Consider, in this connection, the reservations put forward by Jung in his preface to *The Psychology of Dementia Praecox:* "Fairness to Freud, however, does not imply, as many fear, unqualified submission to a dogma; one can very well maintain an independent judgment."[2] And later, having sent the little book to Vienna, Jung explained to Freud why certain interpretations of unconscious life appeared to him in a different light with regard to the emerging theories of psychoanalysis: "I. my material is totally different from yours. . . . II. my upbringing, my milieu, and my scientific premises are in any case utterly different from your own. III. my experience compared with yours is extremely small. IV. both in quantity and quality of psychoanalytic talent the balance is distinctly in your favour. V. the lack of personal contact with you . . . must weigh heavily in the scales."[3]

One should also keep in mind that Jung, before meeting Freud, had already, with his studies on the processes of association, delineated the spheres of interest to which he would devote the rest of his life.[4]

Jung and Freud knew from the beginning that their viewpoints differed, but why should a difference of opinion be an obstacle to friendship or collaboration?[5] Given the atmosphere of the time and the revolutionary impact of psychoanalytic hypotheses, even conflicts in theory were likely to be felt on both sides as personal attacks. Nevertheless, the wish to trace everything back, despite the evidence, to a theoretical divergence is reductive, to say the least. One might even say that it reveals the anxiety aroused by the mere suspicion of an emotional conflict.

Take, for instance, this remark by Marie-Louise von Franz: "The separation was necessary, broadly speaking, because Freud concentrated on the physical and biological background of the unconscious . . . while Jung conceived the psyche in terms of polarity. . . ."[6] Is one to believe in the *necessity* of a separation simply because they were looking at the unconscious from different perspectives? In fact, every time an author tries to demonstrate the scientific reasons for this separation, he is unable to bring forward a single plausible element, since there are indeed no reasons that can withstand a calm and objective examination.

It remains only to turn to the psychological reasons, meaning in this case the intricate emotional relationship that existed between two rivals who had the misfortune to dip their hands into the incandescent magma of the unconscious at a time when it was almost entirely unknown and therefore charged with peril.

At the time of his first letters to Freud, Jung was thirty-one years old. He had been at the Burghölzli, the psychiatric hospital in Zurich, since 10 December 1900, and in 1903 he had married Emma Rauschenbach, the daughter of a manufacturer. His first child, Agathe, was born in 1904, and the second, Gret, in 1906. He had to his scientific credit his dissertation, *On the Psychology and Pathology of So-Called Occult Phenomena*, published in 1902, and his experimental researches on word association.[7] Furthermore, Jung had already been working for three years on *The Psychology of Dementia Praecox*, a distillation of the wealth of experience gained inside the Burghölzli. Freud could, in a certain sense, already consider himself famous with *The Interpretation of Dreams*,[8] and in fact the growing number of his adversaries served to confirm his importance.

Jung, of course, had been bitten by the analytic virus, and despite their geographical distance, he was sending Freud dreams to be analyzed. Oddly enough, it would seem that Jung did not always reveal to Freud that he himself was the dreamer. From one letter it emerges that he only later acknowledged that the dream pertained to himself.

Let us now take a look at what was probably the first dream sent to Freud by Jung. It appears in *The Psychology of Dementia Praecox* and is accompanied by a footnote in which Jung, not without humor, says: "The personal and family circumstances of the subject are well known to me."⁹

Here is the dream in its entirety:

"I saw horses being hoisted by thick cables to a great height. One of them, a powerful brown horse which was tied up with straps and was hoisted aloft like a package, struck me particularly. Suddenly the cable broke and the horse crashed to the street. I thought it must be dead. But it immediately leapt up again and galloped away. I noticed that the horse was dragging a heavy log along with it, and I wondered how it could advance so quickly. It was obviously frightened and could easily cause an accident. Then a rider came up on a little horse and rode along slowly in front of the frightened horse, which moderated its pace somewhat. I still feared that the horse might run over the rider, when a cab came along and drove in front of the rider at the same pace, thus bringing the frightened horse to a still slower gait. I then thought now all is well, the danger is over."¹⁰

Jung gives what I consider a masterly interpretation of this dream, and even the corrections later offered by Freud do not substantially alter its meaning. But Freud interprets some details that the dreamer himself may have perhaps deliberately overlooked, such as Jung's statement that he has been happy with his wife from every standpoint, to which he added in parentheses, "not merely from optimism." Making this point may have helped Jung to deny other feelings. Indeed, in the rest of his letter to Freud, Jung stresses that "the rationalistic explanation, 'sexual restraint,' is, as I have said, merely a convenient screen pushed into the foreground and hiding an illegitimate sexual wish that had better not see the light of day."¹¹

Throughout the exchange of letters between Jung and Freud, it is generally Jung, for reasons not hard to fathom, who reveals himself to Freud, and not vice versa. In many of his statements—such as "[I] ask you to let me enjoy your friendship not as one between equals but as that of father and son"¹²—Jung virtually places himself in the hands of his more illustrious colleague, thereby developing, however, precisely those feelings of ambivalence that in general accompany any true analytic treatment. Unless we keep these details in mind, certain aspects of their relationship will appear incomprehensible, as will the violence of the passions that pitted one against the other in the course of almost seven years of correspondence. Consider also that in the first phase of a confidential relationship like the analytic one, the patient unconsciously asks to be dominated, even if simultaneously he is fighting to re-establish equilibrium in a situation in which he feels crushed. On the other hand, in the Freud-Jung relationship the parts had already been fatally assigned.

Let us return for a moment to Jung's dream. Among the various interpretations, the wish to be high up and to achieve success by his own work is obvious. Jung perceived the difficulties of an academic career, especially through his contact with Bleuler, toward whom in his letters (he never mentions him in his autobiography[13]) he expresses a veiled contempt. The only road open to Jung was that of the nascent psychology of the unconscious, and Freud's support seemed absolutely indispensable, at least in the beginning. Throughout the period of their correspondence, Jung suffered from apprehensiveness; he was often mistaken about how Freud would evaluate his scientific contributions. He feared that the judgment on *The Psychology of Dementia Praecox* would be negative;[14] Freud instead insisted that the book represented "the richest and most significant contribution to my labours that has ever come to my attention."[15] The first part of *Transformations and Symbols of the Libido*[16] also aroused many doubts in Jung as he awaited word from the Master, who finally declared, "In it many things are so well-expressed that they seem to have taken on definitive form and in this form impress themselves on the memory. . . . But it is the best thing this promising author has written, up to now, though he will do still better."[17]

If in the face of such enthusiastic expressions of appreciation the young Jung still allowed himself to be overcome by doubt, his reactions would be even more complex in situations where the transference ambivalence can in any case often gain the upper hand. By a strange quirk of destiny, it was precisely one of the first "control cases" submitted to Freud by Jung that was to have an important effect on his metapsychological hypotheses.[18] In a letter of 23 October 1906, his second in the correspondence, Jung informs Freud of a "difficult case." It concerned a twenty-year-old girl student who since the age of fourteen had been displaying certain symptoms classified as hysterical. The matter was eventually to become complicated to such a degree that Jung, Freud, and several others were to be involved in it.

Until recently there has been little information available about this patient,[19] but the fortunate discovery of the supporting documents has made it possible to reconstruct in broad outlines the story of Jung, Freud, and Sabina Spielrein.

II
THE WORLD OF
A CHILD

THE DATA I have collected on Sabina Spielrein are based on a clinical paper presented by Jung in September 1907, on the letters between Freud and Jung concerning Spielrein's illness and subsequent analytic career, on Spielrein's own diary, and on one of her clinical papers in which she describes some problems of child psychology, drawing directly on her childhood memories. In addition, I cite the opinions of certain individuals who knew her personally. A further source would be the clinical file on Sabina Spielrein's treatment at the Burghölzli Hospital in Zurich. This medical report, presumably drawn up by Jung himself, was not available to me.

Sabina Spielrein was born of a wealthy Jewish family in Rostov-on-Don in 1885. Her father was a businessman; her mother, though a housewife, had received an education at the university level. Her grandfather and great-grandfather had been rabbis, much respected in the sphere of the family and in the community in which they had exercised their calling. Sabina was the eldest child; a younger sister died, leaving three younger brothers, Isaak, Jean, and Emile.[1]

From early childhood Sabina revealed a thriving imagination and a rich inner world. She thought of herself as a goddess, sovereign of a powerful realm, and felt herself in possession of a great strength that would allow her to achieve anything she wanted. She was, however, aware of her fantasies and able to distinguish them from reality. One day she has her first hallucination: she sees two kittens on the dresser in the adjoining room. From that moment on she experiences anguish and is assailed by night terrors, during which she feels threatened by horrifying animals. In addition, she has a dismaying apprehension that she may be forcibly torn away from her parents and afflicted with serious diseases. Like all children up to the age of three or four, she wonders where babies come from, and never tires of digging large holes in the ground to find out what lies on the other side. They tell her that it is God who sends babies to earth, and so she, too, is seized with the yearning to be able to make a baby. An experiment by a chemist uncle fires her imagination, and she pretends to be an alchemist, mixing every kind of material that comes to hand. "I spread leftover food and drink on the table, then carefully mixed it all together, making a great mess, because I wanted to see what would come out of it. It gave me great joy when one color changed into another or a new form or consistency resulted. I will never forget the combination of happiness and anguish that overcame me when a piece of cloth, through the mysterious power of some liquid, was transformed into paper. I couldn't believe my eyes. I had a lot of little bottles with 'secret' liquids, 'magic stones,' and the like, from which I was expecting the great creation."[2]

Sabina traces the vision of the two kittens to an old woman who had told her jokingly that she, too, might perhaps give birth to a kitty. In her article, she goes back to the Freudian theory of sexuality to show how and why kittens, babies, and illnesses could have been connected.

In describing her childhood preoccupations, Spielrein omits certain important elements, the very ones that lay at the roots of her later psychological trouble. At about the age of three or four, little Sabina began to retain her feces, until the impossibility of holding them any longer forced her to defecate. Later she would sit on her heel in such a way as to block the anus, hampering defecation for as much as two weeks. After her seventh year she gave up these practices in favor of masturbation. While sitting at the table she could not help thinking of defecation, and anyone she saw was imagined as engaging in that act. In addition, her father's hands had a special meaning: simply seeing them aroused her sexually. With the passage of time the situation worsened to the point that, at about the age of eighteen, she was no longer able to look at anyone. Attacks of depression now began to alternate with fits of weeping, laughter, and screaming.[3]

It was in this condition that Sabina Spielrein probably attended the girls' high school; when she graduated, her parents apparently thought of taking her to Zurich so that she could study medicine and undergo medical treatment as well.

Our first information about the state she was in goes back, as I said, to 23 October 1906, the date of the letter in which Jung informs Freud that he is applying the Freudian method to the treatment of a hysteric: "Difficult case, a 20-year-old Russian girl student, ill for 6 years."[4] Sabina Spielrein must therefore have manifested her symptoms in an alarming fashion at the age of fourteen. In his report to the First International Congress of Psychiatry and Neurology in 1907, Jung was to designate the case as one of "psychotic hysteria."[5]

Freud responds to Jung's description of the case as follows: "I am glad to hear that your Russian girl is a student; uneducated persons are at present too inaccessible for our purposes. The defecation story is nice and suggests numerous analogies. Perhaps you remember my contention in my *Theory of Sexuality* that even infants derive pleasure from the retention of faeces. The third to fourth year is the most significant period for those sexual activities which later belong to the pathogenic ones. . . . The sight of a brother being spanked arouses a memory trace from the first to second year, or a fantasy transposed into that period. It is not unusual for babies to soil the hands of those who are carrying them. Why should that not have happened in her case? And this awakens a memory of her father's caresses during her infancy. Infantile fixation of the libido on the father—the typical choice of object; anal autoerotism. The position she has chosen can be broken down into its components, for it seems to have still other factors added to it. Which factors? It must be possible, by the symptoms and even by the character, to recognize anal excitation as a motivation. Such people often show typical combinations of character traits. They are extremely neat, stingy and obstinate, traits which are in a manner of speaking the sublimations of anal erotism. Cases like this based on repressed perversion can be analysed very satisfactorily."[6] After this reply, by which Freud offers his analytic contribution, Sabina Spielrein is never again mentioned in the correspondence in the context of her illness. Instead she was to be the center of a distressing question over which even Freud seemed to lose his bearings.

From Jung's letter explaining the case to Freud, it is unclear whether the girl was still being treated at the Burghölzli or had already become Jung's private patient; from Spielrein's autobiography we can deduce that she was in the hospital and that it was there that she had met Jung. The difficulty of establishing a probable date arises. From the diary we know that a few experiments in association conducted with Binswanger included Sabina's own contributions, and that Jung, already fascinated by the intelligence of this Russian girl, had suggested to her that she become a psychiatrist. Many of his studies on association had been done between 1904 and 1905, which would lead us to suppose that the girl had been admitted to the hospital in those years. Abraham, in two letters to Freud, gives some information that may help to pin down the period that Sabina spent in the hospital: in speaking of anal eroticism, he shares Freud's views and points out that the description "fits a case of hysteria analysed by Jung with which you will be acquainted from his description."[7] And when, some time later, Freud, who was working on The History of the Psycho-Analytic Movement, asked Abraham to send him some data on what had been done at the Burghölzli in relation to psychoanalysis, Abraham replied that although he had arrived at the hospital in December 1904, there had been some attempts before then, and among them "a case of hysteria had been analysed by Jung (definitely 1904)."[8]

It seems quite unlikely, given the restricted nature of the material, that Abraham is referring to two different cases. This makes it almost certain that by the year 1904 Sabina had entered the Burghölzli and was being treated by Jung. Indeed, the present director of the Burghölzli has confirmed that Sabina Spielrein was a patient there from 17 August 1904, to 1 June 1905. Probably the treatment was still going on in 1906. Later, as can be seen from the letters that Jung wrote to his patient, on being released from the hospital she must have been well enough to be able to pursue a private analysis. Sabina had enrolled in medical school at the University of Zurich on 28 April 1905, and finished her studies and received her diploma in May 1911,[9] with a dissertation, prepared with Jung's help, entitled "The Psychological Content of a Case of Schizophrenia," which was published in 1911 in the *Jahrbuch*.[10] The work was later amply cited by Jung in *Transformations and Symbols of the Libido* (both the 1911–12 edition and the revised one of 1952).[11]

Spielrein, obviously in response to Jung's suggestions and possibly those of Bleuler, had undertaken a detailed examination of all the material offered her by an intelligent paranoiac woman patient. The patient's speech seemed to make no sense, but Spielrein's keen observation, making use of word associations and other productions of the psyche, in a short time succeeded in grasping the meaning and decoding the apparent absurdity of her verbalizations. Only after this deciphering did Spielrein look at the data in the hospital file, where she found confirmation of her conclusions about the meaning of the language used by the patient. The method adopted in this case by Spielrein to demonstrate the parallel between the patient's thought mechanisms and the thought patterns fundamental to mythological formulations also bears an utterly Jungian stamp.

This paper by Spielrein, quoted with many expressions of esteem by Jung, is no longer included in the specialized literature on the subject; it was probably a casualty of the ostracism that subsequently struck Jung.

Spielrein was later driven by the vicissitudes of her relationship with her teacher and analyst to leave Zurich for a stay of about nine months in Vienna, where she met Freud and was able to participate in the famous Wednesday meetings. But even earlier, after studying the content of the psychoses, she had begun to formulate her hypothesis on the death instinct. And according to Jung, it was precisely the study of *Transformations and Symbols of the Libido*, in particular the chapter on "The Dual Mother," that stimulated his pupil in this direction.

Published in 1912, also in the *Jahrbuch*, "Destruction as the

Cause of Coming into Being"[12] was Spielrein's second notable work. None of her subsequent contributions, continuing until 1931, match it in concentration and originality of thought. In this paper she anticipated, almost literally, the concepts that Freud was to express in 1920 in *Beyond the Pleasure Principle*. Freud honestly admits it, even though he declares that he had not understood very well what Spielrein meant.[13] A shaky defense of Freud is attempted by the editors of the *Minutes of the Vienna Psychoanalytic Society:*

"At first glance it might seem that, under Jung's influence, Dr. Spielrein had formulated, many years before Freud, the hypothesis that instinct life . . . consists of two opposing drives—the life instinct and the death instinct. Closer scrutiny, however, discloses that she does not express this theory at all, but rather believes that the sexual instinct—that is, the life instinct, the creative instinct itself—contains a destructive component."[14]

Today this criticism can be accepted only with reservations, because the fact is that in 1920 Freud was simply improving on Spielrein's basic idea, which at the time of the Society meetings he had rejected with much vehemence. Besides, this is certainly not the only instance in which Freud developed ideas that were not his own, giving them, however, a definition consistent with his hypotheses. Despite the opinion expressed by Freud, Spielrein's article does not seem to me all that obscure. At the end of her discussion she states that her examples demonstrate "clearly enough that, as certain biological facts show, the reproductive instinct, from the psychological standpoint as well, is made up of two antagonistic components and is therefore equally an instinct of birth and one of destruction."[15]

This second effort of Spielrein's also met with very little response and is at present scarcely remembered in studies of the origins of the death instinct in Freud's thought.[16] The article was, however, reviewed at some length by Paul Federn, who gave a substantially positive critique of it, stating that "apart from its objective correctness, the paper seems to me, thanks to the author's sensitivity for emotional relationships, a contribution as well to the analysis of the mystical modality of thought that is so significant for humanity."[17]

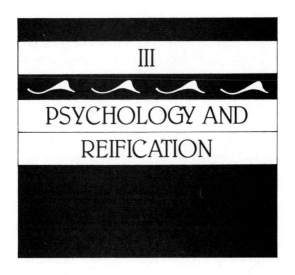

III

PSYCHOLOGY AND REIFICATION

SABINA SPIELREIN'S two most important papers, on schizophrenia and the death instinct, clearly show Jung's influence. Let us now look at their significance within their author's affective structure.

I share the view of those who maintain that any psychological theory, regardless of its actual validity, in some way expresses a concern of its author. As early as 1913, Jung, in his attempt to understand the coexistence of several theories, was essentially surmising the diversity of psychological types; he was to arrive at a precise formulation of the hypothesis in 1921.[1] I believe that Jung, with his typological theory, by far anticipated the modern method, which consists in tracing to the author's complexes the roots of his metapsychological formulations. More recently, G. E. Atwood and S. S. Tomkins have taken up this subject and have stated: "The psychobiographical investigation of personality theory actually represents only one branch of a larger discipline which would study the role of subjective factors in the structure of man's knowledge in general."[2]

I must stress, however, that the aim of such an investigation is not to belittle a theory but, rather, to offer it the subjective support that guarantees its link with human experience. In other words, any psychological concept that can take its place in the sphere of metapsychology represents the deepest and most nagging concern of its author. Again according to Atwood, "the reification involved in metapsychological theory-building serves specific defensive and/ or reparative functions for the theorist in question."[3]

Following Freud and Jung, Spielrein had immediately understood that even the most dissociated thought has a meaning if one can only uncover the intricate frame of reference that underlies it. From Jung's report and the testimony of Spielrein herself, we know she had been suffering so gravely that it had been necessary to hospitalize her. Without access to the clinical files of the Burghölzli, one can only surmise that the diagnosis of psychotic hysteria made by Jung refers to a genuine schizophrenic episode. In a note included in the *Minutes of the Vienna Psychoanalytic Society*, mention is made, in connection with the presentation of the first part of her paper on the death instinct, that Sabina Spielrein had in the course of her medical studies suffered a psychotic episode.[4] Helene Deutsch still remembers Sabina Spielrein as a gifted person, if mentally disturbed;[5] Jean Piaget, who was in fact analyzed by Spielrein, primarily stresses her analytical and symbolical capacity and makes no mention of her psychological troubles. It is possible, however, that the period of a few months that Piaget spent with Spielrein was too short to allow him to see her personality in perspective; oddly enough, Jean Piaget ignores this encounter completely in his autobiography, and only later refers to it, in an interview on psychoanalysis, but without giving the name of his analyst:

Q. Were you ever tempted to undergo analysis?
A. But I *have* been analyzed! After all, when people are talking about something, you have to know what they're talking about. I had a training analysis with a woman who was a direct pupil of Freud. Every morning at eight, for eight months. In Geneva, with a woman pupil of Freud's who was from Eastern Europe and had been analyzed by him. Of course I've been analyzed, otherwise I wouldn't talk about it!
Q. And why did you break it off?
A. I broke if off because I was— The things I saw all interested me very much, it was extraordinary to discover all my complexes. But my analyst, realizing that I was immune to the theory and that she'd never succeed in convincing me, told me it wasn't worth the trouble to go on.

Q. So fundamentally you were putting up resistance?

A. Yes, but only from a theoretical standpoint, not in the practice of analysis. The psychoanalyst had been sent to spread the doctrine in Geneva by the International Psychoanalytic Association. That was in 1921. I was quite happy to be the guinea pig, and I can assure you that it all interested me very much, but the doctrine was another matter. It didn't seem to me that the salient facts pointed out by the psychoanalyst had necessarily to be interpreted in the way she insisted I take them. It was she who broke off the analysis.

Q. And how might this have put her in difficulty in the practice of analysis with regard to you?

A. Since we weren't dealing with a therapeutic analysis and not even a training one, and since I had no intention of becoming a psychoanalyst, but it was only a question of propaganda, in the best sense of the word, of spreading the doctrine, in short, she decided it wasn't worthwhile to waste an hour a day with a fellow who refused to swallow the theory.[6]

In the Piaget interview there are a few inaccuracies: Spielrein was never analyzed by Freud, and I do not believe that she went to Geneva to carry out a program of proselytism at the instigation of the International Psychoanalytic Association.[7] Her wanderings are more likely due to inner anxiety and to an inability to put down roots in foreign countries, though she several times expressed her hatred for her homeland. Spielrein's strange behavior with Piaget can in part be explained by the enthusiasm of the neophyte, even if one cannot exclude a character trait that is unusual, to say the least.

Over the distance of time it is hard to judge Spielrein's mental state. The most likely possibility is that she experienced a brief psychotic episode, which had promptly receded, thanks to Jung's intervention. In any case, even after her recovery her personal "contact" with the world of psychosis must have been considerable, without her being so overwhelmed by it as to take on the typical characteristics of the psychotic state. Indeed, when we examine Spielrein's diary or her scientific papers, we immediately see that she is seeking a "truth," while in the world of the psychotic this kind of search is generally lacking. The psychotic lives his experience without being concerned with what is true. In psychosis, moreover, the structure of interpersonal relations is dyadic; a third witness is always lacking. In Spielrein's situation, the witness was always present, even when, in love with Jung, she was to call on Freud to mediate. Her love for Jung may also suggest the sudden appearance of a single psychotic episode, of brief duration.

Bleuler pronounced his opinion on Sabina's condition when he wrote in a letter of recommendation: "She is a little nervous, but has worked diligently."[8]

There is, however, a significant observation by Freud, a sufficiently revealing one that traces to personal matters Spielrein's professional contributions: ". . . her destructive drive is not much to my liking, because I believe it is personally conditioned. She seems abnormally ambivalent."[9]

Even Jung, forgetful of the situation in which he had been involved, calls her paper on the death instinct "overweighted with her own complexes."[10]

These statements bring us back to the theme of the subjectivity of certain psychological arguments. Spielrein succeeded in confronting, on a metapsychological level, the problem of her schizophrenia, not letting herself be destroyed by it but giving it a conceptual framework. She was attracted by the idea that schizophrenic thought was similar to mythological thought. Hence schizophrenia did not mean isolation from the world and the impossibility of being understood, but, rather, a way of understanding the world and of expressing oneself. Let us go back for a moment to her childhood memories: "I was a Goddess ruling over a powerful realm; I possessed a strength that I called 'Portum-strength,' a name derived from the French verb *porter*, meaning 'to fly.' This nonexistent verb was probably the result of the mingling of two words: *partir* and *porter*. A strength, therefore, by which I was carried away. By this strength I was able to know and achieve everything I wanted. And even if I did not believe directly in the reality of my fantasies, it was something too beautiful for me not to believe in it at all. Had not 'Abraham' ascended into the sky in flesh and blood? So why couldn't the same miracle happen to me as well? Meanwhile I possessed a strength unknown to anyone else and I was surely the chosen of the Lord. My parents knew nothing about this part of my inner life, despite the fact that I was convinced I hid nothing from them; besides, this thing did not seem to me so important, and I was afraid of being laughed at by the grownups."[11]

Notable in these memories is the presence of an inner world of which the parents are not aware. If on the whole this experience is fairly common, what is not common is the way in which it is transformed during the development of the personality. In Spielrein's case, the feeling of alienation was experienced in an unusually dramatic manner, for added to her secret sense of omnipotence were her obsessive ideas concerning defecation and her excitation in looking at her father's hands.

Her fantastic child's world is thus linked to a mythological world, and to a religious idea like that of Abraham. She can thereby declare that if we find pleasure in approaching the myth, it is because it evokes past experiences, collective as well as personal ones.

The patient presented to us by Spielrein is an inexhaustible source of discoveries, for her psychosis and dreams have impressive points of contact with mythology. Thus schizophrenia emerges from its isolation and can be better understood when one reflects, for example, on the blood of Christ or the "spermatic bath" of Persian mythology. Furthermore, Spielrein points out how her patient always speaks in the plural ("we test"), a device that enables one to sidestep personal complexes in favor of collective and therefore unifying phenomena. It is precisely from the strength of the personal complex that is transformed into a collective complex that all art forms, according to Spielrein, are derived.

In this interpretation of schizophrenia, which obviously springs from personal sources, Spielrein sets in motion both her defensive and her restitutive needs. Defensive because in this way her isolation and her childhood secrets can be referred to a boundless universe, and her psychological illness becomes not a hardship but the manifestation of an ancient language that, interpreted in a modern fashion, enlivens art and poetry. Restitutive because her narcissism and her omnipotence would be able to offer the world from which she is isolated a rapport on much broader terms.

Spielrein's paper on the death instinct seems more complex. Published in 1912, in the fourth volume of the *Jahrbuch*, it was conceived around 1910. As in her previous essay, Spielrein makes reference to Jung, and specifically to a passage in *Transformation and Symbols of the Libido*—"This passionate longing has two sides: it is the power which beautifies everything, but, in a different set of circumstances, is quite as likely to destroy everything"[12]— while Jung, in a note added to the revised edition of 1952, remarks, in connection with the "Terrible Mother" who represents death, that "This fact led my pupil Dr. Spielrein to develop her idea of the death-instinct, which was then taken up by Freud."[13]

Spielrein had been introduced to Freud on 11 October 1911 and had begun to attend the meetings after moving to Vienna.[14] And on 25 November 1911, in the presence of eighteen members, including Freud, Federn, Rank, Sachs, Stekel, and Tausk, she gave a report illustrating her ideas on the death instinct. The discussion, as described in the *Minutes*, immediately became animated. Tausk, for example, promptly pointed out the metaphysical nature of the report, in which, contrary to psychoanalytic methodology, which proceeds by induction, she had applied the deductive method instead. He stressed, however, that the idea of resistance to sexuality being based on destructive elements was one worthy of consideration.[15] Federn, noting the recurring mythological references, warned those present of the possibility that myths were created not by healthy people but by sick ones, and that this might explain the similarity between madness and myths. Freud, for his part, objected to the free and easy use of mythology, which the author might have borrowed from Jung: "The presentation itself provides the opportunity for a critique of Jung. . . ."[16]

The next day Freud communicated his impressions to Jung: "Fräulein Spielrein read a chapter from her paper yesterday . . . and it was followed by an illuminating discussion. I have hit on a few objections to your . . . method of dealing with mythology, and I brought them up in the discussion with the little girl. I must say she is rather nice and I am beginning to understand."[17]

The feeling one gets, however, from reading the *Minutes of the Vienna Psychoanalytic Society* is that the problem, interesting as it may have been, was not perceived in its true light. This must have been largely due to the psychological modality of Spielrein herself, who could not have kept the "complex-ridden significance" of her paper from shining through. This sort of performance can have a sufficiently negative effect on an audience, even arousing resistances that while scarcely justifiable on the intellectual level, are much more so on the emotional one. Eighteen years after this famous gathering, Freud felt obliged to write: "I remember my own defensive attitude when the idea of an instinct of destruction first emerged in psycho-analytic literature, and how long it took before I became receptive to it."[18]

Let this brief quotation from Freud on the idea of the destructive impulse suffice, although the criticisms that emerged in analytic circles would require more extended treatment.[19] What concerns us here is to understand how a death instinct came to be surmised. Why should an author have the need to assume a polarity of life and death instincts? Here Spielrein's psychological propensities can offer as much insight as the content of her paper. She states, for example: "I have therefore come to the conclusion that the basic characteristic of the individual consists in being 'dividual,' i.e., divisible." Or: "The depths of our psyche know no 'I,' but merely its sum, namely 'We.' "[20] On the other hand, in the description of her childhood memories, Spielrein says that although she had been aware of the difference between reality and fantasy, "in that period I did not want to hear fairy tales told by others—I was able to produce enough of them by myself."[21] If we try to connect these propositions, we can conjecture on the one hand Spielrein's narcissistic dimension and on the other an ability to depersonalize herself (telling herself fairy tales), which was later to be constructed over her own schizophrenia and that of her patient. The child Sabina persuades herself that the good Lord was able to create a human being by an act of will—"therefore, in my fantasies, I transformed myself into the omniscient and omnipotent Goddess. With earth, with mud, with any material I could get my hands on, I tried to create people but was unable to infuse them with life."[22] These sentences would seem to reveal that psychotic childhood situation known as omnipotence-impotence: in telling herself fairy tales she demonstrates her omnipotence, while her attempt to become a goddess and to impart life to a human being dramatically points up her own impotence.[23] But this impotence also overflows into her paper on the death instinct. In speaking of schizophrenia, she says: "the predominant feeling in this state is that the world is transformed, fearfully extraneous, like a theatrical performance; simultaneously there emerges the idea 'I am completely extraneous to myself.' Thoughts become depersonalized, they are something 'done' to the patient precisely because they come from the depths that lie outside the I, the depths that have already made the I a 'We' or, rather, a 'They.' " But how to get out of this state of possession? At issue is a true problem of obsession, in which "one is aware of the enemy in oneself, and it is actually our loving ardor that forces on us the ironclad necessity of doing something we do not want to do. . . ."[24]

How can such insights be related to little Sabina's world? From the age of three on, she grapples with the problem of defecation, with masturbation, with the obsessive notion that all the people around her are defecating. She is in the grip of a violent neurosis. Her remarkable intelligence probably sustains her, and she clings to her world of fantasy, while within her psychological structure are formed modalities that will later be projected onto her metapsychology. Meanwhile she will be obliged to admit that "it would be, however, incorrect to maintain that the psychic world of the hysteric is richer than that of the patient afflicted with dementia praecox—in dementia praecox we perhaps find more significant thoughts."[25] And why? Because it is precisely when the ego is overpowered that we find ourselves dealing with archaic patterns of thought, which in a certain sense elucidate a fundamental line as the prototype of any other kind of thought. But then what seems to be destruction is not in reality destruction, because man, or a part of man, must die so that something else can be reborn. "Destruction as the cause of coming into being" thus has a meaning, just as the terrible illness that had struck Sabina as a little girl must have had a meaning.

The struggles undergone by Jung during a difficult period in his life are also significant for an understanding of how Spielrein worked on her own psychological disturbances with a view to developing them theoretically.[26] The sense of the destruction and end of the world is typical in schizophrenia. But if this sense is combined with a solid intelligence, and also sustained, as in Spielrein's case, by meeting a man of such undoubted worth as Jung, the tragic journey may end quite differently. Yet one can also understand a purely emotional resistance to the hypothesis that life is born of destruction—that destruction lies at the base of life and rebirth. It is a hypothesis that cannot remain pure abstraction, since each individual must try it on himself. And not everyone is prepared to accept such a risk. Whether she liked it or not, Sabina Spielrein was forced by fate (is there any other word for it?) to look madness in the face, inside a psychiatric hospital. Since we do not yet know the particulars, we can only assume that the girl found herself isolated in her terror; after all, she was no longer able to look at anyone. My clinical experience has taught me what the mental patient's world is like, and I have often reflected on how much more terrible his condition must have been when—as was the almost unquestioned practice in Sabina Spielrein's time—"psychiatry teachers were not interested in what the patient had to say, but rather in how to make a diagnosis or how to describe symptoms and to compile statistics. . . . Patients were labeled, rubber-stamped with a diagnosis, and, for the most part, that settled the matter. The psychology of the mental patient played no role whatsoever."[27] In these circumstances, the patient sank still deeper into his fantasy world, eliminating the world of the Other and living his own human drama eternally with himself alone. Sabina actually covered her eyes with her hands—not even the world of images could get through, since all of her anxiety was projected onto them, transforming them into terrifying symbols. She was later to say: "A woman who abandons herself to passion . . . experiences all too soon its destructive aspect. . . . One must imagine oneself as being somewhat outside bourgeois customs to understand the feeling of enormous insecurity that overtakes the man who entrusts himself unconditionally to fate. To be fruitful means to destroy oneself. . . ."[28] Letting oneself go, loving and giving of oneself, are experienced in her fantasy world as destruction. Here lies the key to the mystery of Sabina, in the recesses of her childhood, when people probably responded to her expansive moments with reminders of the traditional canons of propriety, with the castration of feelings. Sabina's mother had found no satisfaction in marriage, and love was a sentiment unknown to her.[29] Sabina, as the eldest child, would have borne the brunt of these arid motions of the heart, and must have conceived from the beginning the fear of abandonment and of love. The anal regression to which she fell victim probably represented a desperate message, which her father and mother in remote Rostov-on-Don were incapable of interpreting correctly. "In my attacks of anguish it seemed to me that an unknown force was trying to take me away from my parents. I often had the feeling of flying away, against my will. Animals and diseases, which I imagined in the form of living beings, were trying to 'do me harm' and drag me into the fearful darkness of death."[30] The anguish of being carried off was nothing but the wish to escape from her parents. But losing her parents also signified the journey into the darkness. Thus little Sabina slowly built up her psychosis.

In her autobiographical references she often speaks of the "plague" as a disease that pursued her—plague destroys the skin, and thus the protective covering of her ego. So the only response is to take refuge in herself, to reject the terrible world that surrounds her and seek, if possible, within her fantasy that corner of happiness to which every child is entitled. But through the gaps in the fingers that covered her face, she must have glimpsed a young man who seemed to be taking an interest in her. She was not mistaken.

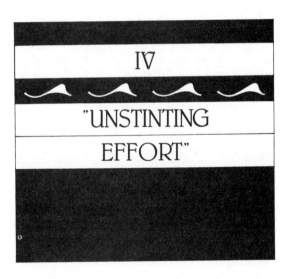

IV

"UNSTINTING EFFORT"

JUNG HAD BEEN WORKING at the Burghölzli since 1900. At the time of his meeting with Sabina he was about thirty years old, while his patient would have been eighteen or nineteen. In *Memories, Dreams, Reflections,* Jung succeeds in evoking his state of mind at that period. Unlike his colleagues, who were engaged in psychiatric statistics and the classification of symptoms, he was beginning to ask questions about the meaning of mental illness. But to ask oneself such questions involves first of all adopting a special attitude in the presence of patients and acknowledging that they have their own codes that need to be deciphered.

The mental patient's world is made up of divisions and watertight compartments. Any attempt by the patient to include himself and his own mode of being within a broader universe—for instance, that of other people—is doomed to fail, since the connections and inferences he makes follow not common logic, but logic of another kind that, taken as a whole, has great significance and involves suffering and tragedy. It is not easy for the psychiatrist to start reconnoitering a different way of thinking. When Jung was about to embark on the difficult path of deciphering madness, the only precedents he had to go on were a few suggestions derived from the publications of Freud and his own interpretative monograph on the so-called occult phenomena. But he may have had in his favor an extraordinary anima dimension that allowed him to look deeper into women than the austere Freud had been able to do. As we read in *Memories, Dreams, Reflections:* "From my encounters with patients and with the psychic phenomena which they have paraded before me in an endless stream of images, I have learned an enormous amount—not just knowledge, but above all insight into my own nature. And not the least of what I have learned has come from my errors and defeats. I have had mainly women patients, who often entered into the work with extraordinary conscientiousness, understanding, and intelligence. *It was essentially because of them that I was able to strike out on new paths in therapy.*"[1]

Why should Jung make such a statement at the end of his life's journey? Precisely because—as he acknowledges in his autobiography, which is also his self-analysis—the most delicate sector (rigorously concealed) of his life had been the gash through which he had discerned and experienced his unconscious, or, as he liked to say, his inner demon.

According to Paul J. Stern: "Jung's magnetism for female neurotics of all shades was remarkable. . . . Part of Jung's secret was that he empathized strongly with the aspirations of women who were or felt misunderstood; undoubtedly, his extreme, almost 'feminine' sensitivity also contributed to this peculiar sex-appeal. In any case, women were his first, most enthusiastic, and most fanatic disciples."[2] Even Jung's wife, in a "secret" letter to Freud, wrote of her husband: "Naturally the women are all in love with him."[3]

We are speaking, then, of deep psychic knowledge. It is something that cannot take place without reciprocity. Jung would never have been able to descend into Sabina's world without her imperceptibly taking possession of him. It should be clear that true seduction is always psychological and never physical. Seduction is like an odorless gas that has been inhaled, whose effects make themselves known only when poisoning has occurred. In view of Jung's youth, his relative lack of experience, the state of emotional fragility in which he found himself at that time, and above all the fact that he had not, for obvious reasons, been analyzed, it is not surprising that his new way of looking at and approaching his patients should have led him into a thorny situation. We analysts start from a fundamental premise: we feel ourselves capable of confronting any situation, even when the circumstances are completely new and previous analytic experiences can no longer serve as a possible reference point. This presumed certainty comes to us, in great part, from our analytic training, which serves essentially as a compass by which to orient ourselves in moments when we might lose our bearings. Here an example may be useful. Some time ago I was urged to accept a young girl for psychological treatment. I had inner misgivings, but finally I yielded to pressure and accepted the girl in therapy. After a few sessions I learned that she had more than once attempted suicide. My initial reluctance probably stemmed from a subliminal perception of the patient's ego disturbance. As was to be expected, she again tried to kill herself. The doctor on duty at the hospital telephoned me and asked me to come to the emergency ward. As soon as the girl, who was lying in bed, saw me, she smiled, wanted me to take her hands, and asked me how I had been able to abandon all my patients in order to come to her. The rules of the analytic game lie precisely in the interpretation of everything that happens and not only in the analyst's office, and so on that occasion, as on others, I did not feel I was breaking any rule if, in the face of the patient's actions, I behaved in other than the usual way. If we were to try to understand together the meaning of her gesture and to interpret it correctly, we could begin to do so immediately, even outside the office. This opinion is shared by Maffei, who states that when there is a correct interpretation of anything that happens, one has then been able to ensure that "despite the attacks it suffers, the analyst's power of interpretation remains complete and never ceases to be at the patient's side."[4] Within the bounds of possibility, analytic training allows the analytic relationship to be kept constant, so that the patient is always offered a reference point, even in the stormiest moments, when everything seems plunged into darkness and patient and analyst have the feeling of no longer understanding anything. But unlike the patient, who has entered treatment for the precise purpose of reconstructing his identity, the analyst has an ego in which to recognize himself. This, however, does not always happen, and Jung's initial experience is proof.

In my description of the psychotic world, I spoke of the sense of exclusion felt by the patient. Maffei correctly links this exclusion to the psychotic's sense of potency, since "this potency of the psychotic is the potency of one who, in remaining outside the game of life and never compromising himself, will never be able to stand up to others and measure his own worth."[5] But the price to be paid for this omnipotence acquired by fleeing the world is the impossibility of obtaining any outside recognition. To be sure, the world is frightening because it is terribly practical, and because the aggression of others can burst forth at any moment, but if we do not stand up to it and take the risk of being overcome, we cannot evaluate our own capacities, and we therefore become impotent. "Omnipotence-impotence are the extremes of the psychotic world."[6] Now, "what afflicts the omnipotent-impotent is an experience that finds no room, finds no possibility of expansion, it is a series of extremely alarming and terrible phantasms—and the therapist may easily gloss over this problem and not develop an interest in it, limiting himself to a superficial recognition. If the encounter is to be useful, it is necessary instead to give the omnipotent-impotent a true and profound confidence, without being discouraged by the sullenness and harshness he displays and which actually conceal a possibility for development."[7]

Jung intuitively felt the need to give a true and profound confidence to his psychotic patients. From the beginning of the century he had been treating schizophrenia by psychotherapy,[8] without, however, being able to avail himself of the insights, and especially of the training analysis, that have evolved since then. The nature of the transference was not understood, in particular psychotic transference and psychotic countertransference. But these problems must be examined later.

In all probability Jung was the only one at the Burghölzli who approached his patients with the principles he described in detail in his noted psychiatric papers. He succeeded in bringing to conclusion the case of Babette, a patient famous for her utter lack of attractiveness. Babette had been presented also to Freud, who had been unable to refrain from calling her "this phenomenally ugly female."[9] Obviously the patient's fearful and indescribable ugliness had not kept Jung from finding her delusions "lovely" and the things she said "interesting."

Jung's patient Sabina was a young Russian girl from a good family, educated, who hoped to accomplish great things. In a touching moment of narcissism, she describes her sense of her body as follows: "down to the waist I am not embarrassed; I took pleasure in having the contours of a grown woman, I was happy that my skin is soft, my curves lovely and well developed. Even if I have a very ordinary face, I can still be attractive."[10] Helene Deutsch recalls something of Sabina's physical appearance: "She was short, rather thin, and more or less a brunette."[11]

Jung's inquiring spirit must have driven him irresistibly toward the girl, whose sole expectation was perhaps to become attached to someone. Indeed, how many times has anyone with a psychotherapeutic practice been witness to the deep libido bond of his patients, whose single wish is to possess him completely? In this case we can speak of psychotic transference. In a normal transference situation, the symbolic dimension of the relationship is more or less grasped by the patient. It is, of course, a question of degree, but, at least in the neurotic mode, the absolute need for the analyst is always experienced by the patient with doubt and suspicion, not only through its contingent analytic cultivation, but above all through the establishment of a therapeutic alliance that goes back to some integral part of the ego. In a psychotic transference things are much different. In the first place, the libido attachment is enormously greater, almost animalistic. A patient of mine expressed the idea by saying that the analyst was part of her bloodstream, just as heroin comes to form part of the drug addict. I do not know whether Freud was referring to this type of transference when he spoke of certain situations as not yielding to analysis.[12]

In the psychotic transference the symbolic dimension of the relationship does not touch the patient in the least, and he deifies the object of his transference to the point of causing actual disturbances in the analyst. To state it more clearly and to refer to a now classic model, it is not *as if* the analyst were the father; he *is* the beloved father. This lack of symbolization ensures that what emerges from the relationship is not experienced as a repetition, but is a genuine feeling that the patient tragically lives as such, with untold suffering and with such reality that, should the storm subside, he carries in his heart for the rest of his life the image that the analyst, by his presence, has allowed him to arrive at and make concrete.

Sabina, according to Jung's description, "could no longer look anyone in the face, kept her head bowed, and when anybody touched her stuck her tongue out with every sign of loathing."[13] This psychotic modality is significant. In the experience of therapy, as every analyst knows, the patient's way of looking is highly indicative. In particular, the schizophrenic patient never observes the therapist directly, or, rather, if he does, his eyes seem to stare past or through the other person. In general, it can be said that when a schizophrenic is unable to look at someone directly, he is primarily possessed by the fear of losing himself in the other (and hence by the wish to do so). Perhaps more than in any other person, this desire in the schizophrenic to merge himself is the desire for the earthly paradise, the utopia that every man who constructs his own ideology ardently yearns for. This fusion, however, also involves the destruction of the other, and such a result cannot always be accepted. So instead of merging himself and facing the risk of this annihilation, the schizophrenic patient tries to do harm only to himself.[14] The therapist must, however, be capable of looking this reality in the face and *not* be afraid of his patient's fear. If he does not fear being killed or being madly loved, the therapist allows the patient to confront, for the first time in his life, what before was impossible: to try to destroy, knowing that the love object will not be eliminated. Psychosis demands something more than neurosis. Maffei writes: "The capacity not to be swayed by panic generally emerges in the therapist from the fact that within his psyche, because he is not omnipotent-impotent and because of the analysis he has had, a kind of ego identity is created in which the therapist recognizes himself and which can therefore resist possible ego-dystonic impulses. . . ."[15] There is also another consideration: the father whom the patient sees in his analyst is not the father of a child who has now become an adult, but is the father as first perceived, that is to say of the little child, and thus an all-powerful person in relation to that child.

The beginning of the relationship is always circumspect, and Jung tells us how he approached the psychotic patient without preconceived judgments: but what is the *other person*, the patient, going through? He knows only his inner devastation, he knows his unlimited power but also his deep and wretched fragility.

As already mentioned, Jung's technique was based primarily on certain intuitions and on a charismatic personal dimension; he was not, in my opinion, equipped to take on Sabina's psychosis. Here the psychotic countertransference comes into play. I shall take this concept to mean the analyst's emotional response to the conscious and unconscious material offered him by the patient. This is not to say that in working with psychotics the analyst necessarily has a psychotic emotional response, but it may happen, as it did in Jung's case, that the other's psychosis may dislodge some psychotic nuclei that often even a good analysis does not succeed in bringing to light. Expert analysts acknowledge with chagrin that certain patients teach them much about their own nature.[16] And now to the Spielrein case itself.

Jung's first communication to Freud about Sabina's case is dated 23 October 1906, but, as already noted, the beginning of the psychological treatment must fall within the year 1904.[17] Jung later gives another veiled piece of information concerning a hysterical patient and a line of poetry that kept recurring in her mind, without disclosing that it had to do with the same case. It was still Spielrein, but the communication received from Jung surely did not allow Freud to connect the two letters. Then on 7 March 1909, about two and a half years later, Jung is forced to make a bitter confession to Freud—without, however, revealing that he was referring to the patient of the two previous letters. After explaining to Freud that he finds himself in a dreadful situation, he goes on: ". . . a woman patient, whom years ago I pulled out of a very sticky neurosis with unstinting effort, has violated my confidence and my friendship in the most mortifying way imaginable. She has kicked up a vile scandal solely because I denied myself the pleasure of giving her a child. I have always acted the gentleman towards her, but before the bar of my rather too sensitive conscience I nevertheless don't feel clean, and that is what hurts the most because my intentions were always honourable. But you know how it is—the devil can use even the best of things for the fabrication of filth. Meanwhile I have learnt an unspeakable amount of marital wisdom, for until now I had a totally inadequate idea of my polygamous components despite all self-analysis. Now I know where and how the devil can be laid by the heels. These painful yet extremely salutary insights have churned me up hellishly inside, but for that very reason, I hope, have secured me moral qualities which will be of the greatest advantage to me in later life."[18]

Jung speaks of *unstinting effort* [*grösster Hingabe,* literally "greatest devotion"]. The phrase seems to express Jung's boundless need to come to grips with his anima dimension.

Immediately after the treatment began, Jung, to judge by the modest silence in his letters to Freud, must have perceived that things were not going in the right direction and that his "unstinting effort" had precipitated him into what I have called psychotic countertransference. It is possible that Jung talked to Freud about his predicament on the occasions when they met, but since it does not turn up in the correspondence the possibility may be set aside. In the psychotic countertransference, especially when it cannot be analyzed by an outside observer, the suffering psychotic patient is slowly transformed into an elusive image, "the treasure beyond one's grasp"—consisting of the patient's world, his most heated fantasies, his enchanting detachment from the world, his contempt. All this becomes, in the view of the youthful Jung, that lost paradise of an accord marvelous to the degree that it cannot be attained or deciphered. And all this passion flowed inexorably like a river toward Sabina, who was slowly but surely making progress toward recovery.

We know that psychotics, precisely because of their particular modality, are able to read us with true perspicacity. We may surmise that in his relationship with Sabina Jung initiated an "analysis" of his own. After all, Jung, by his own testimony, at the beginning of his career often used his sessions with his patients, especially if they were psychotic, to discuss his dreams. One such case was young Honegger, who represents a dark and painful page in Jung's life; another was Gross, also an unpleasant episode in his experience.[19]

But with Sabina things were different because she was a woman. She could more easily strike Jung's unconscious, his anima, and the possibilities of resistance were reduced virtually to naught. Let us put ourselves in his place: the girl we have before us has been destroyed by her psychosis and we hope to be able to draw her out of the inferno. Imperceptibly she makes us feel that we are indispensable to her, that her intelligence, her sensitivity and culture, her feminine charm as a young woman, and her self-declared inner demon are all for us, because she trusts us. We then become that daily drug necessary for her life, and in that moment we feel ourselves to be creators of life and hope.

In the situation in which Jung found himself, Sabina must have expressed a typical image of the anima, attracting and repelling, wondrous and diabolical, exciting and depressing. But Jung could not have known this. The only thing he could have been aware of was the "unstinting effort" he was offering this girl. She must have aroused in him, for the first time in his life, a typical sentiment that might go by the name of love. I express myself uncertainly because the problem that now opens up before us is a vast one.

There is to my mind no text of Freud's more ambiguous than the one devoted to transference love. The ambiguity arises not so much from the delicacy of the subject as from the underlying Freudian thesis according to which transference love is always seen as a form of resistance. But Freud does not succeed in convincing even himself, since in his paper he feels the need to convey the idea that in normal conditions love has more or less the same characteristics as are met with in the kind of love activated by analysis.[20] Actually, the problem is not all that difficult. Any love, in whatever situation it develops, is based on a transference. If this love is placed at the service of resistance, that is another matter. An obvious supposition is that there also exists a countertransference love, which cannot be distinguished from the analogous feeling in nonanalytic situations. It becomes, however, a psychotic love when the analyst is unable to perceive that his loving rapture, real as it is felt to be, is availing itself of circumstances in his life characteristic of *mana*.

In investigating this subject further we can, strange though it may seem, find enlightenment in Hegel, who in his youth wrote some excellent pages on love.

Hegel says: "True union, or love proper, exists only between living beings who are alike in power and thus in each other's eyes living beings from every point of view; in no respect is either dead for the other."[21] In the analytic situation, especially at the beginning, no symmetry can exist. Clearly, it takes more than the analyst's will to place himself on a level of equality and eliminate the asymmetry of the relationship, since the reality lies in that very asymmetry. The disparity between patient and analyst is responsible in the first place for a psychological process described by Melanie Klein, the projective identification that consists in expelling and situating in the analyst parts—both good and bad—of one's self, with the omnipotent wish of being able to control them. In this state the bond created between the patient and the analyst acquires, in certain cases, an almost indestructible strength.[22] This bond would seem to approach love, but it differs from it because the intensity of the feelings projected by the patient onto the analyst makes the latter by far the stronger of the two. One can suppose that in patriarchal society as well, where power is purely male, the love of the woman for the man is based primarily on projective identification and that a relationship therefore develops in a situation of inequality with a typical characteristic: it always excludes the other and acquires all the connotations of a narcissistic relationship. Certainly anyone who has intensely experienced such a relationship knows, despite its negative aspects, that it exerts an incredible spell, since it places the individual, even if in an illusory way, at the center of the world. In these moments one experiences a state of complete abandonment and, above all, of mutual dependence. When this happens in analysis, we have a true symbiotic relationship, from which one can emerge only at the cost of severe suffering. Béla Grunberger seems to have hit the mark when, in attempting to describe the characteristics of the "good" analyst, he is obliged to admit that "mastery of the unconscious borders on the illusion of narcissistic omnipotence, and if we grant that the readiness to regress to that stage and find oneself in familiar surroundings is often referrable to a structure that is more or less susceptible to regression, one that is fragile in the face of certain practical tasks as well as sensitive to the messages coming from the unconscious. . . ."[23] This means that in the moment of maximum identification with the other it is precisely the reality principle that is lacking, with consequences that can easily be imagined. In the pages of Sabina's diary there are many references to her intuitive affinity with Jung—for example, unbeknown to each other, their appreciation of Wagner. Such affinities are described by almost all people in love with each other: it is as though their intuition of the things of the world were simultaneous. Another typical aspect of love is its being an end in itself: every person in love cherishes the illusion of being able to enclose himself in the circle of his love. When Jung confesses to feeling insecure in the girl's presence, in reality he is revealing another typical, almost "ontological" condition of being in love—that of feeling weak and defenseless in the presence of a sentiment that may overwhelm us.

But that is not all. This love between Jung and Spielrein emerged within an analytic relationship, where, at least in the initial exchanges, the analyst does not appear weak. Not only in concrete matters, but also in the symbolic world of the patient, he is experienced as a mysterious god, untouchable and unknowable, and later as an understanding, beloved father who brings protection and salvation. If this situation gives way to one in which the analyst speaks of himself and discloses his human suffering, it is as though a pact has been broken. In these moments the patient may feel that she is losing an illusion for good, losing an earthly paradise, and she ceases, perhaps abruptly, to be a child. This means that the patient is forced to remove her gaze from her own inner world and look at the analyst, becoming aware, in most cases, of the sorrow and fear that he, too, experiences. In a certain sense, the god abandons its customary abode in the depths of the patient's soul and, having been killed, is resurrected on solid ground. In place of the god there is now a human being who suffers and loves as she does.

It is a difficult and risky transition, one in general to be avoided, but inevitable when the analyst is fragile in his feelings. The patient is most often thrown into confusion by it. She places herself on two different levels; one part tries to remain a child, protected by the warmth of the analyst's omnipotence, while the other is already straining toward the new experience—a part, it should be emphasized, that never before had the courage to press forward or ask questions, and in general was content to observe, feel, and secretly daydream. The patient is being asked to grow up and become a woman. This request is heard with awe and panic.

Pascal writes that the first thing God inspires in the soul, when he deigns to touch it truly, is an intuition, a new knowledge, a new light, that brings fear and confusion. It is the path of those who are summoned, halfway between the elect of heaven and the rejected of hell, the path of those who seek God but have not found Him, a hidden God, always present and always absent, whose existence is simultaneously certain and uncertain, hope and risk. The same thing happens in analysis when certain pacts are broken: anxiety, emotion, and confusion take possession of the patient, who comes to know, in Freud's words, the truth of the uncanny. It is the fright and anguish we feel when faced with something new and foreign and at the same time old, well known, and familiar. The uncanny implies ambivalence, ambiguity, conflicting judgments.

The relationship between Jung and Spielrein was uncanny. It was the birth of a god who is like the aroma described by Baudelaire: it can be enjoyed but is never completely there, it is both the body and the negation of the body. And Jung was to write as follows in *Memories, Dreams, Reflections:* "Whatever the learned interpretation may be of the sentence 'God is love,' the words affirm the *complexio oppositorum* of the Godhead. . . . I have again and again been faced with the mystery of love, and have never been able to explain what it is. . . . Here is the greatest and smallest, the remotest and nearest, the highest and lowest, and we cannot discuss one side of it without also discussing the other. No language is adequate to this paradox. Whatever one can say, no words express the whole."[24]

But it is also true that every patient, at the beginning of analysis, exists in a state of emotional aridity, or in any case of suffering. It is as though there were a prohibition, of the kind imposed on children. It exists and is gradually transformed into the impossibility of establishing contact with the world and with life. Put briefly, it is the prohibition of living. The patient finds herself locked as though for punishment in her own body, which like herself is forced to move around in the world. This leads to fear and alienation, lack of self-confidence, the inability to grasp reality. It is the kind of estrangement of which one can even be unaware, for ostensibly one desires relations with other human beings while in reality one seeks spaces in which to prolong the silence. Annihilated to the depths, the patient is not even aware that the need to survive makes her take sides with the oppressor. While living, she chooses to commit suicide through life. The analyst is generally the first person to take care of her, the first who can be counted on for forgiveness. The encounter has the flavor of magic, a mystery filled with hopes, the expectation of a good god by whom one can be nourished. It is almost the birth of a holy secret that slowly allows one to begin living again. It is like appropriating the strength and courage of the analyst in order to face up to and accept the truth about oneself. One grows through the analyst's patience, his understanding, his sense of justice, and what is experienced as his unbounded wisdom.

The beauty of the feeling that issues forth is also linked to the inherent obstacle of the analytic relationship, since this appears to be sacred and inviolable. But this is precisely the point. Is the difficulty, as in the love of Tristan and Isolde, "simply a *pretext* needed in order to enable the passion to progress, or is it connected with the passion in some far more profound manner? If we delve into the recesses of the myth, we see that this obstruction is what passion really *wants*—its true object."[25] It is as though patient and analyst had to understand each other's existence through the obstacle. "Thereupon to love is no longer to flee and persistently to reject the act of love. Love now still begins beyond death, but from that beyond it returns to life. And, in being thus converted, love brings forth our *neighbour*."[26]

It would seem that for the patient the price to be paid for emerging from herself, from her concentrated navel-gazing, is to go through a state of love and passion that is all the more violent the longer she has remained in the silence of the love that nullifies everything. It is a rather high price, since the violence of the feeling is "a kind of naked and denuding intensity; verily, a bitter destitution, the *impoverishment* of a mind being emptied of all diversity, an obsession of the imagination by a single image. In the face of the assertion of its power, the world dissolves; 'the others' cease to be present; and there are no longer either neighbours or duties, or binding ties, or earth or sky; one is alone with all that one loves."[27] In this situation, love amounts to coming together to commit a crime, a pact in which one becomes an accomplice of anything that can happen in life, and where sexual union is above everything else. Once one feels this, it is perhaps possible to accept the other's fear as well, his sorrows and compromises, but each must stand naked before the other, and love the other also for his delinquency.

There is yet another characteristic of the analytic state of love. One almost has the impression that this love ought never to end, and the lovers have the sense of the infinite rather than of transience. Thus in the analytic relationship, more than elsewhere, the libido is bound to its objects, and their loss is the cause of indescribable suffering[28]—so that when the analyst falls in love, one can even suppose that in a certain sense he is incapable of sooner or later vanishing for his patient, since his falling in love contributes still more to keeping the ties intact. So one might also say that the analyst's supreme task is to learn to die for his patient. Hegel writes: "To say that the lovers have an independence and a living principle peculiar to each of themselves means only that they may die."[29]

Was it really love that bound Spielrein to Jung? Can the whole episode be understood in the light of the transference? *Non liquet.*

But it is time to return to the subject of transference love. So let us ask ourselves: what counterresistance on the part of the analyst does this type of love help to support? Most likely the course of the analysis reaches a moment painful to the analyst, and love in this case might indicate the way to bypass a temporary inability to communicate. Certainly one needs courage to face such a situation, and Jung, with sure instinct but unaware of the dangers involved, chose (or was chosen by) this path. He let himself go completely, and this unhappy woman, obsessed by disgust and the notion of the feces that everywhere surrounded her, became a graceful feminine image who, in a boat on the Lake of Zurich, revealed to Jung the world of feeling and of overwhelming love, free of that bourgeois hypocrisy that forces the man and woman to live an everlasting and humiliating lie. Sabina would seem to have been a woman for whom love did not imply calculation or the demand for promises that are broken the moment they are made, a Dionysiac woman, vibrant with feeling, who understood and forgave everything while offering Jung a forceful spur for his spiritual growth.

In September 1907 Jung presented his clinical experience of Sabina to the First International Congress of Psychiatry and Neurology, at Amsterdam. It was a case that enabled him to explain the Freudian theory of hysteria to the public. One can suppose that at that date, if for no other reason than good taste, the situation was still under control, at least on Jung's side. It is difficult to imagine that had he been emotionally involved, he would have found it possible to present the object of his emotions to a scientific audience. Jung probably realized he was in love with the patient at the beginning of 1908, as shown by the letter dated 26 June 1908 in the correspondence with Sabina.

The first group of letters, all from 1908, introduce us directly to the problem, while the others, which run from 1910 to 1919, take on a more impersonal and didactic tone. Jung's emotional separation from Sabina, which probably began in 1909, was to be accentuated, as we will see later, in the following years.

By 1908 Sabina had already been out of the hospital for three years. She must have made a fairly good recovery, for she was able to attend the lectures at medical school on a regular basis. It would be natural that even after being discharged from the hospital she continued to see Jung, and that her love and affection for him should remain unchanged. As we know, Sabina was a sensitive and intelligent girl. What could she ever have written to Jung to upset his unconscious so drastically? There can be no doubt that it was a love letter, but its contents must have touched precisely the most unhappy chord in Jung's life. Perhaps his marriage to a worthy daughter of the Swiss bourgeoisie no longer offered him the "Pindaric flights" of feeling that, by his own admission, were decisive in his life. Unlike Freud, who at the age of forty, after marriage had exhausted its *raison d'être,* looked forward to nothing but death,[30] Jung, feeling anything but resigned, did not let the opportunity slip. "You cannot imagine how much it means to me to have hopes of loving a person whom I must not condemn, and who does not condemn herself, to being smothered in the banality of habit."[31]

Certainly Jung did not lack other occasions of the kind offered by Sabina; his polygamous tendencies are also shown by a dream. One can suppose that Jung was always on the lookout for the problem of the persona, but with Sabina he must have been taken completely by surprise. Indeed, as he confesses in a letter: "I notice how much more attached I am to you than I should ever have thought. I happen to be terribly suspicious and always think others want to exploit me and lord it over me. It is only with great diffi-

culty that I can actually muster that belief in man's natural goodness which I so often proclaim. Which certainly does not apply to
my feelings for you!"[32] He must also have had some doubts, especially since, as Sabina's analyst, he would have known her destructive aspects, but the thought is immediately rejected.

At the time, however, Jung may have been justified, since Freud's
essay "Negation" (1925; *Standard Ed.*, 19) had not yet been published. Jung speaks also of his distrust of other people, and explains
part of this attitude in a letter to Freud,[33] but these reservations
might also be the indication of a paranoid element which always
marked Jung's actions. Even in *Memories, Dreams, Reflections* it
is easy to spot this typical psychological modality, which, inciden-
tally, was not lacking in Freud's personal psychology, either.[34]

But Jung's *nekyia*, his journey through the unconscious, had
scarcely begun. He had completely blotted out Sabina's ambivalence, and quite soon was to be forced to write a dramatic letter,
the most moving one in the whole correspondence, which shows
him vulnerable and defenseless, and signals his capitulation to the
girl. Four months after the letter in which he had confessed to
having no fear of abandoning himself to the new experience of love,
Jung writes one that is full of passionate emphasis. "I am looking
for a person who can love without punishing, imprisoning and
draining the other person; I am seeking this as yet unrealized type
who will manage to separate love from social advantage or disadvantage, so that love may always be an end unto itself, not just a
means for achieving another end."[35] Most likely Jung had deluded
himself into thinking that he was creating a particular kind of
"paradisiacal" situation in which sentiment would be free to express itself without heeding certain rigid rules that generally hinder
love's expression. It is a difficult state to achieve, since in the dual
relationship there is always a disequilibrium that tends to be
righted by the introduction of elements that seemingly have little
to do with love but actually form an integral part of it. Jung certainly had the right to expect from Sabina a love that was "boundless and without reservations," but he should also have expected
that she would unconsciously set in motion all her destructive
mechanisms to strike him where he was most vulnerable. Jung
writes: "It is my misfortune that my life means nothing to me

without the joy of love, of tempestuous, eternally changing love."[36] He sees that it is a misfortune because the more "tempestuous, eternally changing" love is, the higher is the price to be paid.

Sabina's diary may provide a key to the tragedy that was looming over Jung's head. Sabina refers repeatedly to Jung's family, to the bourgeois aspect of his marriage. Probably in her "final scene," the girl had screamed at Jung what she thought of his wife, and had demanded in no uncertain terms that he free himself and come to live with her. It is not for us to sit in judgment on the behavior of Jung, who was apparently caught up in a typical respectable bourgeois marriage; what concerns us is the psychological trap into which he had so obviously fallen. On the one hand, he could not manage without Sabina, and on the other, he had no intention of leaving his wife—this situation was damaging to him on both sides. The words with which his letter closes—"Return to me, in this moment of my need, some of the love and guilt and altruism which I was able to give you at the time of your illness. Now it is I who am ill"—are indicative of his state of mind. He was a man begging for mercy, in a condition that can arise only if the beloved (or the person thought to be the beloved) has become a terrible drug.

Jung must have felt compelled to face up to the contradiction between his capacity to penetrate the hearts of others and his incapacity to love, to have real contact with people; for the love he proposed to Sabina was to be a pure love, "whose true and innermost prerequisite for life is freedom and independence."[37] What Jung suggested may indeed have been an advanced and enlightened program, but in reality it could not be carried out, for it skirted the frontier of the impossible; in other words, it meant not wanting a relationship. After all, Jung was demanding all this of a twenty-three-year-old girl who, moreover, had been seriously ill. A further complication was that she had been his patient and had therefore experienced the relationship in a situation of dependence—a situation in which it is not easy to view objectively the gestures, the words, and especially the promptings that come from the analyst.

The reader must try to enter deeply into the emotional atmosphere into which Spielrein had fallen. Here was a girl who had been very ill and was well aware that she had been able to emerge from her madness only with Jung's help. She was desperately in love with her savior. The consequence was that the beloved man was desired in his totality. But we know how cruel analysis can sometimes be! "The treatment must be carried through in a state of abstinence."[38] But dissatisfaction in analysis pertains not only to love—it is much deeper, more cruel, less reducible. The way of analysis is *par excellence* speech, symbolization. But the symbol is by its nature dissatisfactory. As Hegel attests, consciousness is always dissatisfied. All language is a boundary: the speaker is the intermediary between the expressible and the inexpressible, between the word and silence. Dissatisfaction, the tension between *usage* and *potentiality*, between the *body* of the word, public and expressible, and the always broader *shadow* of intention, of the intimate, individual, no longer utterable resonance, can be said to be typical of all language. All the more so of language in analysis. This constant effort to understand one another, to give form, public usage, or linguistic play to the shadow-images of intention is truly frustrating and cruel. The word, the *logos*, is the gift of Apollo, the god of indirection, of refined and deferred violence. Like the bow or the dart, the word is a mortal challenge by the god. The ambiguity of the riddle is the supreme weapon of Apollonian violence, the most fatal arrow launched from his bow. Apollo's darts are thoughts![39] But the riddle indicates the source of reason, the impulse to interpret, the obscurity of the word as an incentive to continue the struggle.

Thus psychoanalysis, this ritual of the word, is an agon, a contest of thought. Its cruelty is cerebral. Those who expose themselves to the test, like the ancient sage before the riddle of the god, accept a mortal risk. Dissatisfaction is the crux of analysis because language, the symbol, the word are all dissatisfactory. Often, to endure the trial, people seek help in the language of bodies, which is simpler, softer, less cruel. This is an escape, a resistance, of course. But perhaps it is only a *consolamentum*, a small consolation, a mutual gift of warmth and encouragement in order to be able to face the cruelty of abstinence and dissatisfaction.

But could Sabina have understood these subtle, secondary aspects of analysis? It is not easy to accept the symbolic value of love. She was therefore justified in demanding everything, since "a pure heart is not ashamed of love; but it is ashamed if its love is incomplete; it upbraids itself if there is some hostile power which hinders love's culmination."[40]

Toward Jung she felt a fond sentiment of love and gratitude, accompanied, however, by that wish for destruction that characterizes any ambivalence of feeling. A man placed in this situation can, at least for a short while, do what he likes, for he is actually in a very strong position with respect to the woman he has saved. He can in practice permit himself anything, but precisely because he has this unlimited power, his moral integrity and feelings ought to be absolutely steadfast.

Idealization on the part of the patient cannot be brought abruptly into contact with a reality in which the ideal features of the analyst's conduct would come up against concrete necessities. One can conceive a legitimate disengagement in which the patient's inner image of the analyst becomes diminished and stripped of that quality of *mana* that is so necessary at least in the first period of the analysis. It is obviously not a conscious wish, but this is the reality, and any analyst who has encountered the same experience as Jung knows very well the bitterness and dismay of the situation. Perhaps the problem can be put this way: Jung in the beginning devoted himself ardently to his patient's salvation, and he succeeded fully, judging by the later career of Sabina Spielrein. But the price of his success was to fall in love with her. The reason Jung did not retreat was that he was under the illusion of having found that combination of pure feelings that had so far been denied him, even in his marriage. Sabina, for her part, loved Jung very much, not only for the salvation that he represented for her, but also because, being a cultivated and intelligent woman, she immediately understood the spiritual stature of the man. The child Sabina, however, also wanted other things, which Jung did not succeed in giving; Sabina's attitude was such that Jung was forced to behave in an abominable way, with an utter lack of taste. Everything collapsed for Sabina, at least for the moment, not only externally but also in her endopsychic world. This meant she had *necessarily* to seek other support, someone to whom she might recount the beautiful but at the same time devastating affair. One factor made this need especially compelling: while Spielrein allowed herself to be swept along by her love, Jung seemed to express himself as though he still had control within the sphere of his passion.

By now it has been ascertained that a very important difference exists in the analytic relationship between those periods in which one actually loves a person outside the analysis and the periods when one instead feels an overpowering need to fall in love. If, for example, the analyst is in a love situation, what is given the patient is something "left over," something "extra" from his own life. The important things are therefore "outside the analysis." Under these circumstances, of course, the risk of involvement is much reduced.

If the analyst is in love, the analytic relationship is placed in a different situation, because, in the course of love, our lives seem to acquire a sort of universal justification. When the analyst does not love, a confusion between analytic space and personal space almost automatically arises, because when we find ourselves predisposed to fall in love, we always hope that any human being who approaches may be just the person with whom to establish an emotional relationship. It seems clear that when Jung met Sabina he was not happy emotionally. He felt the presence of the Other, he must have hoped and yearned, but he neither knew how nor was able to steer the relationship in the direction he desired. Only the mature analyst can handle such situations skillfully. The analytic pact ought to be kept, despite the search for the Other, despite pain and frustration. Many analyses have this characteristic. The important thing is to understand that affective forms are often a defense with respect to professional duty. Jung, innocent of the pitfalls of the situation, made the mistake of going outside the analytic pact. Here death comes into play: if the analyst is happy and his love is outside the analysis, then he is "dead" for his patient. If instead he wants to experience love in the analytic relationship, then death is imparted by the dissolution of the analysis.

This was the picture that Sabina had before her, and only a man could help her.

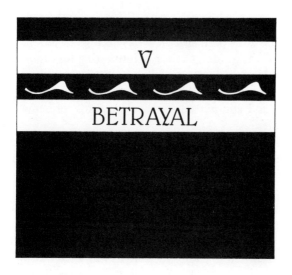

V

BETRAYAL

THIS NEW ASPECT of the situation can be followed through the letters between Freud and Jung and between Spielrein and Freud. One must take into account the solidarity among analysts that dictates, especially if they are friends and collaborators, that they share with each other, with due caution, any element that might disturb an analytic relationship.

The young woman's letter of 30 May 1909 is surely the first one she wrote to Freud. In it Spielrein requests an appointment in such a way as not to arouse suspicion, but Freud's intuition immediately connects the letter with Jung, even if he does not associate the name Spielrein with the mess his friend had previously got himself into. Jung replies at once to Freud's query. For the first time he gives Spielrein's name in writing to Freud and reveals, in accordance with some self-analysis of his own, the reasons for the complicated situation. After explaining that he had felt bound to the patient by gratitude and affection, while knowing that the cure might not last, Jung writes: ". . . I prolonged the relationship over the years and in the end found myself morally obliged, as it were, to devote a large measure of friendship to her, until I saw that an unintended wheel had started turning, whereupon I finally broke with her."[1]

He goes on to declare that he has even been the victim of persecution on the girl's part, since she has been going around spreading slander about him. Jung's letter is interesting for other reasons as well. He alludes to his having fallen in love unconsciously. And he accuses his former patient Otto Gross, with whom he had had tranference and countertransference problems, of being the cause of his troubles.[2]

But later on Jung retracts his accusations against Spielrein and quite honestly discloses the background of his behavior, which, as he himself has the courage to admit, "was a piece of knavery which I very reluctantly confess to you as my father."[3]

For his part, Freud, very diplomatically and, it must be said, with consummate astuteness, offers Spielrein the only honest and therapeutic advice: "Still, if on the basis of the above assumptions I might be permitted to address a word to you, then I would urge you to ask yourself whether the feelings that have outlived this close relationship are not best suppressed and eradicated, from your own psyche I mean, and without external intervention and the involvement of third persons."[4]

In reporting this letter to Jung, Freud congratulates himself by saying: "My reply was ever so wise and penetrating; I made it appear as though the most tenuous of clues had enabled me Sherlock Holmes–like to guess the situation (which of course was none too difficult after your communications) and suggested a more appropriate procedure, something endopsychic, as it were."[5]

This is the attitude of the two analyst physicians toward the patient Spielrein. But the moment has come to examine the Russian girl's own attitude toward being in love. A letter, presumably written between 10 June and 20 June 1909, offers a painful confession that in my view displays more dignity and sense of responsibility than the all-too-human letters of Jung and Freud. In a way Jung and Freud are afraid. Having summoned the demons, they seem to be in agreement in wanting to dismiss them. Note these phrases in which Jung refers to his relationship with Spielrein: "whereupon I finally broke with her;"[6] and, in the same letter, "I need hardly say that I have made a clean break."[7] Apart from the scant truth of these statements, inasmuch as Jung, as we shall see, was soon to resume his relationship with Spielrein, though in a different form, they betray an unabashed rage whose only justification can be Jung's youth and relative lack of experience.

Be that as it may, what we are witnessing is a sick young girl's struggle against Jung and Freud, and it is gratifying to acknowledge that it was the girl who, with shrewdness and perseverance, would win the battle, since both Freud and Jung later claimed her as a pupil! Freud writes: "The way these women manage to charm us with every conceivable psychic perfection until they have attained their purpose is one of nature's greatest spectacles."[8] Indeed, no one can deny a patient's right to fall in love with the analyst; for his part, the analyst has only one duty: to face up to the problem.

Let us now examine the Russian girl's lengthy self-defense. Sabina did not intend, at least consciously, to ask Freud to intervene for the purpose of bringing about a reconciliation. She had already drawn her own conclusions, based on the circumstances—namely, the necessity of breaking with Jung on the emotional level. But with her subtle psychological intelligence she saw that this separation neither could nor should entail the destruction of her love. Perhaps analysts will never sufficiently understand the real importance that they assume for their patients. In the end even the most insignificant analysts—and such exist[9]—succeed in creating in their patients a situation that, much as one may call it "transference," has an objective drama and consistency; if the analyst happens to be famous and of true stature, then the relationship generates heightened conflicts.

Sabina grasped this intuitively. She was a little girl, as she says herself, who ran around the hallways of the Burghölzli with her hair in a braid down her back. Dr. Jung was her friend, and he let her help him with one of his early papers about his experiments on association. Later he was moved to say to her, "Minds such as yours help advance science. You must become a psychiatrist."[10] Such expressions leave an indelible mark, and Spielrein, in the fight against her illness, finally succeeded in carrying out Jung's prediction. But all this cannot fail to produce an infinite tenderness toward the person who holds out such a light in the darkness of insanity.

And so we witness the girl's noble defense of the man she loves, as she pardons and tries to understand even his most disconcerting reactions. The girl is terrified by the idea that Jung might be called a scoundrel, and at this stage who if not Freud can go beyond appearances and bourgeois patterns? "So my last hope of salvation was to speak with a person who deeply loves and respects him, who possesses a profound knowledge of human nature, and when I received your last letter, unfavorable though it was to me, tears came to my eyes: 'He loves him! What if he could understand all this!' "[11]

The youthful Jung's exuberance is revealed in his confessions to the girl when, perhaps under the influence of the dubious Gross, he preaches polygamy and praises Sabina's independent spirit. But did the girl never imagine that fear or some other such feeling would force Jung to beat a retreat? An anonymous letter, which Sabina suspects was written by Jung's wife, informs Sabina's parents of the situation. They demand an explanation from Jung and the answer promptly arrives, a letter that is a genuine *coup de théâtre*, a sensational and unexpected change of mask. Jung writes to Sabina's mother that he is not there to gratify her daughter's sensuality and that he wishes to be free of her and her demands.[12] In view of the bond that had united the girl to Jung, and in view of what he had meant and continued to mean to her, such a letter, which fell into Sabina's own hands, is an upsetting document, and it is hard to see how it even came to be written, except as an outgrowth of Jung's difficulties in object relationships. We must not forget his more humane and passionate letters, which, though arising from what I have called psychotic transference, still reveal his deep involvement with the patient. The strangest part of this letter, and one that almost altogether eludes one's understanding, is the passage in which Jung defines the difference between the services of a physician and friendship. While the latter has virtually no limitations, "the patient may expect her doctor to give her all the love and concern she requires. But the doctor knows his limits and will never cross them, for he is *paid* for his trouble. That imposes the necessary restraints on him. Therefore, I would suggest that if you wish me to adhere strictly to my role as doctor, you should pay me a fee as suitable recompense for my trouble. In that way you may be *absolutely certain* that I will respect my duty as a doctor *under all circumstances.*"[13]

These sentences were of course written not before treatment began (and even then they would have reflected debatable opinions), but after Jung and Sabina had already known each other for about five years! The thought that anyone should contemplate holding his feelings in check by such formal devices is indeed astonishing. It is also true, however, that Jung makes amends for his conduct, the proof of which is the letter written to Freud on 21 June 1909, in which he acknowledges his sins, due primarily to his "stupidity."[14] But the patient, understanding and intelligent as she is, cannot help being appalled by arguments of this kind; Jung then makes things worse by saying that he has made the mistake of being too kind to her, and letting it be understood that the period of affection, compliments, and unbounded esteem was not all that genuine. I doubt that a patient can suffer any blows more savage than these. The analytic situation of seventy years ago is the same as today. The analysand cannot imagine that the powerful analyst could be mistaken. One structures one's own ego, of course, not only through frustrations but through gratifications as well, and if these are then abruptly removed, as happened in this case, there is again the possibility of a retreat into illness. But here the patient was Sabina Spielrein, a young woman steeled by suffering, and therefore capable of doing battle.

Spielrein's discourse strikes me as fundamentally honest and consistent. After they had fallen irreparably in love, she became aware of Jung's depression and indecision, but what primarily concerned her was the possibility of maintaining the relationship: "His profoundly sensitive soul was more important to me than anything else."[15] These are beautiful words, and they reveal, at least in this situation, the fact that Sabina saw things more deeply than Jung. But of course Jung was Sabina's analyst, and she could not have succeeded by herself in formulating the other person's point of view. Thus she did not know that "Occasionally one must be unworthy, simply in order to be able to continue living."[16]

The attitude of her parents, on a visit to Zurich, is surprising, considering the period. For instance, her father said, "People have made a god out of him, and he's nothing but an ordinary human being. I'm so glad she [Sabina] boxed his ears! I would have done it myself. Just let her do what she thinks necessary; she can take care of herself."[17]

One could, of course, look at the problem from another standpoint. The poor sick child—and she must have been very seriously sick—now appeared capable of standing up to her own analyst, and such an analyst! Perhaps the change was a tribute to Jung's therapeutic skill. For this very reason Sabina was unable to be at peace with herself for thinking how much she had loved Jung and how badly he had behaved toward her, the woman who had offered him her whole soul. Showing her his diary, he had said to her: "Only my wife has read this . . . and you!"[18] Revenge, which is usually called for in such cases, seems to have been far from Sabina's mind, and she was doing her utmost to keep Jung from becoming "an unmitigated scoundrel." That is, she understood, with profound intuition, that she could not destroy within herself the wonderful image, the warm nucleus, of what had once been her beloved analyst.

In her letter to Freud, Sabina rejects the idea that Jung's possible love for her might have been a shift from Freud's daughter to herself, and thinks that it can be traced back to another Jewish girl, the famous S.W. described by Jung in his dissertation. This paper was based on some experiments carried out between 1893 and 1900 with a girl, the initials S.W. being used to conceal a cousin of Jung's, Helene Preiswerk. A book by Helene's niece has recently brought to light the deep bond that united Jung with his little fourteen-year-old cousin, suggesting that it was very close, albeit unconsciously, to love.[19] To judge by Sabina's letter, Jung may actually have been conscious of it. Sabina writes: "In the course of an analysis it turned out that so-and-so many years ago Dr. Jung had been fond of a dark-haired hysterical girl called S.W., who always described herself as Jewish."[20] Sabina's deduction that the shift must have been from this girl to herself is confirmed by Jung, who writes to Freud: "then the Jewess popped up in another form, in the shape of my patient."[21]

Sabina's long letter thus demonstrates her wish to preserve the image of Jung intact, and Freud must have understood this. Indeed, in the earliest letters in our possession, Freud maintains an attitude of impartiality. But after Sabina's trip to Vienna, where she attended the famous Wednesday meetings and during which she read the first part of her paper on destruction, Freud's tone begins to change. In a letter of 20 August 1912, Freud, informed that Sabina Spielrein has married Dr. Scheftel, gives this fact a very positive interpretation: "As far as I am concerned, that means that you are half cured of your neurotic dependence on Jung."[22] Here Freud, too, drops the mask and suggests to Spielrein a perverse modality in relation to her love. At this delicate moment, the friendship between Freud and Jung was already beginning to totter. At the time Freud offered Sabina his first "real" interpretation of the affair, he had not yet given up addressing Jung as "Dear friend" and replaced it with the salutation "Dear Doctor."[23] But then everything started to collapse, and Freud, in his letters to Sabina, was no longer restrained by his old and dubious friendship. On 20 January 1913 he writes to Spielrein: "My personal relationship with your Germanic hero has definitely been shattered. His behavior was too bad. Since I received that first letter from you, my opinion of him has greatly altered."[24] Freud's hostility toward his former friend is still greater when, in successive letters to Sabina, he insinuates that she loves Jung because she has not discovered the hatred that she ought to bear him,[25] and he attributes certain paranoid ideas directed at himself to the girl's bad conscience for not having freed herself from her idol.[26] And this leads him to the conclusion: "You are still in love with Jung . . . you cannot be really angry with him, see in him still the hero hounded by the mob. . . ."[27]

At this point we can make a curious observation and derive from it a series of considerations. After the break with Jung, Freud seldom attacked his old friend on the plane of theory. Freud's letters to Spielrein or, for example, to Abraham show that he found an outlet primarily at the personal level. One almost has the impression that the attacks on a private level indicate a certain fear of theoretical discussion.

The reader can better evaluate Freud's attitude by keeping in mind that Jung had been Spielrein's analyst. But the situation offers further complications when we consider that in the beginning Jung was kept in the dark about the correspondence between Spielrein and Freud.

Jung may even have been able to accept what was going on behind his back, but I am convinced that a large dose of aggressivity
had built up in him at the unconscious level. One may object that
Jung himself had taken the initiative in communicating the progress
of the clinical case to Freud. If, however, one carefully analyzes the
way in which the matter was raised in discussion, one realizes that
emotional factors obscured its outlines. Freud, indeed, so fails to
grasp the situation that in referring to Spielrein, at a time when
everything should have been quite obvious, he asks, "Is she a for-
eigner by any chance?"[28]

I have illustrated elsewhere how a schizoid tendency, prevalent
among analysts, prevents them from tolerating any interference in
what can be called a symbiotic relationship.[29] And in this case
there had really been interference, an intrusion, whose consequences would not be long in manifesting themselves. It is not by
chance that Freud divines the imminent tragedy when, in the letter
quoted above, he hastens to add: "Don't find fault with yourself for
drawing me into it; it was not your doing but hers. And the matter
has ended in a manner satisfactory to all."[30] Unfortunately, as we
know, the matter ended in quite another way.

Within the context of this discourse, I must include one more
episode, somewhat resembling that of Sabina, at least in its formal
outlines.

Sabina was treated by Jung, who had fond feelings for her that
were reciprocated; later the situation became critical and Sabina
turned to Freud for advice. Emma Jung had also been analyzed by
Jung,[31] and she obviously had an emotional relationship with her
husband. At a certain point she felt the need to write to Freud,
without Jung's knowledge, and express her worries to him. The
brief correspondence was supposed to be kept a secret, but Jung
found out about it. Emma informed Freud: "At any rate he now
knows about the exchange of letters, as he was astonished to see
one of your letters addressed to me; but I have revealed only a little
of their content."[32]

There are several similarities: for the second time Jung is betrayed with the complicity of Freud. How could one imagine that
these two episodes, even considered in their bare outlines (betrayal
on the part of the patient), could remain without consequences for

the man who has made himself an accessory to these betrayals? Obviously Jung himself had not realized how much aggressivity was building up in him, to be released at the first opportunity.

We can now linger over Freud's attitude, as it can be gathered from his letters. At an early stage he joins with Jung "against" Sabina Spielrein; later, when the two men are on the verge of a break, he takes Sabina's part against Jung. And Sabina? Freud's resentment against Jung will not allow him to be objective, and unfortunately causes him to forget a few elementary rules of the analytic relationship. When a certain type of connection has been generated between analyst and patient, there is no alibi or charisma that would serve to justify intervention. Freud even succeeds in accepting hypothetically the idea that Sabina Spielrein might undertake an analysis with him in order to eliminate the tyrant![33] But just as Sabina resisted Jung's attacks, she also succeeds in resisting Freud's. In fact, she even tries to mediate between the two by sending Freud a letter that Jung wrote her, and writing on this same letter some of her observations: "In spite of all his wavering, I like J. and would like to lead him back into our fold. You, Professor Freud, and he have not the faintest idea that you belong together far more than anyone might suspect. This pious hope is certainly no treachery to our Society! Everyone knows that I declare myself an adherent of the Freudian Society, and J. cannot forgive me for this."[34]

This letter dates from 1914, and Spielrein seems to be beginning to achieve an autonomy of her own. Having received her degree in 1911 and published a few papers, including the already mentioned "Psychological Content of a Case of Schizophrenia," "Destruction as the Cause of Coming into Being," and "Contributions to the Knowledge of the Child's Psyche," and after having married and, probably in September 1913, had a child, a daughter to whom she gave the name Renate, she resumes contact with Jung by letter. She is no longer the little girl with the long braid down her back. She is now a grown woman. From 12 September 1910 to 30 October 1919, Jung writes about twenty-nine letters that show how the conflict between the two was eventually to be cleared up and how Sabina Spielrein was able to keep faith with her determination to continue her friendship with Jung.

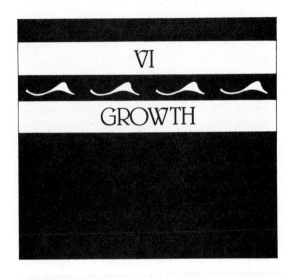

VI

GROWTH

THE WEIMAR CONGRESS, organized by Jung and opening on 11 September 1911, was supposed to include Sabina Spielrein among its participants, as Jung himself informed Freud,[1] but we know from a calm and lengthy letter written by Jung to Sabina that she had found a "psychosomatic" pretext for not going to Weimar. The storm having passed, Jung this time resumes the tone of the therapist and of a man whose mind is not clouded by ungovernable passions: "I allow myself to write to you so frankly and admonish you because after long reflection I have eliminated from my heart all the bitterness against you which it still harbored. To be sure, this bitterness did not result from your dissertation . . . but from earlier, from all the inner anguish I experienced because of you— and which you experienced because of me. . . . Freud will certainly accept you. He has spoken of your dissertation several times, proof that you have made an impression on him. . . . Approach him as a great master and rabbi, and all will be well."[2]

In this passage Jung seems ready to accept the idea that Sabina is "betraying" him even bodily by going to Freud; it is not so much that he seems resigned but that he appears to have "grown." One also gathers from the letter the extent of the suffering that the affair had caused Jung. It is not, however, clear that he was aware of his responsibility. In any case, there is the mention of mutual torment—a small indication, perhaps, of Jung's capacity to expose himself in the first person.

It was during this period that Sabina submitted her second paper to Jung, the one I have often referred to, "Destruction as the Cause of Coming into Being." Jung's judgment is again positive, but at the same time he communicates to his young friend his perplexities over the second part of his own essay on the libido. Indeed, writes Jung, "The more I write in my own style, the greater becomes the danger of misunderstandings, for inwardly I am quite alien to the spirit of the Viennese School, though not to the spirit of Freud."[3]

Jung seems, however, to resume his role of therapist when he tries to make Sabina understand that the perception she has of him is deceptive, in that it remains tied to a completely personal bias. But the correspondence now embarked on with Sabina wavers constantly between scientific evaluations and expressions of emotion. Spielrein's new paper allows him to find surprising connections with the second part of *Transformations and Symbols of the Libido*, but his compliments alarm Sabina, who expresses in her diary the fear of being robbed of her ideas.[4] Jung is obliged to reassure her: "The study is extraordinarily intelligent and contains excellent ideas, whose priority I am happy to acknowledge as yours."[5] Jung also speaks of the paper to Freud a few weeks later, and it is surprising to see how what he writes to the Master in Vienna differs from what he had written to Sabina: "I was working on Spielrein's paper just before my departure. One must say: *desinat in piscem mulier formosa superne* ["What at the top is a lovely woman ends below in a fish"—Horace, *Ars Poetica*]. . . . She has read too little and has fallen flat in this paper because it is not thorough enough. . . . Besides that her paper is heavily overweighted with her own complexes."[6] Clearly, Jung, too, in certain circumstances, expresses personal analytic judgments on subjects that ought to have been criticized only on the theoretical level. That the things he says to Sabina differ from what he reports to Freud is open to various interpretations, especially when one thinks of the honesty that Jung invokes in his letters. But these wavering judgments and feelings should not surprise us. Jung's real analysis was still in progress, and so we can record a series of statements

that conflict among themselves during the years of his development. For example, I have already quoted a passage from the correspondence between Freud and Jung in which the latter makes an
urgent emotional request: "The undeserved gift of your friendship
is one of the high points in my life. . . . The reference to Fliess—
surely not accidental—and your relationship with him impels me
to ask you to let me enjoy your friendship *not as one between
equals but as that of father and son.*"[7]

But five years later his attitude has changed, for in writing to
Sabina and explaining his delay in answering her letter, he says: "I
was completely discouraged, since at that time everyone attacked
me, and in addition I gained certainty that Freud would never understand me and would break off his personal relations with me.
He wants to give me love, while I want understanding. *I want to
be a friend on an equal footing, while he wants to have me as a
son.* For that reason he ascribes to a complex everything I do that
does not fit the framework of his life."[8]

A number of considerations come to mind. For one thing, Jung,
who rightly reproaches Freud for judging him on the basis of his
complexes, falls into the same trap when he calls Spielrein's paper
"heavily overweighted with her own complexes." But what is even
more striking is the change in Jung's attitude toward Freud after
five years of correspondence. The need to be a son diminishes and
the idea of being treated as an equal is put forward. But Freud's
response was to be inflexible: "Accordingly, I propose that we abandon our personal relations entirely."[9]

At the outset I expressed the opinion that the break between
Freud and Jung took place primarily for psychological reasons. The
only constellation that could have kept the two men together was
the submission of the one to the other, as indeed happened with
Freud's early pupils. Independent spirits within the psychoanalytic
movement paid dearly for their need to dissent, to oppose their
own point of view to the *Diktat;* some—inconceivable as it may
seem—even paid with their lives.[10] Under the guise of scientific
disagreement the problem of supremacy is always lurking, and it is
obvious that the role of follower or epigone was not one that appealed to Jung. Freud, moreover, did all he could to bring about the
rupture. For example, let us not forget that he had proposed to

Sabina that she come to Vienna so that he could help her overcome her dependence on Jung,[11] at a time when the salutation in his letters to Jung was still "Dear friend."

Having learned from this experience, Jung, in resuming his relations with Sabina, and though he still considers her his pupil—as she herself acknowledges in a letter[12]—adopts a respectful tone toward her that shows him in a new, somewhat touching light. He argues with her almost on equal terms, and when he offers criticism he does so with due caution, even when Spielrein's attitude might have evoked some resentment in him: "*The tone of your letter touched me to the quick, for I see that you, too, despise me.* Respect for the human personality and its motives should not be undermined by psychoanalysis. Because I fight for it, I must suffer much."[13]

Jung here, with great delicacy, introduces one of the most radical criticisms of psychoanalysis that he ever formulated. He actually warns Spielrein that it is dangerous to confuse knowledge of causes and motivations with *knowledge*. The error becomes a more serious one when we realize that the problem involves the human personality, which Jung already saw as irreducible to any particular past, however complex and rich in events.

Oddly enough, Jung's letter was sent to Freud by Sabina, with some added remarks of her own.[14] This new instance of "acting out" by Spielrein is indicative of how she was trying to keep her distance from both poles of attraction, despite some of her declarations of loyalty to Freud, who, however, pointed out to her many times by letter the persistence of her ambivalence and her difficulty in making "a clear decision."[15]

But Sabina persevered in her ambivalence and, while feeling herself to be Freud's pupil, sent her dreams to Jung. In interpreting one of Spielrein's dreams, Jung states that certain images contained in her unconscious represent Jung himself in the form of hieroglyphics, which, as symbolic images, she should be able to interpret. Here we again have the endopsychic liquidation of the conflict, which in Jung's terms, however, primarily suggested the effort Spielrein ought to make to understand the symbolic language of her unconscious. "You can derive a special insight from that if you are successful at deciphering."[16]

Jung knew that Spielrein considered herself a pupil of Freud and that she figured in the list of Freudian analysts,[17] and a touch of sarcasm appears every so often in his letters. I do not, however, take this to be a reproach, but, rather, regret or bitterness toward a woman who had just begun to understand many things and achieve some results, but was in danger of being compromised by an irremediably rationalistic set of formulations. Jung believed that beyond a certain level one could express onself only in an irrational, symbolic sense, but he was also aware that communication at the level he proposed might encounter resistance on Sabina's part. This is why, according to Jung, in a dream that Sabina had probably written him about, she is *in reality* "crying in vain for the sun and the sun's golden magic, for the verdure of noon and the scent of the earth."[18]

And at this point Jung indulges in a lengthy outburst: "Yes, my dearest lady, I have been slandered and mocked and criticized quite enough, and that is why I cling to my runes and all the pale, skimpy little ideas of which I gave a hint in my libido study. . . . I will not hand over my secret to see it trampled to death by those who do not understand."[19]

But Sabina remained undaunted, and during 1917 and January 1918 she wrote several long letters to Jung in which she expounded her theoretical formulations. In her final letters we can trace her effort to reconcile Freud's theory of the instincts with that of Adler, until she reaches the conclusion that the instinct for self-preservation may well be contained in the instinct for preservation of the species. Jung's answer, beyond confirming on the whole Spielrein's reasoning, points out how she has been moved by her particular typology to study the instinct for self-preservation, which in Jung's view is not entirely insignificant, considering the autonomy of the ego and the forces of repression. Of course, repressed sexuality is a source of artistic inspiration, but—Jung asks Spielrein—how does one grasp the particular quality of one author as compared to another? And this is why Freudian psychology "is merely 'empirical,' finding only moving objects in the world, but no living subjects."[20]

In the dialogue that developed between Spielrein and Jung one can see an ecumenical attempt on the part of the pupil of Jung and Freud. Spielrein had already had the strange idea of becoming the translator of both men. Freud himself was amazed by it and pointed out to her, "People generally do that sort of thing only if it is in keeping with their own principles."[21] Sabina now tried at all costs to make Jung in particular understand the points that he had in common with Freud. "You see neurosis *chiefly* as a process of regression. Freud sees *chiefly* inhibited development. If one chooses such a general definition, both are clearly right. You say that an unfulfilled life goal leads to neurosis, i.e., to regression. Freud says that as a result of inhibited development a person does not find his mission in life, i.e., *cannot sublimate sufficiently.* Where do you see a contradiction here?"[22]

Apart from the correctness of Spielrein's observations, we ought to ask ourselves what could have been the motivation that drove her to a unified vision of the two theories. To be sure, any attempt at synthesis can be taken as a difficulty in accepting conflict, and Sabina Spielrein's whole life, even down to the very content of her papers, represents a wish to reconcile opposite positions. She perceived, for example, the rivalry between Bleuler and Jung; later she tried to intervene as a mediator with Jung; her two closest women friends were a Jew and a Christian; the child she had dreamed of having by Jung, and to whom she would have given the name Siegfried, may have represented, according to Freud's interpretation, a Semitic-Christian hero; schizophrenia she saw not as a meaningless illness but as another form of expression; finally, she denied the existence of destruction, viewing it as a symbol of rebirth. And there are other examples as well.

Roughly speaking, this ecumenical need expresses a difficulty in confronting torments when they are not experienced dialectically, that is to say seen as moving forward in one way or another, but are instead seen as paralyzing and destructive. It is hard to imagine how a person can be incapable of tolerating conflict, but a clue to this particular aspect of Spielrein's life can be obtained through a hypnagogic vision that she had in 1904:

"... I find myself thinking of various things I plan to do; these musings yield a hypnagogic figure, a polygon, along whose perimeter I 'creep' ... the polygon changes into a wire mesh; I try to scramble up it, but each time a silent, dark-haired girl seizes me by the feet and drags me down. ... I see a beetle that has fallen into a spider's web; I touch it with my finger, and each time it must begin again from scratch or at least is set back considerably in its efforts." Spielrein, in analyzing the dream, associates: "You would like to climb, and the devil seizes you by the feet and drags you down."[23] Sabina had had this vision at a moment when she was feeling drained and very tired. She was thinking of all the things she would have to do, and these can be represented by a series of points joined by a continuous but not straight line. If we add that this jagged line tends to return to its point of departure, we have described the perimeter of a polygon. At this time Sabina was probably a patient in the Burghölzli and under treatment with Jung. The image of the polygon may have indicated, in this delicate situation, the impossibility of continuing. Indeed, the more each segment of the polygon's perimeter "departs" from the starting point, the closer it inevitably gets back to it. The other images are even more obvious. There is an attempt to emerge from the psychological prison, but her "shadow" as an endopsychic figure restrains Sabina and makes her efforts vain. There is no relationship with the dark-haired girl except one of hostility; that is to say, the conflict is paralyzing and leads back to the starting point. The beetle and the image of the spider web express the same conflict and the uselessness of her efforts, while the association with the devil implies her desperate struggle with her psychosis. Her mental state could obviously also have expressed itself in other ways, but the fact that it chose these images may, speaking entirely hypothetically, offer us an idea of the basic problems. Even the anal fixation and the resistance to releasing her feces can be interpreted as an inability to accept separations.

The result, then, is Spielrein's reluctance to align herself with one side or the other. To function in the field of psychology one must not necessarily be a partisan, but I do maintain that to espouse a psychological theory involves taking a position. To take a position, however, signifies "embracing" a system of ideas that cannot easily coexist with others. And this is why the last letters to Jung come close to being a proselytizing mission. Spielrein asks Jung not to abjure his ideas but, rather, to see the important aspects of Freud's theories that might help confirm the theses of Jung himself. "It is very possible that Freud will never understand you when you propose innovative theories. In his lifetime Freud has accomplished such extraordinary things, and he has enough to keep him occupied for the rest of his days, simply working out the details of his vast edifice. You, on the other hand, are still capable of growth. You can understand Freud perfectly well if you wish to, i.e., if your personal affect does not get in the way. The Freudian theories were, are, and will remain extraordinarily fruitful. To reproach Freud with one-sidedness seems very unfair to me, since each of us, and particularly one who constructs a mighty world-edifice, at first appears a king; then, when people have had enough and want to free themselves from his sphere of influence, he is denounced as one-sided and distasteful. You should have the courage to recognize Freud in all his grandeur, even if you do not agree with him on every point, even if in the process you might have to credit Freud with many of your own accomplishments. Only then will you be completely free, and only then will you be the greater one."[24]

This passage, presumably written in 1918, indicates how Spielrein attributed to Jung an emotional grudge that prevented him from understanding Freud's teachings. I myself think Jung had understood Freud's ideas very well, but Spielrein's view, dimmed by her fear of conflict, moved her to argue for an ideal meeting of the minds that would, she hastened to point out, cause Jung to become even greater.

In 1918 Jung had just emerged from a profound self-analysis that had brought him to the brink of tragedy. He had come out of it completely renewed, having discovered, this time in a wholly independent way, the demon that inspired him. Perhaps Sabina's letters gave him a sense of the work he had done with her when she was merely an inmate in a psychiatric hospital. Now this same girl was discussing his theory and Freud's with him on an equal footing. Jung did not think of her as an ex-patient or a girl toward whom he had once felt tumultuous emotions. After the passage of years, she may have represented the reification of some of his profound needs, which probably would never have emerged had they not been stimulated by a dramatic situation.

During years of solitude Jung conceived his metapsychology. It is not hard to imagine that in a curious way the hypotheses of persona, shadow, and anima represent the distillation of these old experiences. I have already stated my view that metapsychology expresses an exacting problem of its author's. In this case, any attentive reading of the phenomenological description of the anima and the shadow takes us immediately back to those early years of desolation and suffering, years in which love and unstinting effort served only to force out of Jung his unconscious determinants. By now he is so well aware of this that he can speak of it explicitly in one of his last letters to Sabina: "*The love of S. for J.* made the latter aware of something he had previously only vaguely suspected, that is, of a power in the unconscious that shapes one's destiny, a power which later led him to things of the greatest importance. The relationship had to be 'sublimated' because otherwise it would have led him to delusion and madness (the concretization of the unconscious). Occasionally one must be unworthy, simply in order to be able to continue living."[25]

Anima and shadow emerge from this letter in a striking way. Jung also explains to Spielrein why they never fulfilled their love, for as he sees it, to have experienced his own inner dimension at that time would have meant to be swept away by the unconscious.

These are practically the last words, as far as we know, that Jung wrote to Sabina. The word "love" had not been suppressed, since Jung could hardly have forgotten his feelings, but by now this word had acquired a much more universal significance for him. His unconscious *nekyia* had revealed to him the eternal truth of the general similarity among men. Jung, however, had tried to confront his experience and, like Montaigne, had painfully realized that "each bears in himself the entire form of the human condition."[26]

VII

THE SCIENTIFIC
PAPERS

IT IS TIME to return to the external events of Sabina Spielrein's life, and they can be summarized as follows. Arriving in Zurich in 1904 to enroll in medical school, she was admitted to the Burghölzli Hospital and placed in treatment with Jung. Until 1911 she lived in Zurich, where she took her degree and published her first scientific paper, derived from her dissertation, "The Psychological Content of a Case of Schizophrenia."

Meanwhile the essay "Destruction as the Cause of Coming into Being" was ripening, and it was to be published in 1912. Having broken off relations with Jung, Sabina went to Vienna, where she remained from October 1911 to March 1912. At the end of this period she moved to Germany, and lived in Berlin and Munich. Later she returned to Switzerland, living in Lausanne, Châteaux d'Oex, and Geneva until 1923. Then, deciding to return to Russia, she applied to the Russian Psychoanalytic Society, which accepted her in the autumn of that year. Sabina thereupon resettled in Rostov-on-Don, the city of her birth, where all traces of her vanish in 1937, a year in which her name still appears in the Russian Society's list of analysts. As far as we know, Spielrein up to that date had published about thirty papers, some of them very short, which

I will now try to examine as a body, referring to the more important ones.

We have already seen that her first published work, apart from ample citations by Jung, has practically disappeared from the literature, as have references to Jung's own pioneering work. One might mention an extensive presentation of the paper that appeared with a delay of about nine years in a psychoanalytic journal.[1] This first paper by Spielrein, as was inevitable, makes frequent reference to Jung's thought.

I have also discussed "Destruction as the Cause of Coming into Being." I might add that, like Sabina Spielrein's first essay, it has undeservedly fallen into oblivion, even though the ideas contained in it were later taken up by Freud. In this connection, Marthe Robert states that in Spielrein's article "the conception of the death instinct was anticipated almost in detail."[2] The article was amply reviewed by Federn, while a note appeared after thirteen years in *The Psychoanalytic Review*.[3] "Contributions to the Knowledge of the Child's Psyche" also appeared in 1912. This paper seeks to confirm the hypotheses presented by Freud in the case of "Little Hans." In this third paper as well there are numerous allusions to Jung.[4]

A year later Spielrein published a few brief contributions: "Mother Love," "Unconscious Dreaming in Kuprin's *Duel*," "Self-gratification in Foot Symbolism," "The Dream of *Father Freudenreich*," and "The Mother-in-law."[5] It is interesting to note that "Kuprin's *Duel*" is actually a communication from Jean Spielrein, Sabina's brother and a graduate in philosophy.

In the brief article "The Mother-in-law," Spielrein sets forth a distinction between the psychological modalities of man and woman. According to Spielrein, the typical female capacity for identification with others represents "the reason why women, who in intelligence and imagination are certainly not inferior to men, have not for so long a time created artistic productions on an equal level."[6] For Spielrein, the genesis of a work of art requires a great capacity for objectivization, a theory that anticipates those of Erich Neumann on creativity and the feminine.[7]

From 1913 on, Jung's name virtually disappears from Spielrein's articles, a highly significant occurrence when one remembers that relations between the two were to continue for a long time.

Other important papers are concentrated between 1922 and 1923. The report "Considerations on the Various Stages of Linguistic Development: The Origin of the Childish Words Papa and Mama," read at the Sixth International Psychoanalytic Congress, held in The Hague in September 1920, was published in *Imago* in 1922. Spielrein notes in her paper that man has obviously become a social animal thanks to speech, but it is also true that speech is not one of the first forms of expression. Before he is able to speak, the child makes use of other, no less valid, instruments of communication: "Crying is a sure means of understanding between the child and whoever is looking after him. . . . In an early phase the nursling expresses, intentionally or not, its condition or desires through the rhythm, elevation, cadence, and intensity of its cry, i.e., in a primitive melodic language."[8] According to Spielrein, the first words uttered by the child have their origin in the act of sucking, for this procedure, once it is continued away from the mother's body, produces the sound *mö-mö*. This sound is thereafter connected with the act of sucking and may offer a certain kind of pleasure. For Spielrein this phase represents the autistic stage. One then goes on to a second stage, the magical one, in which the child is able to summon the magical object through the word *mö-mö*, since his cry can provoke the actual arrival of the mother. Spielrein also offers an explanation of the origin of the word "papa," which she sees as linked to the moment of satisfaction: *"Pö-pö, bö-bö* . . . seem to correspond instead to the moment when the child, now satiated, plays with the breast, first letting go of it, then seizing it again."[9] That is to say, the word "papa" emerges when the child is satisfied. Spielrein adds the stimulating observation that the word "papa" is related to joy while "mama" is connected with sorrow.

The reader cannot fail to be struck by the importance that the breast and sucking have in Spielrein's paper. She seems to anticipate the studies of Melanie Klein, especially with these words: "The act of sucking is important as no other for the fundamental experiences in the life of the child: he learns to know the blessedness of placated hunger, but he also learns that this blessedness comes to an end and must be won all over again."[10] Here in a nutshell is what was to be the basic proposition in Klein's work: the "good breast" and the "bad breast." A. Lorenzer recently cited this article of Spielrein's at length.[11]

At the Seventh International Psychoanalytic Congress, held in Berlin in 1922, Spielrein delivered a report on the formation of subliminal time. Probably in the wake of Piaget's experiments, she tries to distinguish the sequence in the development of the concepts of space, causality, and time. For Spielrein, the child knows only the present and the immediate future. Only later does the idea of something that no longer exists take shape in the child's mind. As far as time is concerned, the problems having to do with its *direction* are extremely interesting. Identifying direction is an achievement of the conscious mind, which is able to distinguish present, past, and future, whereas in a dream, for example, the direction of time is unclear. One should, however, note that preconscious thought has a greater capacity than conscious thought for reckoning the *duration* of time. According to Spielrein, this is a capacity that our ancestors possessed to a higher degree. The significance of the article is enhanced by the fact that in writing it Spielrein collaborated with Professor Bally, a well-known linguist from Zurich, thus once again anticipating current trends in psychoanalysis.[12]

In 1923, Spielrein finished a rather extensive study entitled "Some Analogies Between the Thought of the Child, That of the Aphasic, and Unconscious Thought." The paper was read in February 1923 to the Zurich Psychoanalytic Society. Availing herself of the association technique (without once mentioning Jung!), Spielrein tries to show the connections that exist between the thought of the child and that of the aphasic. The subject of the experiment is a little girl who speaks Swiss German, very likely her daughter, Renate, or "Renatchen," as Spielrein customarily calls her when speaking of her in her scientific papers.

She begins with the idea that in the natural state the child is entirely spontaneous, making use, in psychoanalytic terminology, of indirect, unconscious thinking (this is another borrowing from Jung without an explicit acknowledgment). While the adult may attain this state artificially by eliminating, as far as possible, external stimuli, the child, continually stimulated by the surrounding environment, "is constantly abandoning one group of ideas to pursue some other that has been suggested."[13] But, Spielrein observes, the fact that the child so quickly abandons a group of ideas does not mean that they have actually disappeared. On the contrary, it may be—and Spielrein upholds this theory—that the group of pre-existing ideas is absorbed into a new group. In support of her point of view, Spielrein subjects her daughter, about two and a half years old, to a test by offering her four general ideas: *eat, Anna, sleep, child/mama.* When the experiment is over, she comes to the conclusion that "the child's thought is not necessarily bound up with one direction. Indeed, we find two opposite directions simultaneously. No sooner does the child arrive at a new idea than his thought reverts to the previous one, which is then grafted onto the new idea...."[14] Spielrein goes on to give more examples in her effort to demonstrate that the mechanism of the child's thought resembles at many points the dreams and thought patterns of the aphasic, but she emphasizes that in the aphasic it is only the mechanism of thought that becomes primitive, since his human experience is certainly richer than that of the child.

With this paper Spielrein in a certain sense bids farewell to the Western world. For reasons that are still unknown to us, the years she spent in Europe, in Switzerland especially, had not answered her needs. In fact, one of Freud's last letters to Spielrein reads in part: "I am in receipt of your letter and really believe that you are right. Your plan to go to Russia seems to me much better than my advice to try out Berlin. In Moscow you will be able to work at the side of Wulff.... Lastly, you will be on home ground."[15] As we know, after this letter, in the autumn of the same year, she was accepted by the Russian Psychoanalytic Society.

VIII

THE
RETURN

THE IDEA OF returning to Russia to carry out the profession of psychoanalyst had presumably come to Sabina from the observation that in that country, even after the Revolution, it would be possible to advance Freud's ideas. It had seemed to many from the beginning that Freud's discoveries were one more means that could help bring about the paradise promised by the Revolution. At present our sources of information on the situation of psychoanalysis in the U.S.S.R. until 1936, the year in which it was outlawed, remain for the most part whatever can be gleaned from the *Zeitschrift*, which regularly published the reports of the various societies. Other detailed information can be found in an article by Hans Lobner and Vladimir Levitin, published in 1978 in the *Sigmund Freud House Bulletin*.[1] The earliest paper, however, appears in the *Zentralblatt* and is signed by M. Wulff, a Russian analyst recognized by Freud himself and the translator of certain of Freud's works. The report traces the situation up to the year 1911, and opens with these words: "So far psychoanalysis has not become widespread in Russia."[2] It is hard to understand what standard of expansion Wulff might be referring to, since in 1911 psychoanalysis could not be said to have penetrated any country in the world, except among those individuals who were fighting to gain recognition for the new psychology.

But in Russia, by contrast, a magazine of a psychoanalytic nature, *Psikhoterapiya*, had been founded as early as 1909; it published articles by Russian authors and translations of foreign ones. The Russian intelligentsia at that time went to Europe to study, and Zurich was one of its favorite destinations. On their return home, these scholars, the doctors in particular, often became spokesmen for the new ideas with which they had come in contact. Among the authors cited by Wulff as pioneers we find Osipov,* head of the university clinic in Moscow, who, having studied in Zurich, had expounded Freud's ideas and those of the Zurich school on various occasions in his Moscow circle. In particular, he devoted an article to Jung in 1908—"The Psychology of Complexes and Experiments in Association at the Zurich Clinic."

Also in Moscow there was Wirubov, who around 1909 had published two papers on Freudian theory and practice. Wulff's survey goes on to list a modest number of scholars who had been involved with Freudian doctrine from a theoretical standpoint.

One interesting item concerns a certain Pewnitzky, a doctor from Odessa, who in 1908 had delivered a lecture on treating states of obsession by the Freudian method, including cases he had personally handled, all of which would suggest that he had already been employing analytic therapeutic techniques for several years in his medical practice. It is clear that these clinical histories, in line with the most direct tradition of Freudian prehistory, were resolved as soon as the childhood traumas were uncovered. Nevertheless, a recent article on the history of psychoanalysis[3] considers that this very lecture, delivered in Saint Petersburg on 13 March 1908, marks the birth of psychoanalysis in Russia. Wulff did not limit himself to reporting on the development of psychoanalytic initiatives, but when possible tried to evaluate their merits as well. He remarked that Wirubov "found in his material confirmation of Freud's views as far as the psychosexual etiology of neurosis is concerned."[4]

*See note 27, page 228.

From one of Freud's letter it was later learned that in 1909 the medical director of the psychiatric clinic in Moscow, Nikolay Nikolayevich Bagenov, had sent him a very sick patient. These are small signs, to be sure, but they are indicative of a certain interest that Russian psychiatric circles were also at that time taking in psychoanalysis. During the same period, F. Berg returned from Zurich expressing admiration and esteem for the works of Freud and Jung.[5]

Also in 1909, Leonid Drosnés, a physician and psychiatrist, and a diligent reader of Freud, attempted to give psychoanalytic treatment. One of his first patients, who later became known as the Wolf Man, was treated by Freud from 1910 to 1914.[6] One might also mention an article on psychoanalysis by the physician Heilmonovich, published in 1910, and in 1911, Sabina Spielrein, back in Russia on a brief visit, gave her first lecture on psychoanalysis in Rostov-on-Don. In any case, according to Lobner and Levitin, "it seems justified to say that by 1910 psychoanalysis did flourish in Russia, and especially in Moscow. The *Psikhoterapiya* printed translations of the most recent papers by Freud, reviews and reports were being sent to the other professional journals, and a considerable number of psychoanalytic authors began to publish original contributions (in addition to those already mentioned, there were J. W. Kannabikh, Jeanne and S. Neiditsch, A. B. Zalkind, and others) ... and already in 1909 Moscow had its first Adlerian (to my knowledge the only follower of individual psychology in Russia), Dr. J. Bierstein, as well as the first follower of Stekel, M. Schapiro."[7]

Another exponent of Russian psychoanalysis around 1911 was Asatiani, who had published an essay on a case of hysterical psychosis in *Psikhoterapiya*. The patient had recovered, but Asatiani, in his comments on the case, points out that in the course of the treatment he had observed neither the emergence of the transference nor the presence of a polymorphously perverse childhood sexuality. Wulff, who had met Freud and had a deeper knowledge of psychoanalysis than his Russian colleagues, remarks that these are not plausible objections, and explains to the reader the points in the case where the author had made mistakes.[8] Asatiani, however, had been to see Jung in Zurich, a circumstance that made it possible for him to give a lecture on "The Present State of Theory and

Practice in Psychoanalysis According to the Opinions of Jung" at the Moscow psychiatric clinic in 1909. The lecture seems to come close to Jung's short paper "Psychic Conflicts in a Child," the contents of which had barely been worked out. Indeed, in Wulff's report on the lecture, we read that the healthy psychic life of the parents is the *sine qua non* for the mental health of the children. If the parents are abnormal, they transmit their own psychological complications to their offspring.[9]

Of course—leaving aside the official stance that the Communist Party was to take about twenty years after the Revolution—there was no lack of opponents. A certain Dr. Feldmann adopted the usual tactic of distorting Freud's opinions by ridiculing them. When he could not actually attack them, he remarked that they were "bold and risky generalizations of points of view that have already been expressed for some time in the general and medical literature."[10] But the "analyses" offered by Feldmann are so puerile and trivial that Wulff justly points out the enormous distance that separates them from correct Freudian theory. And Wulff remarks that anyone who lacks the proper knowledge to carry on a treatment should not presume to present cases to a public that obviously cannot be an informed one.[11]

A report on a clinical case treated by S. Goldouscheff appears in 1914 in the *Zeitschrift* over the signature of S. Repin. Like Feldmann, the writer, after explaining the patient's psychological problem and the hypothesis adopted by Goldouscheff, criticizes the latter's methods in order to stress the mistakes in the treatment, in particular the strong resistances that would obviously have been activated in the patient. Thus the apparent lack of therapeutic success is due not so much to the analytic technique as to an improper use of it.[12]

As for works by Freud translated into Russian, at the time that Sabina Spielrein returned for good to Rostov-on-Don in 1923, Russian versions existed of the *Three Essays on the Theory of Sexuality*, published in 1909; the *Five Lectures on Psychoanalysis*, translated in 1911; and *The Interpretation of Dreams*, which had been offered to the reading public in 1915.[13]

Furthermore, in 1911, Tatiana Rosenthal, who would go on to commit suicide at the age of thirty-six, had returned to Saint Petersburg from Europe. After taking part in some pre-1917 revolutionary movements, she had been a medical student in Zurich (where, for all we know, she may have met Sabina Spielrein). She had happened to read Freud's *Interpretation of Dreams*, was enthusiastic about it, and immediately thought of a possible scientific blending of Freud and Marx. "After 1911, she settled down in Petersburg as a psychoanalyst, firmly determined to spread the teachings of Freud. . . . If psychoanalysis gained a foothold in Petersburg, it is due primarily to her considerable activity."[14] One should also mention a psychoanalytic paper that she wrote on Dostoevsky, and above all her establishment and direction of the Institute for Neuropathic Children. As for the reasons for Tatiana Rosenthal's suicide, unfortunately the information we have is not particularly enlightening.

The turmoil that followed the years of war and revolution makes it difficult, at least for now, to trace the development and spread of psychoanalysis in Russia.

The 1921 *Zeitschrift* provides us with information in articles by Osipov and Sara Neiditsch. The year 1917 saw the death of W. P. Serbsky, director of the university psychiatric clinic. This physician had had an ambivalent attitude toward psychoanalysis, attacking it in its more sensitive areas, such as that of sexuality. His criticisms were the usual ones—that is, "he agreed that sexuality played a definite role in the etiology of the neuroses, but he could not accept such a broad use of the term sexual."[15] In 1911, however, Serbsky had argued that "Freud's theory merits the greatest attention because it forms the basis of a therapeutic treatment that often succeeds in achieving important and even unbelievable successes."[16] Professor Serbsky also deserves credit for allowing many doctors in his clinic to study Freudian theories and to hold seminars on specific aspects of them.

In 1919, immediately after the Revolution, an Institute for Research on Cerebral Pathology was founded, at which Rosenthal also worked, using psychoanalytic methods. In 1920 she was able to deliver a lecture on the importance of Freudian theories for the upbringing of children.[17] In 1921 Wulff and Ermakov officially founded the Russian Psychoanalytic Society in Moscow. But in a country so vast there were other psychoanalytic centers as well, carrying on their work at the local level, and these were likewise reported on by specialized German periodicals. According to Lobner and Levitin, "a few authors of the first hour were no longer active (Feltsman, Bierstein, Berg), and several new ones turned up. Some of these belong to the forgotten past (e.g., K. Benni, L. J. Bielobodorov, S. Goldousheff, A. A. Joffe, J. G. Orshansky, or men like Likhnitsky, Sakhartshenko, J. N. Shreider), whereas others fill pages in the standard bibliographies now."[18] In the beginning the Moscow Society had three aims: educational, medical, and psychological-artistic. As Lobner says: "The Russian Psychoanalytic Society was organized in three sections, the first being Ermakov's on the psychology of art and literature. The second section, which dealt with clinical analysis, was highly important for a number of aspects and was headed by Professor Wulff, secretary of the Society and its training analyst along with Sabina Spielrein (until 1923). In 1922 Ermakov and Wulff founded a State Psychoanalytic Institute, which in the beginning incorporated Vera Schmidt's center for children and later opened a psychoanalytic consultation office under Wulff's direction. The Russian Psychoanalytic Society was the third center for training and psychoanalytic treatment after those of Berlin and Vienna. In 1924 the Institute offered a program of ten seminars and the staff developed supplementary courses at the University and the Psychiatric Clinic, even though Professor Gilyarovsky, the new director of the clinic, did not appreciate psychoanalysis.

"The third section of the Society was dedicated to the application of psychoanalysis in education. As mentioned above, it was centered around V. Schmidt's work, and it soon had the support of Professor Shatsky, the leading Russian pedagogue at that time. A major part of the findings of observations and experimentation with children did not reach publication stage before it was too late, and is therefore lost."[19]

If there is any comment to be made, it concerns the scope that Freudian concepts had attained on Russian soil. One could almost say that the journal *Imago* has summed up the criterion by which the Russian intelligentsia measured Freud's clinical experiments. In particular, education was seen as the proving ground for psychoanalysis, according to the statements of the educator A. S. Griboedov.[20] Naturally, social psychology was also greatly influenced by psychoanalytic teaching, through M. A. Reusser (the equivalent, according to Lobner, of Hans Kelsen in Vienna),[21] as was the history of psychiatry, through Kannabikh, and criminology, through A. E. Borsilovsky.[22]

The year 1921 also saw the birth of the now legendary experiment of a psychoanalytic children's home in Moscow. We should not be surprised by the interest that the new revolutionary authorities were taking in questions of education. At first any idea that held out the slightest possibility for improving the means of education was well received and encouraged. Later, when it was perceived that education of the psychoanalytic kind did not lead toward the fulfillment of Bolshevik hopes and expectations, obstacles were put in the way of its progress. This problem is one of immediate interest, since Sabina Spielrein suffered considerable frustration in this respect after her return to Rostov-on-Don.

Obviously the Bolshevik Revolution had allowed local psychoanalysts to glimpse the possibility of collaborating with institutions to a greater degree than had been possible under czarism. The experiment of the psychoanalytic children's home, probably the first in the world, is a clear example. The home was entrusted to Vera Schmidt, with the support of the educator Shatsky. Schmidt, employing a team of specialists well informed on psychoanalytic doctrine, placed a limited number of children under observation. The home, called the House of Children, was established in 1921, but conflicts with the authorities immediately arose, while strange rumors kept circulating about the sexual education of the little inmates. Bureaucratic difficulties continued to increase, and the House of Children was finally closed.[23]

It was not long before Russian psychoanalysts found themselves face to face with the problem of Marxism. In 1921, for example, a young psychologist named Alexander Romanovich Luria had joined the ranks of Freud's supporters. At that time Luria was a member of the Society for the Social Sciences in Kazan. Though at first an advocate of psychoanalysis, he later, for scientific (or political?) reasons, detached himself step by step from the psychoanalytic movement, thus avoiding one of Stalin's many purges.[24] In 1925 Luria wrote: "The Russian Revolution has placed considerable emphasis on the scientific philosophy of Marxism. . . . Every branch of science is now discussed from this standpoint . . . and the discussion of psychoanalysis in relation to Marxism has been one of the most interesting."[25]

From a historical point of view, it should be recalled that the first psychoanalyst to confront the problem of Marx was Adler: "In 1909 Adler was the only member of the Vienna Psychoanalytic Society who called himself a Marxist, and his contribution to the introduction of Marx's thought was a steady one."[26]

In postrevolutionary Russia, criticisms of psychoanalysis were put forward primarily by Jurinetz, Deborin, and Thalheimer in the Soviet magazine *Unter dem Banner des Marxismus.*[27] As usual, the attacks on Freud were wholly gratuitous, and, according to Lobner, even now it is hard to understand the contradictory accusations that were hurled at the Master in Vienna. In any case, the problem centered, as was logical, on the idealistic premises of psychoanalysis and the materialistic ones of Marxism. In practice, this has been the problem ever since. Yet Russian psychoanalysts made every effort to find points of contact, not so much for reasons of convenience as, rather, because almost all of them had enthusiastically accepted the Bolshevik Revolution. In these years Stalin had not yet concentrated all power in his own hands and a certain freedom of discussion was still possible, one that would become increasingly tenuous and later disappear completely. But implied in this premise of collaboration with the state was the idea that psychoanalysis would thereby achieve its final form; this idea constituted one of the most serious wrongs that could be done to Freud's doctrine, for any such finality is harmful to the advancement of science.[28]

And events were approaching a climax. After the advent of Stalin, the *Zeitschrift* published fewer and fewer reports on the activities of psychoanalysts in the Soviet Union. The last article of importance appeared in *Imago* in 1931; written by Otto Fenichel, it dealt with the criteria for rehabilitation used in a Soviet penal colony. In Fenichel's description, objective and detached as it may seem, one can read between the lines his enthusiasm for a method of re-education that only Bolshevik Russia could have adopted. This method consisted in offering the convicts a possibility for identification. "This is precisely what the community in the Soviet Union offers in an extraordinary manner. The commn ideal that makes identification possible for its members among themselves and with their comrades, the ideal that is not preached by teachers to youth but is lived as a reality, both in the great surrounding world and in the narrow milieu of one's comrades, where one can truly participate in an autonomous way, without pretenses or obstacles."[29]

In any case, as Luria had already pointed out, the debate over psychoanalysis and Marxism occupied the center of the stage for Soviet psychoanalysts. In 1924, a volume published in Moscow sought to provide the connecting link between Marxism and psychology. Among the various articles, two make explicit reference to psychoanalysis and are signed by Luria and the Moscow analyst Friedmann. The latter's article, "The Principal Psychological Conceptions of Freud and the Theory of Historical Materialism," develops, as is obvious from the title, a comparison between the two doctrines, and arrives at the conclusion that "psychoanalysis carries historical materialism forward in the psychological direction on the methodological level. Freud's theory begins its study where historical materialism leaves off in the study of human activity. . . . To put it more exactly, historical materialism shows how the social creates the psychological, while psychoanalysis shows the way in which the biological is transformed into the psychological under the influence of the social."[30] Throughout the article, which expatiates on Marxist theories as well as Freudian ones, the author demonstrates that he does not harbor the slightest doubt about their compatibility, since it is his view that both theories go beyond appearances. On that, but on that alone, I can concur.

Luria's contribution, which forms part of a larger work, tries to show that psychoanalysis has been the first attempt to formulate a human characterological theory on an organic basis. Only in this way, says Luria, "are the foundations laid for a psychology based on Marxist materialism, one that considers the phenomena of psychic life as forms of organic phenomena and does not draw any dividing line between processes that occur in the individual organs of the human body and the psychic reactions to which they give rise."[31]

At first sight these statements by Luria may seem correct (and in any case who can deny that psychic processes have a source in the organic?), but they carry the seeds of their own condemnation by Marxist orthodoxy in that they exclude, or at least minimize, the concept that the formation of consciousness depends on the social world.

In 1934, Otto Fenichel, in an article whose existence is perhaps known to only a few psychoanalysts, took up the connection between psychoanalysis and Marxism, noting that all the sciences, even though they contain bourgeois errors, cannot be rejected by Marxists, who on the contrary should take possession of the natural sciences and remove them from the monopoly of bourgeois culture. The Marxist, according to Fenichel, must bear in mind that for him "psychoanalysis contains the germ of a particularly important natural science, the natural science of the human psyche."[32] Fenichel goes on to say that the objection that one cannot waste time studying the feelings of an individual is wholly ridiculous because the basic human feelings are at the root of everything that happens in society. "Psychoanalysis . . . does not oppose a psychological conception to a dialectical-materialist one, but, rather, adapts psychological facts to the methods of historical-materialist thought and thus places psychology in a determined setting . . . the setting of social processes."[33]

But this problem of the relationship between Marx and Freud has seldom been resolved, since it has never been understood that "one can do justice to Marx and Freud only by recognizing the profound contradiction that they mutually represent."[34]

Only after this has been acknowledged will a certain kind of reconciliation be possible. It should not, however, be a synthesis, for in that case both doctrines would be distorted.

IX

THE

END

BUT IT IS TIME to return to Sabina Spielrein. In 1923, having discussed it by letter with Freud, she was accepted as a member of the Russian Pychoanalytic Society. Other analysts, among them Luria, entered the association at the same time. The news was reported in both the official English-language psychoanalytic organ and the German-language one.[1] Before her departure for Russia, she published two brief reports in the *International Journal,* one on dreams and shooting stars, the other on the symbolism of the automobile.[2]

It is virtually impossible to follow the ups and downs of Spielrein's career after her return. As for her writings, we have another article from 1931, about thirty pages in length and devoted to an experiment in which Spielrein sought to identify and interpret the differences in drawings made by children with their eyes closed and with their eyes open. Published in *Imago,* the article was reviewed in 1938 in *The Psychoanalytic Review.* If one were to analyze the choice of subject, one would see how in this paper—which seems to be the last she ever wrote—the problem of contrasting closed eyes with open eyes emerges as a reflection of the conflict between the unconscious and consciousness and its possible resolution.[3]

Some interesting information about this obscure period in Spielrein's life has been provided by Jeanne A. Lampl–De Groot in Amsterdam:

"All I know is that in Russia she founded a home for infants and children, in the hope of offering them a better life in a community than they could have had in their families. This means that she founded her children's home having in mind the original and idealistic ideas of Soviet society. I do not know how old she was when she died, but in the thirties there were rumors that she was very disappointed that analysis had been banned and that her home for children had had to be closed."[4]

As I have already said, and for the reasons mentioned, psychoanalysis was outlawed in 1936, at the height of Stalinism, and of course all the activities connected with it suffered the same fate. Sabina Spielrein, however, since her return to Rostov-on-Don, had taught at the local university, which unfortunately was in part destroyed during the war; thus all attempts to trace her in the records of that university have so far been unsuccessful.[5]

Her name still appears on the lists of Russian psychoanalysts in 1937. After this date, silence. It is interesting in this connection that the specialized publications in Western countries made no mention of the destruction of psychoanalysis in Russia, just as they made no comment during the years of the Second World War when psychoanalysis was virtually silenced in Italy and Germany.[6]

With Spielrein's disappearance, the story itself comes to an end. The moment has come to determine to what extent the events I have described left their mark on the work of Jung. As I said before, there should be no difficulty in recognizing the many reifications that go back to the painful, dramatic conflicts of those years— conflicts that were of course overcome, but nevertheless decisively influenced his thinking.

It is reasonable to suppose that whenever Jung touched on the subject of the analyst's relations with the patient, his thought, both consciously and unconsciously, was nourished by his former experience, and in *The Psychology of the Transference* the memory of one of the first intense relationships in his life may well have reappeared with renewed ardor. I personally have the feeling that at least the emotional, existential aspect of the transference-counter-transference phenomenon could have been illustrated solely by the events I have recounted. "The doctor, by voluntarily and consciously taking over the psychic sufferings of the patient, exposes himself to the overpowering contents of the unconscious and hence also to their inductive action. The case begins to 'fascinate' him."[7] But Jung rightly emphasizes how this fascination imperceptibly leads patient and analyst toward a state of mutual *unconsciousness*, against which the therapist will try to defend himself by means of the *persona medici*. Connected with the *persona* are the analyst's clinical methods and his feeling of self-importance, that typical doctor's delusion that he already knows everything and is indeed infallible, "yet this lack of insight is an ill counsellor. . . ."[8] How can the harsh words that Jung wrote to Sabina's mother not come to mind? On the other hand, the obvious psychic phenomena that underlie our lives have a disconcerting simplicity. The fundamental lines are virtually always the same, whereas the ways in which these premises develop in our concrete human existence become varied and changeable.

It is clear that Jung would not have been able to write *The Psychology of the Transference* immediately after his encounter with Spielrein, for the simple reason that at the time he did not know the things he was later to observe and study. But when he thought back on his experience over the span of years, the psychic processes he had witnessed were revealed and clarified. To put these conjectures in a more precise context: once the analyst accepts the idea that his work involves psychic contagions, he is forced to take a different attitude toward his patient. "The patient then means something to him personally, and this provides the most favourable basis for treatment."[9]

What Jung is suggesting is that the therapist who bases his work on a sense of infallibility behaves in quite a different way toward his patient from one who believes in psychic contagion. In each case the analyst evaluates the consequences of his behavior differently. In the first modality nothing that happens to the patient has anything to do with the psychic life of the doctor, whereas in the second the improvement or deterioration of the patient has a direct effect on the analyst. This is the sense in which Jung maintains that the patient's destiny involves that of the analyst.

The reasons that may have induced Jung to make this statement are clear. But they become more obvious still when Jung feels the need to declare that "a thing which is not liked and desired generally requires no prohibition."[10] Broad though this sentiment may sound, it must necessarily bring to mind the limitations that Jung had thought to place on his relationship. When we then consider that Jung's observation, in the context of *The Psychology of the Transference*, refers to the problem of incest, the picture should be even clearer. Jung based part of this work precisely on the problem of incest and the particular position it occupies in the sphere of therapeutic treatment. Let us examine his thesis: "The existence of the incest element involves not only an intellectual difficulty but, worst of all, an emotional complication of the therapeutic situation. It is the hiding place for all the most secret, painful, intense, delicate, shamefaced, timorous, grotesque, unmoral, and at the same time the most sacred feelings which go to make up the indescribable and inexplicable wealth of human relationships and give them their compelling power. Like the tentacles of an octopus they twine themselves invisibly round parents and children and, through the transference, round doctor and patient. This binding force shows itself in the irresistible strength and obstinacy of the neurotic symptom and in the patient's desperate clinging to the world of infancy or to the doctor. The word 'possession' describes this state in a way that could hardly be bettered."[11]

One has only to hold these thoughts up to the light to be able to see in them not just the experience of the patient, but also, and perhaps especially, that of the analyst. Jung goes on to say that in a situation like the one he is describing, the doctor's psychic life is all unconsciously subjected to transformation, and analyst and patient are both forced to confront "the daemonic forces lurking in the darkness."[12] The allusion to the devil is certainly not new in Jung's writings, but it acquires a certain conjectural significance when we recall that, in speaking to Freud of his relationship with Spielrein, Jung sadly admits that "the devil can use even the best of things for the fabrication of filth."[13] And what is this filth? Probably not the erotic element, which is the first thing that comes to the layman's mind, but above all the illusions that every analytic treatment engenders in therapist and patient. Jung is very clear in this connection. The relationship is hampered by the unconscious precisely because the latter, through projection, creates an unrealistic expectation, "an atmosphere of illusion which either leads to continual misinterpretations and misunderstandings, or else produces a most disconcerting impression of harmony. The latter is even more trying than the former. . . ."[14]

Spielrein's diary provides an interesting counterpoint to these statements. Indeed, we know that the girl's greatest sorrow came from knowing she had been deceived, or at least disappointed, because of her own vulnerability and defenselessness in the presence of feelings that had been kindled in her for the first time. And what is one to say of the repeated references made by Jung to his own gullibility and weakness? Out of these the drama of the transference is skillfully woven, a drama in which the shadow stands at the head and itself becomes a devil by which we are forced to realize that, much as we may struggle to keep ourselves united, "one becomes two,"[15] or something even more split and multiple.

But naturally this price ultimately has its reward. Once the transference is analyzed, it is possible that the unconscious contents may return to their source. Of course, as Jung acutely observes, the problem is by no means resolved; it has simply been postponed. The libido, which underlies the projection, seeks an object, however, in our case a human relationship that remains, in Jung's view, the most profound meaning of the transference. But once this relationship with the Other is broken, the impulse toward the relationship will emerge with a new beauty and violence and will be channeled into individuation. In explaining this longing, Jung retraces, perhaps unwittingly, his own past: "Individuation has two principal aspects: in the first place it is an internal and subjective process of integration, and in the second it is an equally indispensable process of objective relationship. Neither can exist without the other, although sometimes the one and sometimes the other predominates. This double aspect has two corresponding dangers. The first is the danger of the patient's using the opportunities for spiritual development arising out of the analysis of the unconscious as a pretext for evading the deeper human responsibilities, and for affecting a certain 'spirituality' which cannot stand up to moral criticism; the second is the danger that atavistic tendencies may gain the ascendancy and drag the relationship down to a primitive level. Between this Scylla and that Charybdis there is a narrow passage, and both medieval Christian mysticism and alchemy have contributed much to its discovery."[16]

How Jung himself managed to navigate between the two extremes is still not perhaps entirely clear. But let us leave final judgments to history.

And speaking of history, I should like to suggest to the reader an analogy between this episode in Jung's life and an experience of Johann Christoph Blumhardt, who in the years 1842–43 used exorcistic techniques to treat a possessed girl named Gottliebin Dittus. The case is well documented and demonstrates in a surprising way the dangers and complications generally encountered in the treatment of severe schizophrenia. Gaetano Benedetti, in a detailed study of the incident, has shown that the therapist, availing himself of his psychological intuition alone, succeeded in confronting and curing a patient who would have liked to destroy him. After the experience—and herein lies the most subtle analogy—Blumhardt was a completely changed man with a great faith in Jesus, who had helped him. Not only that, but the young woman he had cured later became one of his most valued assistants.[17]

In Jung's writings it may be possible to discover some direct allusion to Spielrein. In *Memories, Dreams, Reflections* there is an echo. The author describes his encounter with the unconscious: "I knew for a certainty that the voice had come from a woman. I recognized it as the voice of a patient, a talented psychopath who had a strong transference to me. She had become a living figure within my mind."[18]

It is clear that Jung could never have forgotten this important aspect of his life, for in looking back on the memories he compiled with the help of Aniela Jaffé, he feels called upon to state: "But of those relationships which were vital to me, and which came to me like memories of far-off times, I cannot speak, for they pertain not only to my innermost life but also to that of others. It is not for me to fling open to the public eye doors that are closed forever."[19]

But as I have tried to argue, it is precisely in our innermost lives that the historical source of our works is hidden. To critics who may object that the work is more important than the life of the author, one could reply that while this *may* hold true for such creations of the human spirit as great scientific and cosmological theories, it is much less true for psychology, a discipline in which the scholar is driven, even unconsciously, to draw on his own experiences, including the more traumatic ones. To know these events, to understand them and compare them with the relative metapsychology, does not, in my opinion, impugn or impair the validity of the theory. The latter, of course, will derive from the experience of the author, not excluding his personal vicissitudes, but if these are creatively transformed, they become, like art, part of the collective heritage of mankind. The psychologist cannot ignore these premises, especially if he is interested in depth psychology, which—as Freud teaches with his self-analysis and Jung with his descent into the hell of the unconscious—is based essentially on the self-observation of its authors.

Insufficient attention has been paid to Jung's statement in *Memories, Dreams, Reflections*: "The years when I was pursuing my inner images were the most important in my life—in them everything essential was decided."[20] Jung seldom refers to his objective studies on his patients, whose importance he recognizes, however, in another part of the book;[21] he concentrates on the dialogue with his inner images. So when it is Jung himself who makes a statement suggesting that analytical psychology is first of all his *own* psychology, is it not our duty to open those doors that he has jealously and "justly" (justly for him, the protagonist of those events) always kept closed?

This, then, is the dilemma I have faced with the documents that have come into my possession. It has been my judgment that the subject and contents of the documents could be made public, though we are still waiting for permission to publish the correspondence of Jung with Spielrein. It is not my task to deify anyone, but still less to conceal facts and ideas that may, at least on superficial examination, run counter to the prevailing current of thought. There are precedents for such censorship. As we know, Karl Marx had his own opinion of the so-called czarist colossus, and in his farsightedness had understood how Russia, with its immense resources and unlimited boundaries, could be a perennial threat to Europe. But the work in which this view was presented, indeed of which it was the main argument, was for many years kept carefully hidden, since Marx's ideas were not entirely flattering when examined in the light of later developments in the Soviet Union.[22] Such censorship is a deception for all those who believe in Marxism. I am convinced that no one in the world has the right to conceal anything from anybody. There is no stain, no matter how great, that cannot, when placed in the context of a system of ideas, lend clarity and precision to an understanding of the matter at hand.

One can make the same point about Freud in connection with the "cocaine papers." The editors of the English translation of these papers find it curious that although there is a great interest in psychopharmacology, Freud's efforts in this direction are completely unknown. I believe that this omission is due not to chance but to a definite, if not wholly conscious, choice. The one exception is Ernest Jones, who devoted a whole chapter to the subject, in a tone that was not apologetic but discreetly objective.[23] According to Donoghue and Hillman, Freud's experiments with the drug derived not from his desire to make a name for himself but from an archetypal factor, fundamentally involving a search for freedom. And it is from this very standpoint that the writings on cocaine should not be considered "a youthful error to be ignored by his successors and excluded from the body of his works. Rather, it is a youthful mark of his greatness. He had the capacity to be caught up by a powerful collective pattern and yet work his way through to an individual solution. . . . He continued on to realize the same spiritual ambition, but on a psychological level."[24] As we know, Freud was so enthusiastic about the properties of cocaine that he recommended it to everyone, and even the ever-faithful Jones was obliged to write: "In short, looked at from the vantage point of our present knowledge, he was rapidly becoming a public menace."[25] To draw a veil of shame over certain disconcerting aspects in the figure of a great man means ultimately not to have faith in his absolute worth; this faith is demonstrated only by accepting even these negative moments in the long story of his research and scientific endeavor.

One might still object that, unlike the writings of Marx and Freud just mentioned, the Spielrein documents were not written with publication in mind, and as such ought to remain undisclosed.

I do not agree. Any man who raises his voice to say something truly new to his contemporaries, who counters their ideas and convictions with a different vision, cannot be measured by a common yardstick. How many people have been influenced—to keep to the examples cited—by Freud, Marx, and Jung? How many people recognize themselves in their opinions and studies? Any fact, any piece of information that can better illuminate their contributions to science should be known and made known.

Jung's long journey, from his association studies to his *Mysterium Coniunctionis*, is one that spans exactly fifty years of analytic and speculative work. Just as Freud did not remain ensnared by his youthful false steps in search of a hasty glory, so Jung's exuberance and inexperience in treating his first patients did not prevent him from redeeming past errors and incurred risks, and putting them clearly in focus. I repeat once more the analogy: Freud thought that with cocaine he had discovered something that would free man, but in reality man's liberation lay at quite another level, as Freud himself later demonstrated; in his encounter with Sabina Spielrein Jung had the impression that he had found *his* liberation, but as he later realized, for him, too, integration would have to come by quite other paths. As for us, who have flung open secret doors, nothing remains but to live with greater humility.

NOTES

WRITINGS of
SABINA
SPIELREIN

INDEX

NOTES

CW = *The Collected Works of C. G. Jung,* ed. Gerhard Adler, Michael Fordham, and Herbert Read; William McGuire, exec. ed.; trans. R. F. C. Hull (vol. 2 trans. Leopold Stein in collaboration with Diana Riviere). The entire edition constitutes Bollingen Series XX. 1953–67: New York: Pantheon Books and Bollingen Foundation. Princeton University Press: 1967–79.

Freud/Jung Letters = *The Freud/Jung Letters: The Correspondence between Sigmund Freud and C. G. Jung,* ed. William McGuire, trans. Ralph Manheim and R. F. C. Hull. Bollingen Series XCIV. Princeton University Press, 1974.

Jahrbuch = *Jahrbuch für psychoanalytische und psychopathologische Forschungen.* Leipzig and Vienna, 1909–13.

Jones = Ernest Jones, *The Life and Work of Sigmund Freud.* London: Hogarth Press, and New York: Basic Books, 1953, 1955, 1957.

Memories = *Memories, Dreams, Reflections by C. G. Jung,* recorded by Aniela Jaffé; trans. Richard and Clara Winston. New York: Pantheon Books, 1963.

Minutes = *Minutes of the Vienna Psychoanalytic Society,* ed. Herman Nunberg and Ernst Federn; trans. M. Nunberg. New York: International Universities Press, 1962–74. (I: 1906–08; II: 1908–10; III: 1910–15.)

Standard Ed. = *The Standard Edition of the Complete Psychological Works of Sigmund Freud.* Translated under the general editorship of James Strachey, in collaboration with Anna Freud, assisted by Alix Strachey and Alan Tyson. London: The Hogarth Press and the Institute of Psycho-Analysis, 1953–74.

Zeitschrift = *Internationale Zeitschrift für ärztliche Psychoanalyse.* Vienna, 1913.

Zentralblatt = *Zentralblatt für Psychoanalyse; Medizinische Monatsschrift für Seelenkunde.* Wiesbaden, 1911–13.

INTRODUCTION

1. Henri F. Ellenberger, *The Discovery of the Unconscious: The History and Evolution of Dynamic Psychiatry* (New York: Basic Books, 1970), pp. 447–48, 672–732, 889–91.
2. William McGuire, introduction, *Freud/Jung Letters*, pp. xiii–xxxvii. (See list of abbreviations.)
3. Aldo Carotenuto, *Senso e contenuto della psicologia analitica* (Turin: Boringhieri, 1977), p. 131.

PART ONE. DIARY AND LETTERS

I. THE DIARY OF SABINA SPIELREIN (1909–1912)

1. Peter Nansen (1861–1918), Danish writer; his novels depicted the emotional and erotic life of Copenhagen. He enjoyed tremendous success but is now totally forgotten. *The Diary of Julia* dates from 1893.
2. A reference to "Über den psychologischen Inhalt eines Falles von Schizophrenie (Dementia praecox)," *Jahrbuch* 3 (1911): 329–400.
3. In Italian in text.
4. Emma Jung, née Rauschenbach (1882–1955). *(Freud/Jung Letters*, p. 14, n. 4.)
5. Agathe, born in 1904; Gret, born in 1906; and Franz, born in 1908.
6. A reference to "Destruction as the Cause of Coming into Being."
7. Johann Jakob Honegger (1885–1911), a brilliant pupil of Jung who committed suicide. See Hans Walser, "An Early Psychoanalytical Tragedy: J. J. Honegger and the Beginnings of Training Analysis," *Spring* 1974, pp. 243–55.
8. Esther Aptekmann wrote a paper on psychogalvanic experiments as her doctoral thesis with Bleuler. She later returned to Russia. *(Freud/Jung Letters*, p. 455, n. 7.)
9. "Psychic Conflicts in a Child." Published in 1909, it went through several editions. In *The Development of Personality*, CW 17.
10. Marianne (1910–65), who married Walther Niehus. She was one of the editors of Jung's *Gesammelte Werke*, and originally a member of the editorial committee for the publication of Jung's letters. *(Freud/Jung Letters*, p. 353, n. 2.)
11. Most likely Jung's letter of 29 September 1910 and Freud's reply of 1 October 1910. *(Freud/Jung Letters*, pp. 355 ff.)
12. Spielrein is referring to her doctoral dissertation, "Über den psychologischen Inhalt eines Falles von Schizophrenie (Dementia praecox)."
13. A reference to Jung's "The Significance of the Father in the Destiny of the Individual," *Jahrbuch* 1 (1909): 155–73. The article went through several editions and was revised in 1949. In *Freud and Psychoanalysis*, CW 4.
14. Sabina's brother Jean, who was living in Stuttgart, according to a document from the Spanish consulate in Stuttgart.
15. Alexander Mikhailovich (1301–1339), duke of Tver and later grand duke of Vla-

dimir and of all the Russias. He and his son were slain by rival factions.

16. In a letter from Stuttgart dated 1 July 1918, her brother Jean wrote: "Our parents have enough money. Have you received the 4000 crowns that our father sent you? I estimate your inheritance in Rostov at 150-200,000 rubles; it's running no risks. Our father has invested all the money in real estate, which has much increased in value."

17. See the letter from Freud to Jung, 1 December 1911, in *Freud/Jung Letters*, p. 473.

18. This paper was to be entitled "Destruction as the Cause of Coming into Being."

19. By "pair no. 4," Sabina Spielrein means Jung and Freud.

20. For "poetry" we must surmise a metaphorical significance known only to Jung and Sabina. A literary analogy can be found in Proust. Swann and Odette used the metaphor *"faire cattleya"* to express the physical act of possession.

21. Surely after 1906, since his son, Franz, was born in 1908.

22. Freud had six children. See Jones, 1:152.

23. Probably a medicine of the period.

24. See n. 20.

25. Rudolf Ulrich Krönlein (1847–1910), Swiss brain surgeon.

26. Spielrein was accepted in 1911.

27. Spielrein wrote, probably by mistake, "XI" for the month instead of "XII."

28. *The Sandman*, a story by E. T. A. Hoffmann (1776–1822), published in 1816. "The title derives from the fact that the central character of the novella, the sensitive and visionary Nathanael, grew up, in his dark and desolate childhood, under the incubus of a fairy tale told by his nurse, in which a fantastic creature called the Sandman pours sand into the eyes of children until the eyes bleed and pop out of the empty sockets. Certain circumstances led the boy to identify the wicked Sandman as Coppelius, his father's collaborator in alchemy experiments. Coppelius, in different guises, reappears later in his life at exceptional moments, and always as an enemy. In this framework the central action of the story unfolds—the strange love story of Nathanael, now a university student. In the small university town lives the great Italian scientist Lazzaro Spalanzani, who appears, however, as a magician of science, inventor, and creator of a doll, Olympia, resembling a human being and to whom he imparts movement and speech; the hapless Nathanael falls in love with her as with a live woman and, through various fantastic episodes, ends by losing his mind. And it is again Coppelius who destroys him: one day, as Nathanael, having freed himself from the evil spell of Olympia, stands gazing with his childhood sweetheart, Klara, from the top of a tower on the city below, Coppelius bewitches him with a look and drives him to hurl himself over the edge." From *Dizionario letterario delle opere e dei personaggi di tutti i tempi e di tutte le letterature* (Milan: Bompiani, 1955), 4:501–502. Freud also refers to the Sandman story in his paper "The 'Uncanny,' " *Standard Ed.*, 17:227–36.

29. See Hans Lobner and Vladimir Levitin, "A Short Account of Freudism: Notes on the History of Psychoanalysis in the USSR," *Sigmund Freud House Bulletin* 2, no. 1 (1978): 9.

30. Unidentified person.

31. Arthur Schnitzler (1862–1931), physician, dramatist, and writer, exchanged letters with Freud on psychoanalytic subjects. Although gifted with great psychological insight, he was never able to overcome his aversion for the concepts of incest and infantile sexuality. See Jones, 3:84. But consult also *Letters of Sigmund Freud*, ed. Ernst L. Freud, trans. Tania and James Stern (New York: Basic Books, 1960).

32. The date here given in the original for the wedding ("14.I") is rendered quite unreliable by the diary itself (see the entries for 7 January and 28 February 1912). On the other hand, in a letter to Spielrein of 20 August 1912, Freud takes note of the news of her marriage, and thus it surely took place between February 1912 and 11 July 1912 (the date of the present entry). Since in the manuscript the date "14.I" is written so clearly as to exclude any uncertainty in reading, it must be a slip of the pen by Spielrein (perhaps *I* instead of *J* for *Juni*, "June").

II.   LETTERS FROM SABINA SPIELREIN TO C. G. JUNG

1. Unidentified, but probably a professor at the University of Zurich.

2. The complete passage runs as follows: "To the lone-dwellers will I sing my song, and to the twain-dwellers; and unto him who has still ears for the unheard, will I make the heart heavy with my happiness." F. W. Nietzsche, *Thus Spake Zarathustra*, trans. Thomas Common (Modern Library ed.), Zarathustra's Prologue, sec. 9.

3. Wilhelm von Kaulbach (1805–74), celebrated German painter, famous for the cartoon "The Cock Fight." In 1837 he became court painter to King Ludwig I and finished his illustrations for *Reinecke Fuchs*. There is a reference to Kaulbach in *Freud/Jung Letters*, p. 72, n. 3. *Reinecke Fuchs* is a medieval collection of tales in which the hero is a fox.

4. "Über den psychologischen Inhalt eines Falles von Schizophrenie," *Jahrbuch* 3 (1911).

5. In *Freud/Jung Letters*, p. 447, there is confirmation that Spielrein had arrived in Vienna by 11 October 1911.

6. Part I of Jung's *Wandlungen und Symbole der Libido*, *Jahrbuch* 1 (1911). In its revised version of 1952, Jung retitled the work *Symbols of Transformation*.

7. Spielrein is referring to her paper "Destruktion"; see *Freud/Jung Letters*, p. 498. Siegfried was the symbolic name by which Spielrein alluded to her possible child.

8. Leonhard Seif (1866–1949), Munich neurologist and head of the Psychoanalytic Society of that city—see *Minutes* III: 209, 218. He later became a follower of Adler.

9. It should be remembered that Spielrein was writing in German, although her mother tongue was Russian.

10. Wilhelm Stekel (1868–1940), one of the first psychoanalyst disciples of Freud. He had a special talent for the interpretation of symbols. He committed suicide in London. His book was entitled *Die Sprache des Traumes: Eine Darstellung*

der Symbolik und Deutung des Traumes in ihren Beziehungen zur kranken und gesunden Seele für Ärzte und Psychologen (The Language of Dreams: A Presentation for Doctors and Psychologists of the Interpretation and Symbolism of Dreams in Relation to the Sick and Healthy Psyche). Published by Bergmann of Munich in 1911, it went through many editions. Freud on this book: "Stekel's new book is as usual rich in content;—the pig finds truffles, but otherwise it's a mess, no attempt at coherence, full of hollow commonplaces and new lopsided generalizations, all incredibly sloppy" (*Freud/Jung Letters*, p. 404).

11. See "Godfather Death" in *Grimm's Fairy Tales*, trans. Margaret Hunt, rev. James Stern (New York: Pantheon, 1944), pp. 209–12. A poor father hands his last child over to Death, who adopts him as his godson. When the child grows up, Godfather Death lets him become a famous doctor. The doctor's skill derives from the help he receives from Godfather Death, who indicates to him those patients who are going to die and those who will survive. After the doctor has twice tried to deceive Godfather Death, the latter, infuriated, decides to do away with him. Godfather Death seizes the doctor and carries him to an underground cave.

"There he saw how thousands and thousands of candles were burning in countless rows, some large, others half-sized, others small. Every instant some were extinguished, and others again burnt up, so that the flames seemed to leap hither and thither in perpetual change.

" 'See,' said Death, 'these are the lights of men's lives. The large ones belong to children, the medium-sized ones to married people in their prime; the little ones belong to old people; but children and young folks likewise have often only a tiny candle.'

" 'Show me the light of my life,' said the physician, and he thought that it would be still very tall. Death pointed to a little end which was just threatening to go out, and said, 'Behold, it is there.'

" 'Ah, dear godfather,' said the horrified physician, 'light a new one for me, do it for love of me, that I may enjoy my life, be King, and the husband of the King's beautiful daughter.'

" 'I cannot,' answered Death, 'one must go out before a new one is lighted.'

" 'Then place the old one on a new one, that will go on burning at once when the old one has come to an end,' pleaded the physician.

"Death behaved as if he were going to fulfill his wish, and took hold of a tall new candle; but as he desired to revenge himself, he purposely made a mistake in fixing it, and the little piece fell down and was extinguished. Immediately the physician fell on the ground, and now he himself was in the hands of Death."

12. Hermann Swoboda (1873–1963), a famous patient of Freud's, involved along with Weininger and Fliess in a dispute over the priority of the idea of bisexuality. In 1906 W. Fliess published a short book on the question, *In eigener Sache* (Berlin: Emil Goldschmidt, 1906).

13. Aulus Cornelius Celsus (first century A.D.), Roman author of treatises of which only scattered fragments have survived. His *De medicina* has been preserved in eight books, a complete work on medicine and surgery according to the rules of Hippocrates. The quotation is probably from *De medicina*.

14. The *Jahrbuch* was born from the first informal meeting of all those who were interested in Freud's work, at Salzburg on 27 April 1908. The first issue appeared in 1909, the last in 1913. The contents of the five volumes are listed in *Freud/Jung Letters*, pp. 563–67.

15. Spielrein alludes to the problem of "Destruction as the Cause of Coming into Being" in a note in her "Über den psychologischen Inhalt eines Falles von Schizophrenie (Dementia praecox)," *Jahrbuch* 3 (1911); 371, n. 2.

16. Paul Eugen Bleuler (1875–1939), director of the Burghölzli cantonal hospital and clinic. He coined the term "schizophrenia," and from the beginning was open to the theories of psychoanalysis. See his *Dementia Praecox, or the Group of Schizophrenias*, trans. J. Zinkin (1950; orig. ed. 1911).

17. The reference is to *Die Psychologie der unbewussten Prozesse* (Zurich, 1917), the first edition of "On the Psychology of the Unconscious," in *Two Essays on Analytical Psychology, CW* 7.

18. Alfred Adler (1879–1937), first president of the Vienna Psychoanalytic Society. In 1911 he broke with Freud and founded the school of individual psychology.

19. A reference to the secondary gain from illness as described by Freud in *Introductory Lectures on Psycho-Analysis* (1917), *Standard Ed.*, 16: 384.

20. See n. 17.

21. Emil Medtner appears later as editor of a series in Russian of books on analytical psychology, including *Psychological Types* and *The Psychology of Dementia Praecox*. See *General Bibliography of Jung's Writings, CW* 19, p. 140.

22. See the reference in Hans Lobner and Vladimir Levitin, "A Short Account of Freudism: Notes on the History of Psychoanalysis in the USSR," *Sigmund Freud House Bulletin*, 2, no. 1 (1978): 9.

23. The following works by Jung and Freud have been translated into Russian.

C. G. Jung:

1901. "The Content of the Psychoses" (1908).

1924. An excerpt from *Psychological Types* (1921).

1929. Complete translation of *Psychological Types* (1921).

1939. "The Psychology of Dementia Praecox" (1906); "Psychic Conflicts in a Child" (1910); "On the Psychology and Pathology of So-called Occult Phenomena" (1902); "The Content of the Psychoses" (previously published in 1909); four brief articles on word association. These essays were published in a single volume edited by Emil Medtner.

Sigmund Freud:

1910. *The Psychopathology of Everyday Life* (1904).

1911. *Three Essays on the Theory of Sexuality* (1905); *Five Lectures on Psycho-Analysis* (1909–10).

1912. *On Dreams* (1900–1901); *Delusion and Dreams in Jensen's "Gradiva"* (1906–

7); "Obsessive Acts and Religious Practices" (1907); "The Relation of the Poet to Daydreaming" (1907–8); " 'Civilized' Sexual Morality and Modern Nervousness" (1908); "Analysis of a Phobia in a Five-Year-Old Boy" (clinical case of Little Hans) (1908–9); *Leonardo da Vinci: A Psychosexual Study of an Infantile Reminiscence* (1910); "Formulations Regarding the Two Principles in Mental Functioning" (1911).

1913.*The Interpretation of Dreams* (1899–1900); "The Employment of Dream-Interpretation in Psycho-Analysis" (1912); "The Dynamics of the Transference" (1912); "Recommendations for Physicians on the Psycho-Analytic Method of Treatment" (1912); "A Note on the Unconscious in Psycho-Analysis" (1913); "Further Recommendations in the Technique of Psycho-Analysis: 1. On Beginning the Treatment" (1913); "Types of Neurotic Nosogenesis" (1912).

1922.*Introductory Lectures on Psycho-Analysis* (1915–17).

1923."Freud's Psycho-Analytic Method" (1903–4); "On Psychotherapy" (1905); "Character and Anal Eroticism" (1908); "Observations on 'Wild' Psycho-Analysis" (1910); "Fausse reconnaissance (déjà raconté) in Psycho-Analytic Treatment" (1913–14); "The Moses of Michelangelo" (1913–14); "Further Recommendations in the Technique of Psycho-Analysis: 2. Recollection, Repetition and Working-Through" (1914); "On the History of the Psycho-Analytic Movement" (1914); "Observations on Transference-Love" (1915); "Repression" (1915); "The Unconscious" (1915); "Instincts and Their Vicissitudes" (1915); "On the Transformations of Instincts with Special Reference to Anal Erotism" (1915–17); "Some Character-Types Met with in Psycho-Analytic Work" (1915); "One of the Difficulties of Psycho-Analysis" (1916–17); "Mourning and Melancholia" (1917); Metapsychological Supplement to the Theory of Dreams" (1916); "Turnings in the Ways of Psycho-Analytic Therapy" (1918–19); "A Note on the Prehistory of the Technique of Analysis" (1920).

1924.*Totem and Taboo* (1912–13); "Narcissism: An Introduction" (1914); "The Infantile Genital Organization of the Libido" (1923); *The Ego and the Id* (1923).

1925.*Jokes and Their Relation to the Unconscious* (1905); "Contributions to the Psychology of Love" (1910–17); *Beyond the Pleasure Principle* (1920); *Group Psychology and the Analysis of the Ego* (1921).

1927.*Inhibitions, Symptoms and Anxiety* (1925–26).

1928.*The Future of an Illusion* (1927).

24.Jung, "On the Question of Psychological Types" (1913), in *Psychological Types, CW* 6, appendix.

25.Johann Wolfgang von Goethe, "Prologue in Heaven," *Faust, Part One,* trans. Philip Wayne (Harmondsworth, Eng.: Penguin Books, 1949), pp. 41–42.

26.Herbert Silberer (1882–1923), Viennese psychoanalyst interested particularly in symbolism and the analysis of dreams. His most important work, *Probleme der Mystik und ihrer Symbolik* (Vienna: H. Heller, 1914), influenced Jung's studies on alchemy. He killed himself after a disagreement with Freud. See Paul Roazen, *Brother Animal: The Story of Freud and Tausk* (New York: Knopf, 1969), p. 157.

27.It has not been possible to trace this quotation.

28.References to K. A. Scherner, author of *Das Leben des Traumes* (Berlin, 1861), can also be found in Freud's *Interpretation of Dreams.*

29.Vladimir M. Bekhterev (1857–1927), Russian psychophysiologist, author of over 600 published works and 369 speeches and lectures. He is famous for having studied the reflexes of association.

30.Actually, in the handwritten original of this letter, the second P.S. begins with a "17," which is then crossed out and followed by the date "16.I.1918."

31."La structure de l'inconscient," *Archives de psychologie* 16 (1916), which in its final version was to be entitled "The Relations Between the Ego and the Unconscious," in *Two Essays on Analytical Psychology, CW* 7.

32.Alexander Feodorovich Kerenski (1881–1970), Russian revolutionary leader who was overthrown as prime minister by the Bolsheviks in 1917; fled abroad, eventually to the United States, where he continued his political activity against the Soviet regime.

33.Gregor Johann Mendel (1822–1884), considered the father of modern genetics. His study on inherited characteristics, published in the pages of a provincial journal in 1866, was completely ignored by the scientific world. His work was rediscovered in 1900 by Hugo De Vries, Carl Correns, and Eric von Tschermak.

34.The reference may be to Haelius, descendant of Samem-Roumos, title of a sun god of Tyre. See Canon John, ed., *The Mythology of All Races,* vol. V, *Semitic* (New York: Cooper Square Publishers, 1964), p. 54.

35.In Norse mythology, the god Balder had an anxiety dream in which his death was prophesied. Thereupon his mother, Frigg, overwhelmed by grief, extracted from all the creatures in the world the promise that they would do no harm to her son. But mistletoe was not asked and made no promises. A branch of mistletoe later killed Balder. Jung speaks of this myth in *Wandlungen und Symbole der Libido* (1912). In the revised edition, *Symbols of Transformation* (1952), p. 257, Jung again brings up the myth and stresses the similarity between Balder's death and that of Osiris.

III. LETTERS FROM SABINA SPIELREIN TO SIGMUND FREUD

1.This is the third letter written by Spielrein to Freud (see n. 10).

2.Unidentified person.

3.A reference to the letter sent by Jung to Sabina Spielrein's mother. See *Freud/ Jung Letters,* p. 236.

4.Unidentified person.

5.Spielrein was a patient from 17 August 1904 to 1 June 1905.

6.This is an error, since the correspondence between Freud and Jung began on 11 April 1906.

7.An old German folk song.—TRANS.

8.See n. 10.

9.Ludwig Binswanger, "Über das Verhalten des psycho-galvanischen Phänomens beim Assoziationsexperiment," *Journal für Psychologie und Neurologie* 10, no. 1 (1907). "On the Psychogalvanic Phenomenon in Association Experiments," *Studies in Word-Association*, trans. M. D. Eder (New York: Moffat, Yard, 1918), pp. 446–79. Binswanger (1881–1966) was the founder of existential analysis.

10. Freud had replied (4 June 1909) to Spielrein's first letter (see letter of 30 May 1909) by asking her to be more specific about her reasons for wishing to see him. Spielrein's second letter to Freud is surely missing; in it she must have mentioned her troubles with Jung, without going into too much detail. On 8 June 1909, Freud replied that, since he was a friend of Jung's, before receiving Sabina he would have to adhere to the old Latin saying *audiatur et altera pars* ("listen to the other side, too").

11. By these initials Jung indicated Helene Preiswerk, the young medium with whom he carried out experiments, later published as his graduate thesis, "On the Psychology and Pathology of So-called Occult Phenomena" (*CW* 1). See Stefanie Zumstein-Preiswerk, *C. G. Jung's Medium: Die Geschichte der Helly Preiswerk* (Munich: Kindler, 1975); also James Hillman, "Some Early Background to Jung's Ideas," *Spring* 1976, pp. 123–36.

12. Mathilde, Freud's eldest daughter.

13. Otto Gross (1877–1919) studied medicine in Graz and was later Kraepelin's assistant in Munich. His book *Das Freud'sche Ideogenitätsmoment und seine Bedeutung im manisch-depressiven Irresein Kraepelins* (Leipzig, 1907) deals with cases examined in the Munich clinic. Jung devoted a chapter of *Psychological Types* (1921) to the typological ideas developed by Gross in *Die zerebrale Sekundärfunktion* (Leipzig, 1909) and *Über psychopathische Minderwertigkeiten* (Vienna and Leipzig, 1909). Gross, a teetotaler and vegetarian, was then a well-known figure at the Café Stephanie in Munich. Leonhard Frank depicted him as "Doctor Otto Kreuz" in his autobiography *Links, wo das Herz ist* (1952). Frieda Weekley (née von Richthofen, later the wife of D. H. Lawrence) had an affair with him in that period; in her memoirs he appears under the name Octavio. See *Frieda Lawrence: The Memoirs and Correspondence*, ed. E. W. Tedlock, Jr. (London, 1961); see also R. Lucas, *Frieda von Richthofen* (Munich, 1972), pp. 53 ff., and Martin Green, *The von Richthofen Sisters* (New York, 1974). From *Freud/Jung Letters*, p. 66, n. 7.

14. Johann Wolfgang von Goethe, *Faust, Part One*, trans. Philip Wayne (Penguin, 1949), p. 75. Jung used the same quotation in *Symbols of Transformation, CW* 5:234.

15. Antinous August Rauber (1841–1917), a gifted German thinker, attained considerable fame with his studies on anatomy, embryology, and anthropology. In 1866 he held the chair of anatomy at Dorpat. Among his countless works, *Urgeschichte des Menschen* (Leipzig, 1884) and *Die Regeneration der Krystalle* (Leipzig, 1895–96) stand out.

16. "Robber" in German is *Räuber*. Probably a pun on the name Rauber, the anatomist.

17. The attribution of the following fragment to the same letter as the fragment that ends here is conjectural but highly probable.

18. In German *Sabinerin/Sabinerinnen* means "woman/women of the Sabine people," while *Sabinchen* is the diminutive of the proper name *Sabina* (or *Sabine*). The director meant to distort the title in such a way that even an educated German spectator would associate it with girls named Sabina rather than the women of the Sabine people.

19. The attribution of the fragment that follows to the same letter is also conjectural.

20. Unidentified person.

21. Small cakes made with chocolate and dried fruit.

22. *Spielerein* suggests *ich spiele* (I play) + *rein* (clean), while *Spielerei* means "joke." Sabina, instead of stating that her real name is Spielrein (without the second "e"), confirms "with the most serious expression in the world" that she is called "I-play-clean."

23. This paragraph is written on the back of a letter from Jung to Sabina Spielrein of 15 April 1914 and was probably sent to Freud by Spielrein in the same period.

IV.   LETTERS FROM SIGMUND FREUD TO SABINA SPIELREIN

1. Freud mentions this letter in writing to Jung on 7 June 1909 (*Freud/Jung Letters*, p. 230).

2. Freud wrote to Jung: ". . . and [I] suggested a more appropriate procedure, something endopsychic, as it were." *Ibid.*, pp. 234–35.

3. See Jung's letter to Freud on 21 June 1909, *ibid.*, p. 236.

4. Freud is referring to the meeting of the Vienna Psychoanalytic Society on 25 October 1911, during which the philosopher Ludwig Klages had given a lecture on the psychology of handwriting. The discussion that followed had been very vehement. See *Minutes* III: 293–98.

5. Karl Abraham (1877–1925), Berlin psychiatrist and psychoanalyst, worked at the Burghölzli from 1904 to 1907. A close collaborator of Freud's, he founded the Berlin Psychoanalytic Society.

6. *Traum und Mythus: Eine Studie zur Völkerpsychologie (Schriften zur angewandten Seelenkunde*, ed. Sigmund Freud, vol. 4, 1909). See Abraham, *Clinical Papers and Essays on Psychoanalysis* (New York: Basic Books, 1955), p. 207.

7. Ludwig Jekels (1867–1954), Vienna-educated Polish psychiatrist, then at a sanatorium at Bistrai, near Bielitz (Austrian Silesia, now Poland); later in New York. (*Freud/Jung Letters*, p. 134, n. 2.)

8. See Spielrein, "Selbstbefriedigung in Fusssymbolik," *Zentralblatt* 3 (1913): 263. Founded in 1910, the *Zentralblatt* was left to Stekel in November 1912. It continued to be published until September 1914.

9. Paul Federn's critical review of Spielrein's article "Die Destruktion als Ursache des Werdens" appeared in the *Zeitschrift* 1 (1913): 89–93.

10. Friedrich Kraus (1858–1936), professor of medicine at Berlin University, director of the medical clinic at the Charité. (*Freud/Jung Letters*, p. 397, n. 5.)

11. Spielrein had probably informed Freud that she was pregnant.

12.A reference to the Fourth International Psychoanalytic Congress, held in Munich, 7–8 September 1913, during which Jung delivered a paper, "Contribution to the Study of Psychological Types," *CW* 6, pp. 499–509.

13.Sabina Spielrein had given birth to a daughter, to whom had been given the name Renate.

14.Freud is evidently referring to Emma Jung's letter to him 6 November 1911 (*Freud/Jung Letters*, pp. 455–57).

15.Freud makes use of a concept expressed in *Totem and Taboo* (1912): "Another side of the attitude of primitive peoples towards their rulers recalls a procedure which is common in neuroses generally but comes into the open in what are known as delusions of persecution. The importance of one particular person is immensely exaggerated and his absolute power is magnified to the most improbable degree, in order that it may be easier to make him responsible for everything disagreeable that the patient may experience." *Standard Ed.*, 13:50.

16.A reference to the *Jahrbuch*.

17.Oskar Pfister (1873–1956), Swiss Protestant pastor and psychoanalyst; a faithful follower of Freud. He sought to apply the discoveries of psychoanalysis to education. For a short time he wavered between Freud and Jung, and then chose Freud.

18.Otto Rank (1884–1939), one of Freud's favorite pupils. He had a special interest in the psychoanalytic interpretation of art. He was a close friend of the writer Anaïs Nin.

19.Hanns Sachs (1881–1947) joined Freud's group in 1909. In 1932 he moved to the United States, where he founded the review *American Imago*.

20.The *Internationale Zeitschrift für ärztliche Psychoanalyse* was founded by Freud in 1912; the first issue bears the date 1913. Here Freud evidently means the first number of the third volume, published in 1915. The article referred to is "Bemerkungen über die Übertragungsliebe," *Zeitschrift* 3 (1915): 1–11. "Observations on Transference-Love (Further Recommendations on the Technique of Psychoanalysis, III)," *Standard Ed.*, 12: 157–71.

21.*Imago* was founded in 1911; the first issue was published in 1912. The article referred to is probably "Zeitgemässes über Krieg und Tod," *Imago* 4 (1915): 1–21. "Thoughts for the Times on War and Death," *Standard Ed.*, 14: 273–300.

22.Victor Tausk (1875–1919), Croat psychoanalyst famous for his study of schizophrenia. He had taken a degree in law and later in medicine. He committed suicide after a quarrel with Freud. See Paul Roazen, *Brother Animal: The Story of Freud and Tausk* (New York: Alfred A. Knopf, 1969); François Roustang, *Un destin si funeste* (Paris: Les Editions de Minuit, 1976).

23.See n. 8.

24.Probably Jean Spielrein, Sabina's brother, who was living in Stuttgart.

25.*The Psychopathology of Everyday Life* had been translated in 1910, and the *Five Lectures on Psychoanalysis* in 1911.

26.A Russian translation by "Medem" appeared in 1910, according to Alexander Grinstein, *Sigmund Freud's Writing: A Comprehensive Bibliography* (New York: International Universities Press, 1977), p. 76.

27. Nikolai Evgrafovich Osipov (1877–1934), Russian physician who had studied at the Burghölzli. He introduced psychoanalysis in Moscow.
28. A reference to the following articles, all published in 1920: "Das Schamgefühl bei Kindern," *Zeitschrift* 6: 157–58; "Zur Frage der Entstehung und Entwicklung der Lautsprache," *ibid.*, p. 401; "Das schwache Weib," *ibid.*, p. 158; "Verdrängte Munderotik," *ibid.*, pp. 361–62; "Renatchens Menschenentstehungstheorie," *ibid.*, pp. 155–57.
29. Edouard Claparède (1873–1940), Swiss scholar, took an interest in countless aspects of psychology. He had a considerable influence on problems of education.
30. For this question, see Freud, "The Psycho-Analytic View of Psychogenic Disturbance of Vision (1910)," *Standard Ed.*, 11: 214.
31. Raymond de Saussure (1894–1971), son of the linguist Ferdinand, was one of the founders of the Paris Psychoanalytic Society. His book *La méthode psychoanalytique* was banned in France in 1922. See Jones, 3: 97; but also Freud, "Preface to Raymond de Saussure's *The Psycho-Analytic Method*," *Standard Ed.*, 19: 283–84.
32. The therapeutic school of Emile Coué (1852–1926), a pharmacist. His method was founded on suggestion that acted on the imagination.
33. "B" is Hippolyte Bernheim (1840–1919), university professor in Strasbourg, a champion of hypnosis and suggestion. Freud's allusion is to his book *De la suggestion et de ses applications à la thérapeutique* (Paris, 1888), which Freud translated into German.
34. Moshe Woolf (Wulff) (1878–1971), Russian psychoanalyst who received his training in Berlin with Abraham. In 1927 he left Russia and in 1933 settled in Palestine, where he was one of the founders of the Israeli Psychoanalytic Society.
35. Ivan Ermakov (Ermakoro), director of the psychiatric clinic in Moscow, translated various works of Freud. His name appeared on the roster of Russian psychoanalysts until 1930.
36. Undated note.

PART TWO.   THE STORY OF SABINA SPIELREIN

I.   A DIFFICULT CASE

1. Aldo Carotenuto, *Senso e contenuto della psicologia analitica* (Turin: Boringhieri, 1977), pp. 16 ff.
2. C. G. Jung, "The Psychology of Dementia Praecox" (1907), in *The Psychogenesis of Mental Disease*, CW 3, p. 4.
3. *Freud/Jung Letters*, p. 14.

4. Marie-Louise von Franz, *C. G. Jung: His Myth in Our Time*, trans. William H. Kennedy (New York: C. G. Jung Foundation, 1975), p. 61.

5. In this connection I have particularly in mind the friendly relationship between Einstein and Born and their exchange of letters concerning the composition of matter. Though their opinions differed, I find nothing to suggest that they ever became enemies. See Max Born, ed., *The Born-Einstein Letters* (New York: Walker, 1971).

6. Von Franz, *Jung*, p. 61.

7. C. G. Jung, "On the Psychology and Pathology of So-Called Occult Phenomena" (1902), in *Psychiatric Studies, CW* 1; *Experimental Researches, CW* 2.

8. Sigmund Freud, *The Interpretation of Dreams* (1900), *Standard Ed.*, 4 and 5.

9. Jung, "Psychology of Dementia Praecox," p. 57, n. 12.

10. *Ibid.*, pp. 57–58.

11. *Freud/Jung Letters*, p. 15.

12. *Ibid.*, p. 122.

13. To be precise, there is a single reference to Bleuler. See Jung, *Memories*, p. 255.

14. *Freud/Jung Letters*, p. 13.

15. *Ibid.*, p. 17.

16. The title of the 1911–12 edition was *Wandlungen und Symbole der Libido* (Transformations and Symbols of the Libido); the first part appeared in *Jahrbuch* 3 (1911): 120–227. Years later, in 1952, Jung published a thoroughgoing revision, *Symbole der Wandlung* (Symbols of Transformation), *CW* 5.

17. *Freud/Jung Letters*, p. 459.

18. Carotenuto, *Senso e contenuto*, pp. 130–34.

19. See *Freud/Jung Letters*, p. 228; *Minutes of the Vienna Psychoanalytic Society* III (1910–1911): xvii. I have been told by Ernst Federn, in his letter of 10 July 1978, that further information can be found in the German edition of the *Minutes*.

II. THE WORLD OF A CHILD

1. Spielrein, "Beiträge zur Kenntnis der kindlichen Seele," in *Zentralblatt* 3 (1912): 59.

2. *Ibid.*

3. Jung, "The Freudian Theory of Hysteria" (1908), *CW* 4, par. 57.

4. *Freud/Jung Letters*, p. 7.

5. Jung, "The Freudian Theory of Hysteria," par. 53.

6. *Freud/Jung Letters*, p. 8.

7. *A Psycho-Analytic Dialogue: The Letters of Sigmund Freud and Karl Abraham, 1907–1926*, ed. Hilda C. Abraham and Ernst L. Freud, trans. Bernard Marsh and Hilda C. Abraham (London: Hogarth Press and Institute of Psycho-Analysis, 1965), p. 32.

8. *Ibid.*, p. 163.

9. Personal communication, 26 September 1978, by Professor Huldrych M. Koelbing, director of the Medizinhistorisches Institut of the University of Zurich.

10. "Über den psychologischen Inhalt eines Falles von Schizophrenie," *Jahrbuch* 3 (1911): 329–400.

11. Jung, *Symbols of Transformation*, *CW* 5, pp. 139, 140, 141, 153, 237, 281, 288, 301, 302, 328, 353, 376, 409, 412, 437.

12. Spielrein, "Die Destruktion als Ursache des Werdens," *Jahrbuch* 4 (1912): 465–503.

13. Freud, *Beyond the Pleasure Principle* (1920), *Standard Ed.*, 18, p. 55.

14. *Minutes* III: 330, n. 4.

15. Spielrein, "Die Destruktion als Ursache des Werdens," p. 503.

16. Maurits Katan, "Precursors of the Concept of the Death Instinct," in *Psychoanalysis: A General Psychology*, ed. Rudolph M. Loewenstein, Lottie M. Newman, Max Schur, and Albert J. Solnit (New York: International Universities Press, 1966), pp. 86–103.

17. "Sabina Spielrein: Die Destruktion als Ursache des Werdens," review by Paul Federn in *Zeitschrift* 1 (1913): 92–93.

III. PSYCHOLOGY AND REIFICATION

1. Marie-Louise von Franz, *C. G. Jung: His Myth in Our Time*, trans. William H. Kennedy (New York: C. G. Jung Foundation, 1975), p. 61.

2. George E. Atwood and Silvan S. Tomkins, "On the Subjectivity of Personality Theory," *Journal of the History of the Behavioral Sciences* 12, no. 2 (April 1976): 177.

3. George E. Atwood and Robert D. Stolorow, "Metapsychology Reification and the Representational World of C. G. Jung," *International Review of Psycho-Analysis* 4, no. 2 (1977): 197. Concerning Freud, see also Stolorow and Atwood, "A Defensive-Restitutive Function of Freud's Theory of Psychosexual Development," *The Psychoanalytic Review* 65, no. 2 (1972): 217–38.

4. *Minutes* III: 329.

5. Personal communication, 13 June 1978.

6. Jean Piaget (1977), *Intervista su conoscenza e psicologia* (Bari: Laterza, 1978), pp. 114–16. In another interview, granted to the *Corriere della sera illustrato* (3, no. 7 [February 1979]: 9), Piaget says he was analyzed by a woman named De La Fuente, a direct pupil of Freud.

7. This problem is mentioned in Freud's letter to Spielrein of 12 June 1922.

8. Letter, Bleuler to Spielrein, 16 October 1909.

9. *Freud/Jung Letters*, p. 494.

10. *Ibid.*, p. 498.

11. Spielrein, "Beiträge zur Kenntnis der kindlichen Seele," in *Zentralblatt* 3 (1912): 57–58.

12.Spielrein, "Die Destruktion als Ursache des Werdens," *Jahrbuch* 4 (1912): 466. The quotation is from Jung, *Symbols of Transformation, CW* 5, p. 109.

13.*Symbols of Transformation, CW* 5: p. 328, n. 38.

14.In the list of members in the *Zeitschrift* 2 (1914): 413, Sabina Spielrein is shown as living at Thomasiusstrasse 2, Berlin.

15.*Minutes* III: 332.

16.*Ibid.*, p. 335.

17.*Freud/Jung Letters*, p. 469.

18.*Civilization and Its Discontents* (1929), *Standard Ed.*, 21, p. 120.

19.For this problem, see Otto Fenichel, "Zur Kritik des Todestriebes," *Imago* 21 (1935): 458–66.

20.Spielrein, "Destruktion," p. 413.

21.Spielrein, "Beiträge," p. 58.

22.*Ibid.*, p. 59.

23.Giuseppe Maffei, *Il mestiere di uomo: Ricerca sulla psicosi* (Venice: Marsilio Editore, 1977), pp. 13–54.

24.Spielrein, "Destruktion," p. 467.

25.*Ibid.*, p. 475.

26.Jung, *Memories*, pp. 170–99.

27.*Ibid.*, p. 114.

28.Spielrein, "Destruktion," p. 466.

29.Spielrein, Diary, 23 September 1909.

30.Spielrein, "Beiträge," p. 60.

IV.   "UNSTINTING EFFORT"

1.*Memories*, p. 145 (my italics). And Ellenberger makes the following observation: "Sometimes a psychotherapist, who has taken a patient as a special object of study, finds himself engaged in a prolonged, difficult, and ambiguous relationship. This patient is usually a hysterical woman." *The Discovery of the Unconscious: The History and Evolution of Dynamic Psychiatry* (New York: Basic Books, 1970), p. 891.

2.Paul J. Stern, *C. G. Jung: The Haunted Prophet* (New York: Braziller, 1976), p. 63.

3.*Freud/Jung Letters*, p. 467.

4.Giuseppe Maffei, *Il mestiere di uomo: Ricerca sulla psicosi* (Venice: Marsilio Editore, 1977), p. 165.

5.*Ibid.*, p. 14.

6.*Ibid.*

7.*Ibid.*, p. 143.

8.Jung, *Memories*, p. 127.

9.*Ibid.*, p. 128.

10.Spielrein, Diary, 27 August 1909.

11. Personal communication, 14 September 1978.

12. "Observations on Transference-Love" (1915), *Standard Ed.*, 12:159–71.

13. "The Freudian Theory of Hysteria" (1907), *CW* 4, par. 57.

14. Kenneth R. Silk, "The Schizophrenic Stare," *Bulletin [of the] Menninger Clinic* 42, no. 2 (March 1978): 22.

15. Maffei, *Il mestiere di uomo*, p. 145.

16. Jung, *Memories*, p. 145.

17. See p. 140.

18. *Freud/Jung Letters*, p. 207.

19. See Martin Green, *The von Richthofen Sisters* (New York: Basic Books, 1974), p. 43. See also the references to J. J. Honegger and Otto Gross in *Freud/Jung Letters*, pp. 153, 289.

20. Freud, "Observations on Transference-Love."

21. G. W. F. Hegel, *Early Theological Writings*, trans. T. M. Knox (Philadelphia: University of Pennsylvania Press, 1971), p. 304.

22. The concept of projective identification was formulated for the first time in 1946 by Melanie Klein, "Notes on Some Schizoid Mechanisms," *Developments in Psycho-Analysis* (London: The Hogarth Press, 1952).

23. Béla Grunberger (1971), *Narcissism: Psychoanalytic Essays*, trans. Joyce Diamanti (New York: International Universities Press, 1979), p. 197.

24. Jung, *Memories*, pp. 353–54. See also J. Hillman, "On Psychological Creativity," in *The Myth of Analysis* (Evanston: Northwestern University Press, 1972).

25. Denis de Rougemont, *Love in the Western World*, trans. Montgomery Belgion (New York: Pantheon Books, 1956), p. 42.

26. *Ibid.*, p. 68.

27. *Ibid.*, pp. 145–6.

28. Freud, "On Transience" (1916), *Standard Ed.*, 14: 305–307.

29. Hegel, *Early Theological Writings*, p. 305.

30. *Freud/Jung Letters*, p. 456.

31. Letter, Jung to Spielrein, 30 June 1908.

32. Letter, Jung to Spielrein, 12 August 1908.

33. *Freud/Jung Letters*, p. 95.

34. Erich Fromm, *Sigmund Freud's Mission: An Analysis of His Personality and Influence* (New York: Harper, 1959), p. 49.

35. Letter, Jung to Spielrein, 4 December 1908.

36. *Ibid.*

37. Letter, Jung to Spielrein, 30 June 1908.

38. Freud, "Observations on Transference-Love," p. 165. See also *Psycho-Analysis and Faith: The Letters of Sigmund Freud and Oskar Pfister*, ed. Heinrich Meng and Ernst L. Freud, trans. Eric Mosbacher (London: Hogarth Press, 1963), p. 118.

39. Giorgio Colli, *La nascita della filosofia* (Milan: Adelphi, 1975), p. 43.

40. Hegel, *Early Theological Writings*, p. 306.

V. BETRAYAL

1.*Freud/Jung Letters*, p. 228.
2.Martin Green, *The von Richthofen Sisters* (New York: Basic Books, 1974), p. 43.
3.*Freud/Jung Letters*, p. 236.
4.Letter, Freud to Spielrein, 8 June 1909.
5.*Freud/Jung Letters*, pp. 234–35.
6.*Ibid.*, p. 228.
7.*Ibid.*, p. 229.
8.*Ibid.*, p. 231.
9.S. Arieti, ed., *Trattato di psichiatria* (Turin: Boringhieri, 1969), 2:1514.
10.Letter, Spielrein to Freud, 13 June 1909.
11.Letter, Spielrein to Freud, 10 June 1909.
12.The text of this letter can be found in Spielrein's 10 June 1909 letter to Freud. See also *Freud/Jung Letters*, p. 236.
13.Text contained in letter, Spielrein to Freud, 11 June 1909.
14.*Freud/Jung Letters*, p. 237.
15.Letter, Spielrein to Freud, first one dated 12 June 1909.
16.Letter, Jung to Spielrein, 1 September 1919.
17.Text contained in letter, Spielrein to Freud, 13 June 1909.
18.*Ibid.*
19.Stefanie Zumstein-Preiswerk, *C. G. Jung's Medium: Die Geschichte der Helly Preiswerk* (Munich: Kindler-Verlag, 1975). See also James Hillman, "Some Early Background to Jung's Ideas: Notes on 'C. G. Jung's Medium' by Stefanie Zumstein-Preiswerk," *Spring* 1976, pp. 123–36.
20.Letter, Spielrein to Freud, 20 June 1909.
21.*Freud/Jung Letters*, p. 229.
22.Letter, Freud to Spielrein, 20 August 1912.
23.Throughout his correspondence with Jung, Freud used the salutation "Dear friend" until 14 November 1912, when he began to address him instead as "Dear Doctor."
24.Letter, Freud to Spielrein, 20 January 1913.
25.Letter, Freud to Spielrein, 8 May 1913.
26.Letter, Freud to Spielrein, 15 May 1914.
27.Letter, Freud to Spielrein, 12 June 1914.
28.*Freud/Jung Letters*, p. 238.
29.Aldo Carotenuto, "Psicopatologia dell'analista" (1972), in *Psiche e inconscio* (Venice: Marsilio Editore, 1978), pp. 179–96.
30.*Freud/Jung Letters*, p. 238.
31.*Ibid.*, p. 289.
32.*Ibid.*, p. 465.
33.Letter, Freud to Spielrein, 20 August 1912.
34.Letter, Spielrein to Freud, written on the back of a letter sent by Jung to Spielrein on 15 April 1914.

VI.   GROWTH

1.*Freud/Jung Letters*, p. 440.
2.Letter, Jung to Spielrein, 21–22 September 1911.
3.Letter, Jung to Spielrein, 24 November 1911.
4.Spielrein, Diary, 26 November 1910.
5.Letter, Jung to Spielrein, 25 March 1912.
6.*Freud/Jung Letters*, p. 498.
7.*Ibid.*, p. 122 (my italics).
8.Letter, Jung to Spielrein, 11 April 1913 (my italics).
9.*Freud/Jung Letters*, p. 539.
10.Silberer and Tausk, for example.
11.Letter, Freud to Spielrein, 14 June 1912.
12.Letter, Spielrein to Jung, 3 December 1917.
13.Letter, Jung to Spielrein, 15 April 1914.
14.Letter, Spielrein to Freud, undated, p. 112 ot the present volume.
15.Letter, Freud to Spielrein, 12 June 1914.
16.Letter, Jung to Spielrein, 13 September 1917.
17.See lists in the *Internationale Zeitschrift für ärztliche Psychoanalyse.*
18.Letter, Jung to Spielrein, 10 October 1917.
19.*Ibid.*
20.Letter, Jung to Spielrein, 30 November 1917.
21.Letter, Freud to Spielrein, 2 August 1919.
22.Letter, Spielrein to Jung, presumably of 27–28 January 1918.
23.Letter, Spielrein to Jung, 20 December 1917.
24.Letter, Spielrein to Jung, presumably of 27–28 January 1918.
25.Letter, Jung to Spielrein, 1 September 1919.
26.Quoted in Blaise Pascal, *Pensieri* [Pensées] (Milan: Mondadori, 1976), p. 17, n. 3.

VII.   THE SCIENTIFIC PAPERS

1.*The Psychoanalytic Review* 7, no. 1 (January 1920): 95–100.
2.Marthe Robert, *The Psychoanalytic Revolution*, trans. Kenneth Morgan (New York: Harcourt, Brace & World, 1966), pp. 330–31.
3.Paul Federn, "Sabina Spielrein: Die Destruktion als Ursache des Werdens," in *Zeitschrift* 1 (1913): 92–93. See also *The Psychoanalytic Review* 12, no. 3 (July 1926): 353–55.
4.See the brief notice in *The Psychoanalytic Review* 1, no. 4 (October 1914): 470.
5.Spielrein, "Mutterliebe," *Imago* 2 (1913); "Selbstbefriedigung in Fussymbolik," *Zentralblatt* 3 (1913); "Traum vom Vater Freudenreich," *Zeitschrift* 1 (1913); "Das unbewusste Träumen in Kuprins Zweikampf," *Imago* 2 (1913); "Die Schwiegermutter," *Imago*, 2 (1913).
6.Spielrein, "Die Schwiegermutter," p. 589.

7. Erich Neumann, "Creative Man and Transformation," in *Art and the Creative Unconscious*, Bollingen Series LXI (New York: Pantheon, 1959); *Amor and Psyche: The Psychic Development of the Feminine: A Commentary on the Tale of Apuleius*, Bollingen Series LIV (New York: Pantheon, 1956).

8. Spielrein, "Die Entstehung der kindlichen Worte Papa und Mama," *Imago* 8 (1922): 346. See also the reviews in the *International Journal of Psycho-Analysis* 1, no. 3 (1920): 359–60, and *The Psychoanalytic Review* 14, no. 3 (July 1927): 338–39.

9. Spielrein, "Entstehung der Worte," p. 365.

10. *Ibid.*, p. 366.

11. Alfred Lorenzer, *Zur Begründung einer materialistischen Sozialisationstheorie* (Frankfurt a. M.: Suhrkamp Verlag, 1972).

12. Spielrein, "Die Zeit im unterschwelligen Seelenleben," *Imago* 9 (1923): 317.

13. Spielrein, "Quelques analogies entre la pensée de l'enfant, celle de l'aphasique et la pensée subconsciente," *Archives de psychologie* 17 (1923): 306.

14. *Ibid.*, p. 314.

15. Letter, Freud to Spielrein, 9 February 1923.

VIII. THE RETURN

1. Hans Lobner and Vladimir Levitin, "A Short Account of Freudism: Notes on the History of Psychoanalysis in the USSR," *Sigmund Freud House Bulletin* 2, no. 1 (1978): 5–30.

2. M. Wulff, "Die russische psychoanalytische Literatur bis zum Jahre 1911," *Zentralblatt für Psychoanalyse* 1, no. 7/8 (April/May 1911): 364. Information on psychoanalysis in Russia can also be found in Jean Marti, "La psychanalyse en Russie," *Critique* 32 (March 1976): 346. For further information, see also Michail Rejsner, "Socialnaya psikhologia i isayniye Frayda," *Pechat' i revolutsiya*, 1925 kn. III, IV, V–VI, and "Frayd i yevo shkola o religii," *Pechat' i revolutsiya*, 1924 kn. I–II. The two essays have been published in Italian with the title *Un giurista sovietico e Freud* (Milan: La Salamandra, 1979). See also the introduction by Fausto Malcovati, pp. 17–25.

3. Lobner and Levitin, "A Short Account of Freudism," p. 7.

4. Wulff, "Die russische psychoanalytische Literatur," p. 367.

5. Lobner and Levitin, "A Short Account of Freudism," p. 8.

6. *Freud/Jung Letters*, p. 495, n. 2.

7. Lobner and Levitin, "A Short Account of Freudism," p. 9.

8. Wulff, "Die russische psychoanalytische Literatur," p. 369.

9. *Ibid.*, p. 369.

10. *Ibid.*, p. 370.

11. *Ibid.*, p. 371.

12. S. Goldouscheff, "Zur Kasuistik der Psychoanalyse," ed. S. Repin, *Zeitschrift* 2 (1914): 182.

13. See pp. 222–23, n. 23.

14. Sara Neiditsch, obituary for Tatiana Rosenthal, *Zeitschrift* 7 (1921).

15. N. Osipov, "Zur psychoanalytischen Bewegung in Moskau," *Zeitschrift* 7 (1921): 386.

16. *Ibid.*, p. 386.

17. S. Neiditsch, "Die Psychoanalyse in Russland während der letzten Jahre," *Zeitschrift* 7 (1921): 382.

18. Lobner and Levitin, "A Short Account of Freudism," p. 10.

19. *Ibid.*, p. 12.

20. *Ibid.*,

21. *Ibid.*, p. 13.

22. *Ibid.*

23. Vera Schmidt, *Psychoanalytische Erziehung in Sowietrussland: Bericht über das Kinderheim-Laboratorium in Moskau* (Leipzig, Vienna, Zurich: Internationaler Psychoanalytischer Verlag, 1924).

24. Lobner and Levitin, "A Short Account of Freudism," p. 13.

25. Alexander R. Luria, "Die Psychoanalyse in Russland," *Zeitschrift* 11 (1925): 397.

26. Lucilla Ruberti, "Il dibattito su psicoanalisi e marxismo negli anni Venti e Trenta," *Critica Marxista* 2 (March–April 1976): 114.

27. Lobner and Levitin, "A Short Account of Freudism," p. 14.

28. In this connection, consult the article by Richard F. Sterba, "Discussion of Sigmund Freud," *Psychoanalytic Quarterly* 47, no. 2 (1978): 182, in which Freud criticizes the therapeutic ambitions of all Marxist psychoanalytic efforts: "Therapeutic ambition is only halfway useful for science, for it is too tendentious. Free investigation is tremendously hampered by it."

29. Otto Fenichel, "Die offene Arbeitskolonie Bolschevo," *Imago* 17 (1931): 530.

30. B. D. Friedmann, "The Principal Psychological Conceptions of Freud and the Theory of Historical Materialism" (in Russian), in *Psichologiya i Marksism*, ed. K. N. Kornilov (Leningrad-Moscow, 1925). I was able to consult the volume through the courtesy of Edizioni Rinascita.

31. Alexander R. Luria, "Psychoanalysis as a System of Humanistic Psychology" (in Russian), in *Psichologiya i Marksism*.

32. Otto Fenichel, "Über die Psychoanalyse als Keim einer zukünftigen dialektisch-materialistischen Psychologie," *Zeitschrift für politische Psychologie und Sexualökonomie* 1, no. 1 (1934).

33. *Ibid.*

34. Joel Kovel, "The Marxist View of Man and Psychoanalysis," *Social Research* 43, no. 2 (1976): 220–45.

IX. THE END

1. See *Zeitschrift* 10, no. 1 (1924): 113; *International Journal of Psycho-Analysis* 5 (1924): 258.

2. Spielrein, "Rêve et vision des étoiles filantes" and "L'automobile: symbole de la puissance mâle," *International Journal of Psycho-Analysis* 4 (1923).

3. Spielrein, "Kinderzeichnungen bei offenen und geschlossenen Augen," *Imago*, 1931.

4. Personal communication, 20 June 1978.

5. Personal communication, 26 June 1978, from A. B. Kogan, professor at the State University of Rostov-on-Don.

6. Actually the *International Journal of Psycho-Analysis* confined itself to eliminating from the roster the lists of analysts in countries where psychoanalysis had been outlawed.

7. Jung, "The Psychology of the Transference" (1946), in *The Practice of Psychotherapy*, CW 16, par. 364.

8. *Ibid.*, par. 365.

9. *Ibid.*

10. *Ibid.*, par. 369.

11. *Ibid.*, par. 371.

12. *Ibid.*, par. 375.

13. *Freud/Jung Letters*, p. 207.

14. Jung, "Psychology of the Transference," par. 383.

15. *Ibid.*, par. 399.

16. *Ibid.*, par. 443.

17. On this case see Henri F. Ellenberger, *The Discovery of the Unconscious: The History and Evolution of Dynamic Psychiatry* (New York: Basic Books, 1970), pp. 18–22.

18. *Memories*, p. 185.

19. *Ibid.*, p. x.

20. *Ibid.*, p. 199.

21. *Ibid.*, p. 145.

22. Karl Marx, *Secret Diplomatic History of the Eighteenth Century*, ed. L. Hutchinson (London, 1970).

23. E. Jones, *Freud* 2: 78–97. See also Robert Byck, ed., *The Cocaine Papers [by] Sigmund Freud* (New York: Stonehill, 1974).

24. A. K. Donoghue and J. Hillman, introduction, in Sigmund Freud, *The Cocaine Papers* (Vienna: Dunquin Press, 1963), p. viii.

25. Jones, 1:81.

WRITINGS of
SABINA SPIELREIN

1911."Über den psychologischen Inhalt eines Falles von Schizophrenie (Dementia Praecox)." *Jahrbuch für psychoanalytische und psychopathologische Forschungen*, 3:329–400.

1912."Die Destruktion als Ursache des Werdens." *Jahrbuch für psychoanalytische und psychopathologische Forschungen*, 4:465–503.

1912."Beiträge zur Kenntnis der kindlichen Seele." *Zentralblatt für Psychoanalyse und Psychotherapie*, 3:57–72.

1913."Mutterliebe." *Imago*, 2:523–24.

1913."Selbstbefriedigung in Fusssymbolik." *Zentralblatt für Psychoanalyse und Psychotherapie*, 3:263.

1913."Traum vom *Vater Freudenreich*." *Internationale Zeitschrift für ärztliche Psychoanalyse*, 1:484–86.

1913."Das unbewusste Träumen in Kuprins *Zweikampf*." *Imago*, 2:524–25.

1913."Die Schwiegermutter." *Imago*, 2:589–91.

1914."Der vergessene Name." *Internationale Zeitschrift für ärztliche Psychoanalyse*, 2:383–84.

1914."Tiersymbolik and Phobie bei einem Knaben." *Internationale Zeitschrift für ärztliche Psychoanalyse*, 2:375–77.

1914."Zwei Mensesträume." *Internationale Zeitschrift für ärztliche Psychoanalyse*, 2:32–34.

1915."Ein unbewusster Richterspruch." *Internationale Zeitschrift für ärztliche Psychoanalyse*, 3:350.

1916."Die Äusserungen des Oedipuskomplexes im Kindersalter." *Internationale Zeitschrift für ärztliche Psychoanalyse*, 1:44–48.

1919."Russische Literatur." *Bericht über die Fortschritte der Psychoanalyse 1914– 1919*, Vienna: Internationaler Psychoanalytischer Verlag, 1921.

1920."Das Schamgefühl bei Kindern." *Internationale Zeitschrift für ärztliche Psychoanalyse*, 6:157–58.

1920."Zur Frage der Entstehung und Entwicklung der Lautsprache." *Internationale Zeitschrift für ärztliche Psychoanalyse*, 6:401.

1920."Das Schwache Weib." *Internationale Zeitschrift für ärztliche Psychoanalyse*, 6:158.

1920."Verdrangte Munderotik." *Internationale Zeitschrift für ärztliche Psychoanalyse*, 6:361–62.

1920."Renatchens Menschenentstehungstheorie." *Internationale Zeitschrift für ärztliche Psychoanalyse*, 6:155–57.

1921."Schnellanalyse einer kindlichen Phobie." *Internationale Zeitschrift für ärztliche Psychoanalyse*, 7:473–74.

1922."Briefmarkentraum." *Internationale Zeitschrift für ärztliche Psychoanalyse*, 8:342–43.

1922."Die Entstehung der kindlichen Worte Papa und Mama." *Imago*, 8:345–67.

1922."Schweiz." *Internationale Zeitschrift für ärztliche Psychoanalyse*, 8:234–35.

1923."Rêve et vision des étoiles filantes." *International Journal of Psycho-Analysis*, 4:129–32.

1923."Die drei Fragen." *Imago*, 9:260–63.

1923."L'automobile: Symbole de la puissance mâle." *International Journal of Psycho-Analysis*, 4:128.

1923."Ein Zuschauertypus." *Internationale Zeitschrift für Psychoanalyse*, 9:210–11.

1923."Quelques analogies entre la pensée de l'enfant, celle de l'aphasique et la pensée subconsciente." *Archives de psychologie*, 18:306–22.

1923."Einige kleine Mitteilungen aus dem Kinderleben." *Zeitschrift für Psychoanalytische Pädagogik*, 2:95–99.

1923."Die Zeit im unterschwelligen Seelenleben." *Imago*, 9:300–17.

1931."Kinderzeichnungen bei offenen und geschlossenen Augen." *Imago*, 16:259–91.

INDEX

ABOUT THE AUTHOR

Aldo Carotenuto, Ph.D., is a professor of the theory
of personality at the University of Rome and a
training analyst for the Associazione Internazionale
di Psicologia Analitica. He is the author of
numerous articles and several books, and the editor
of *Rivista di psicologia analitica* and *Giornale
storico di psicologia dinamica.* At present he is
engaged in research on the history of
psychoanalysis. He is married and lives in Rome.